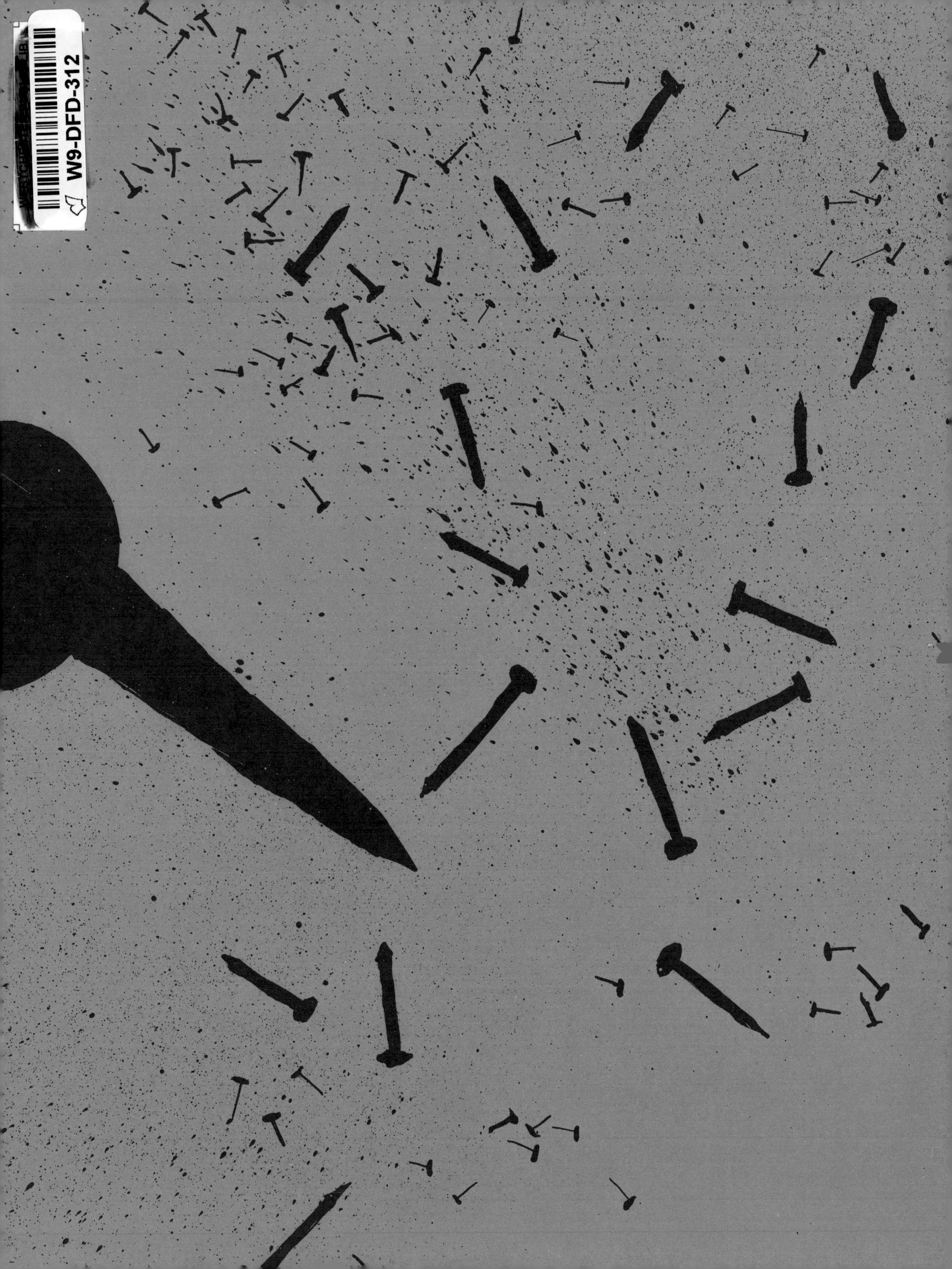

FRANK MILLER'S

HOLY TERROR™

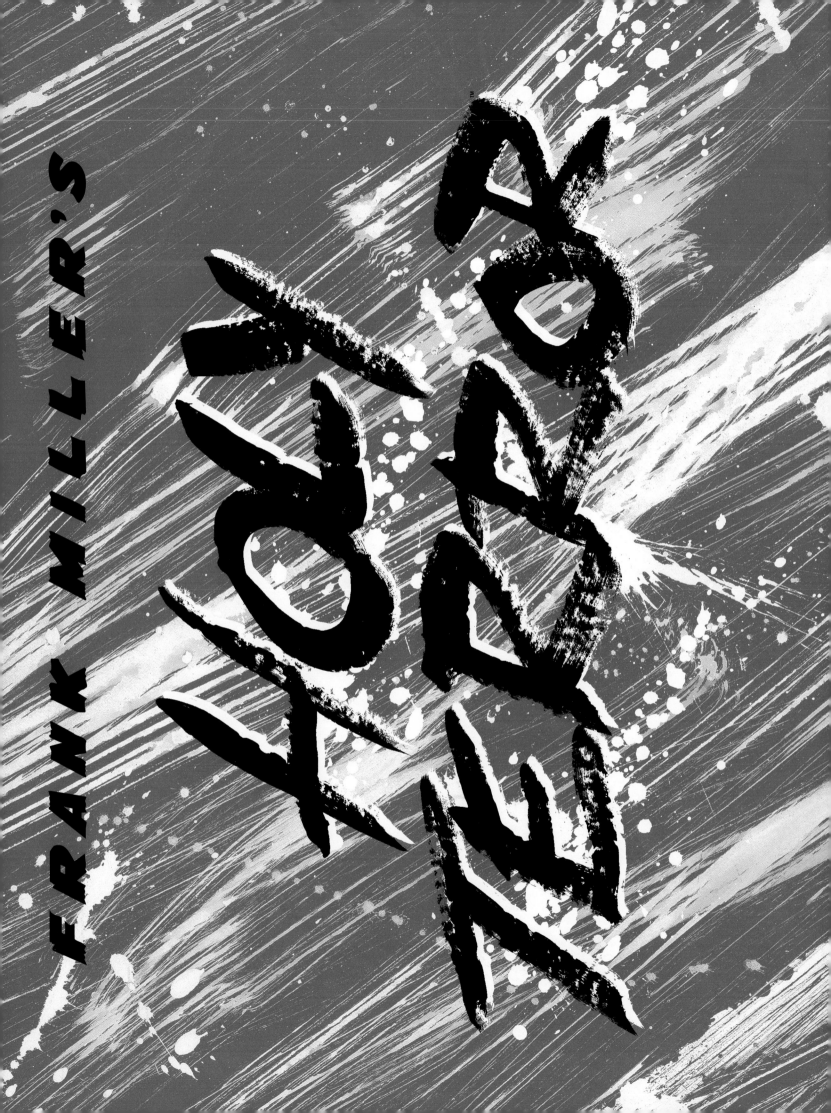

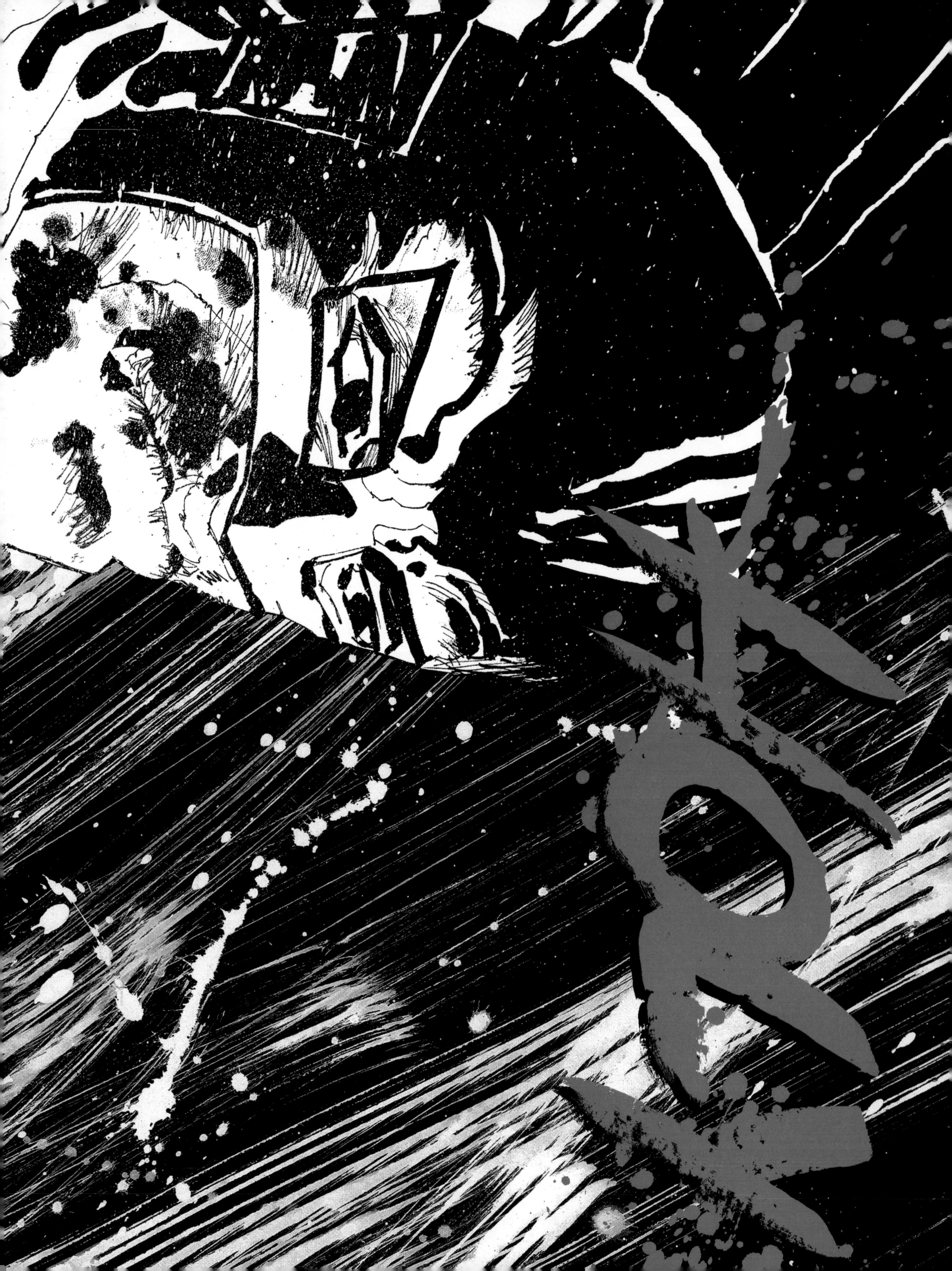

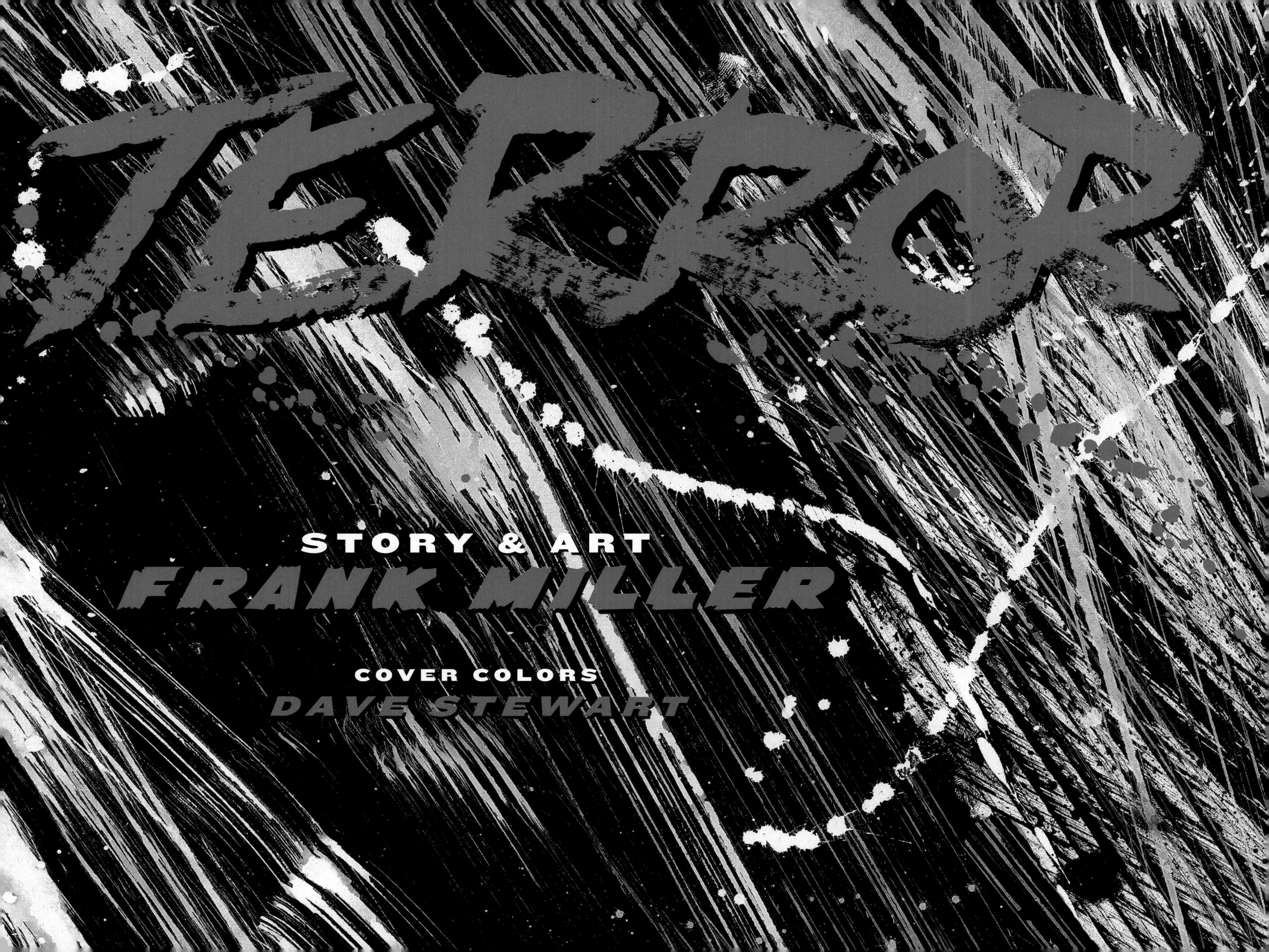
TERROR™
STORY & ART
FRANK MILLER
COVER COLORS
DAVE STEWART

EDITOR
BOB SCHRECK

ASSISTANT EDITOR
GREG TUMBARELLO

LOGO DESIGN
STEVEN MILLER

BOOK DESIGN
STEVEN BIRCH AT SERVO

PRODUCTION
STEVEN BIRCH
CHRISTOPHER SEBELA

LEGENDARY

Published by Legendary Comics, LLC.
4000 Warner Blvd. Bldg. 76
Burbank, CA 91522

BOB SCHRECK Editor-in-Chief
JOSH ELDER Director of Publishing
RICH JOHNSON Consultant

Special thanks to **KIMBERLY COX**

First Printing September 2011
10 9 8 7 6 5 4 3 2 1

ISBN-10: 193727800X
ISBN-13: 9781937278007

Library of Congress Control Number:
2011933316

PRINTED IN CANADA.

IF YOU MEET THE INFIDEL,

KILL THE INFIDEL.

MOHAMMED

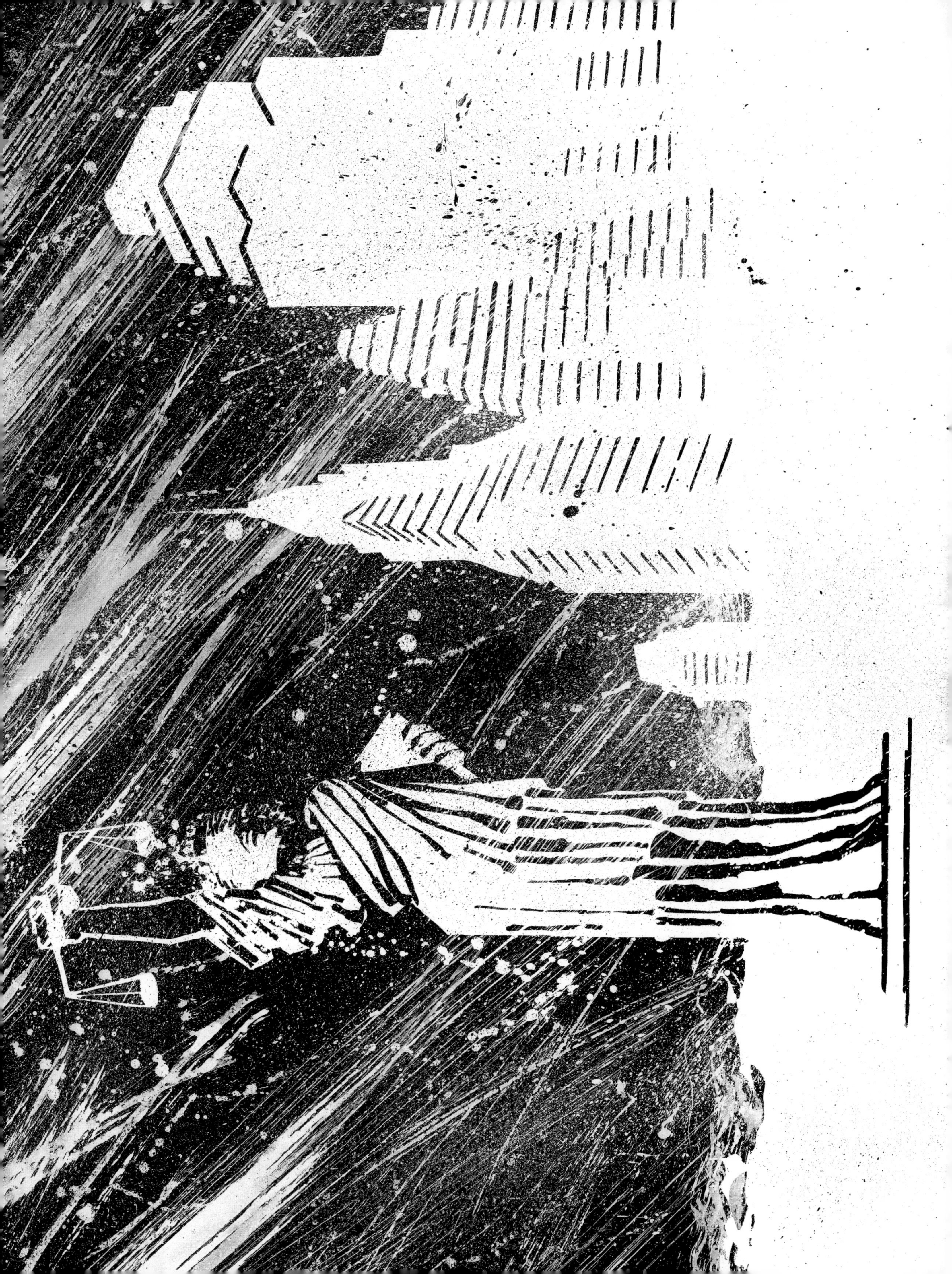

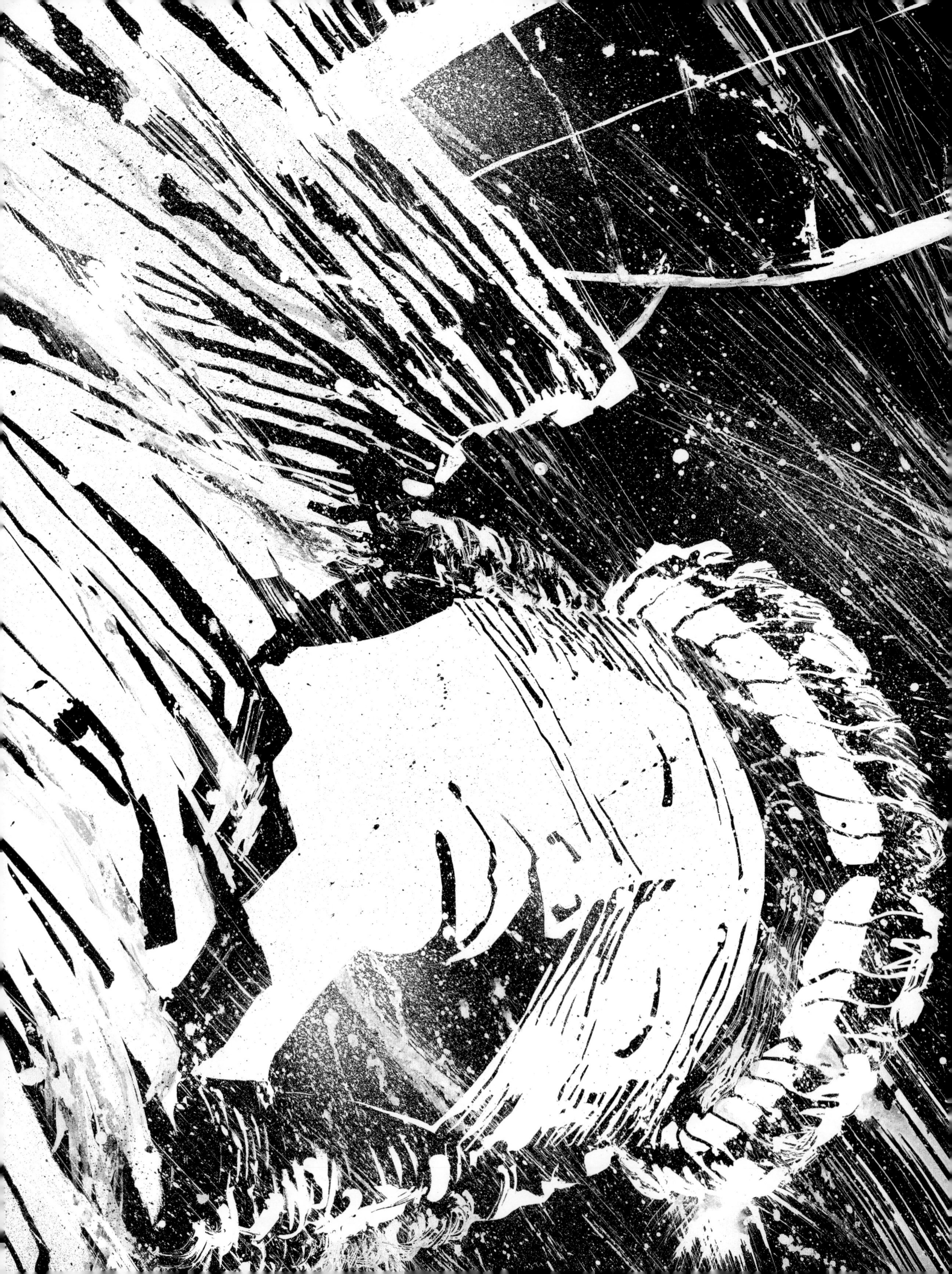

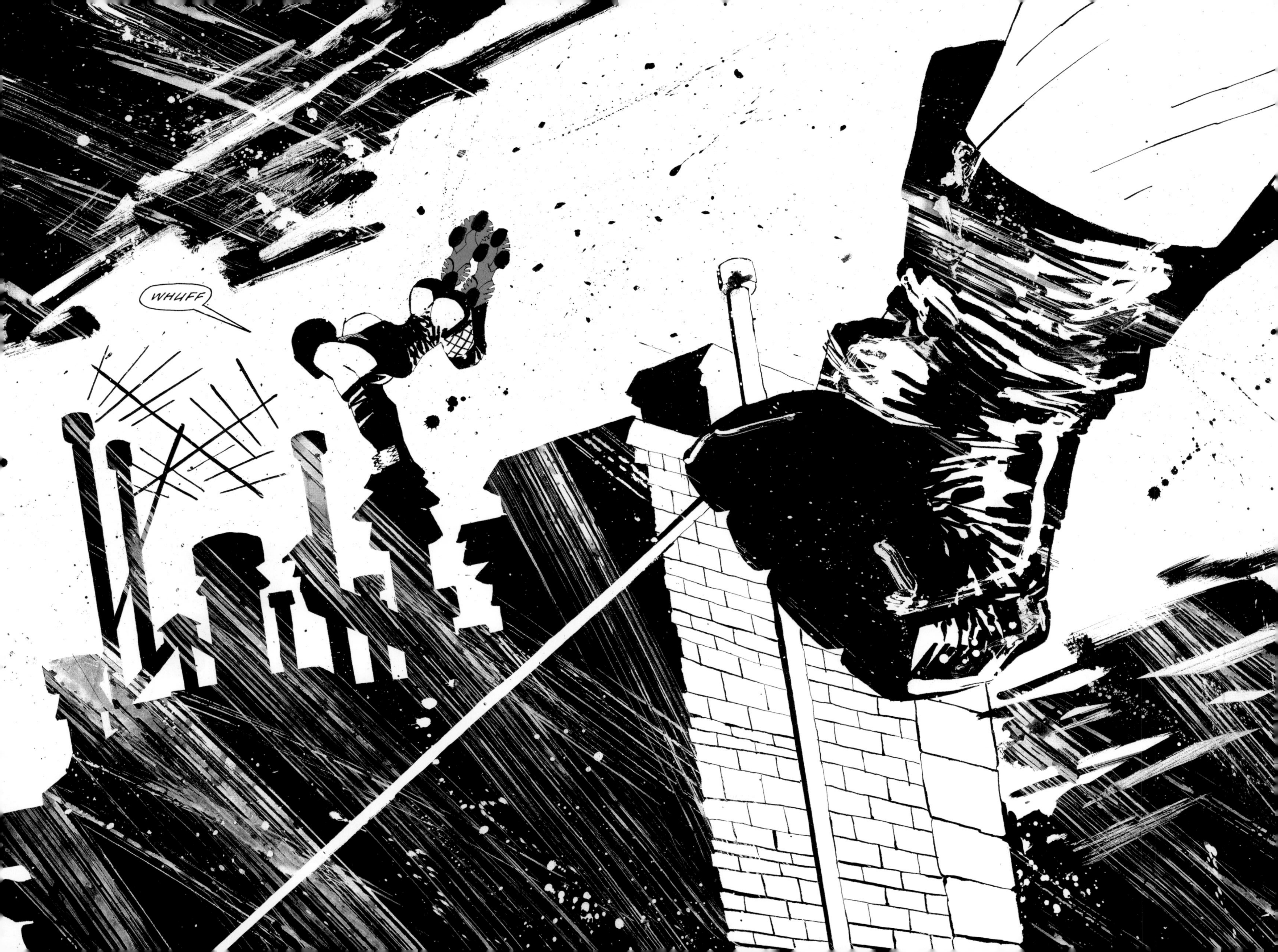
WHUFF

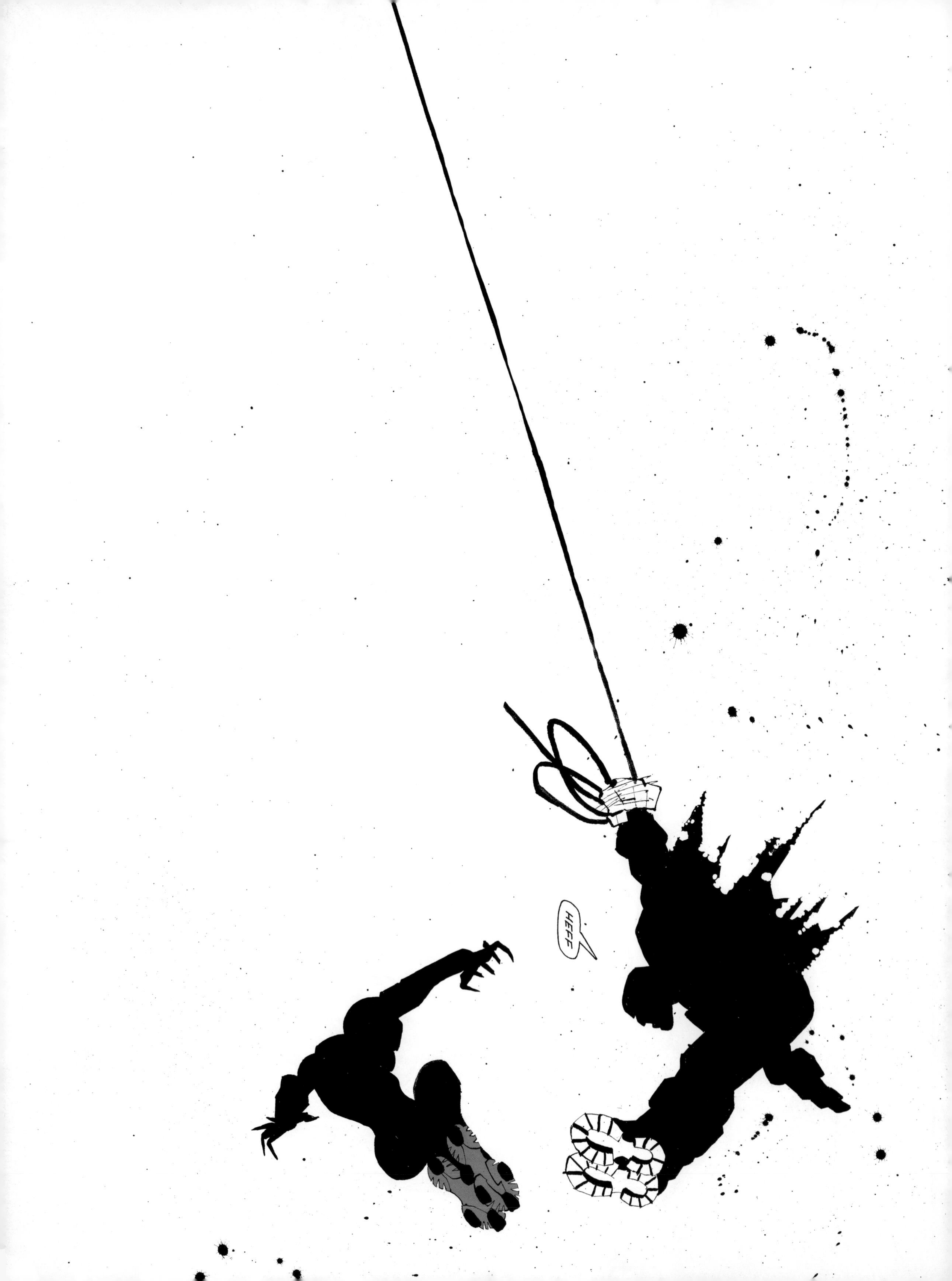
HEFF

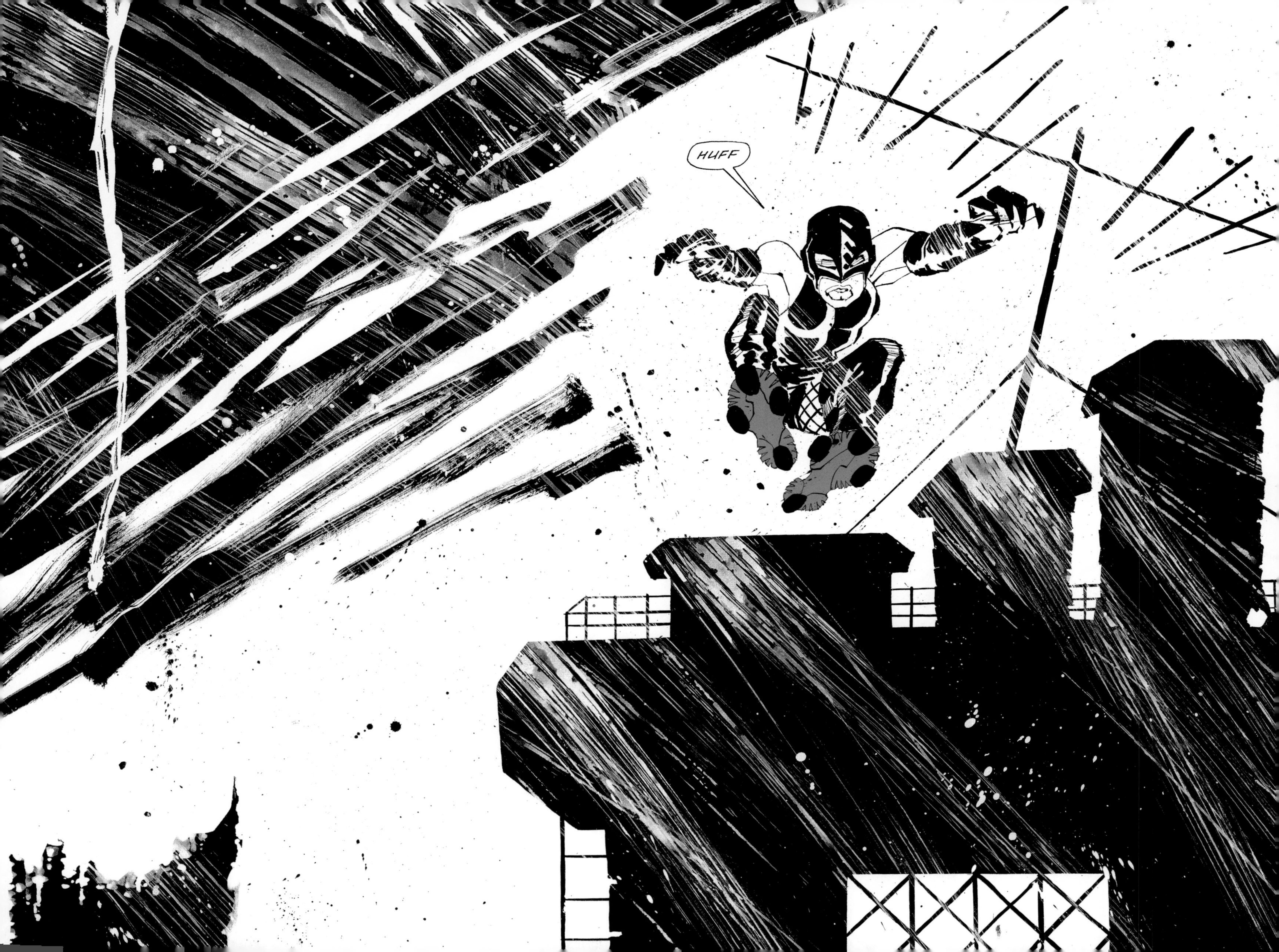
HUFF

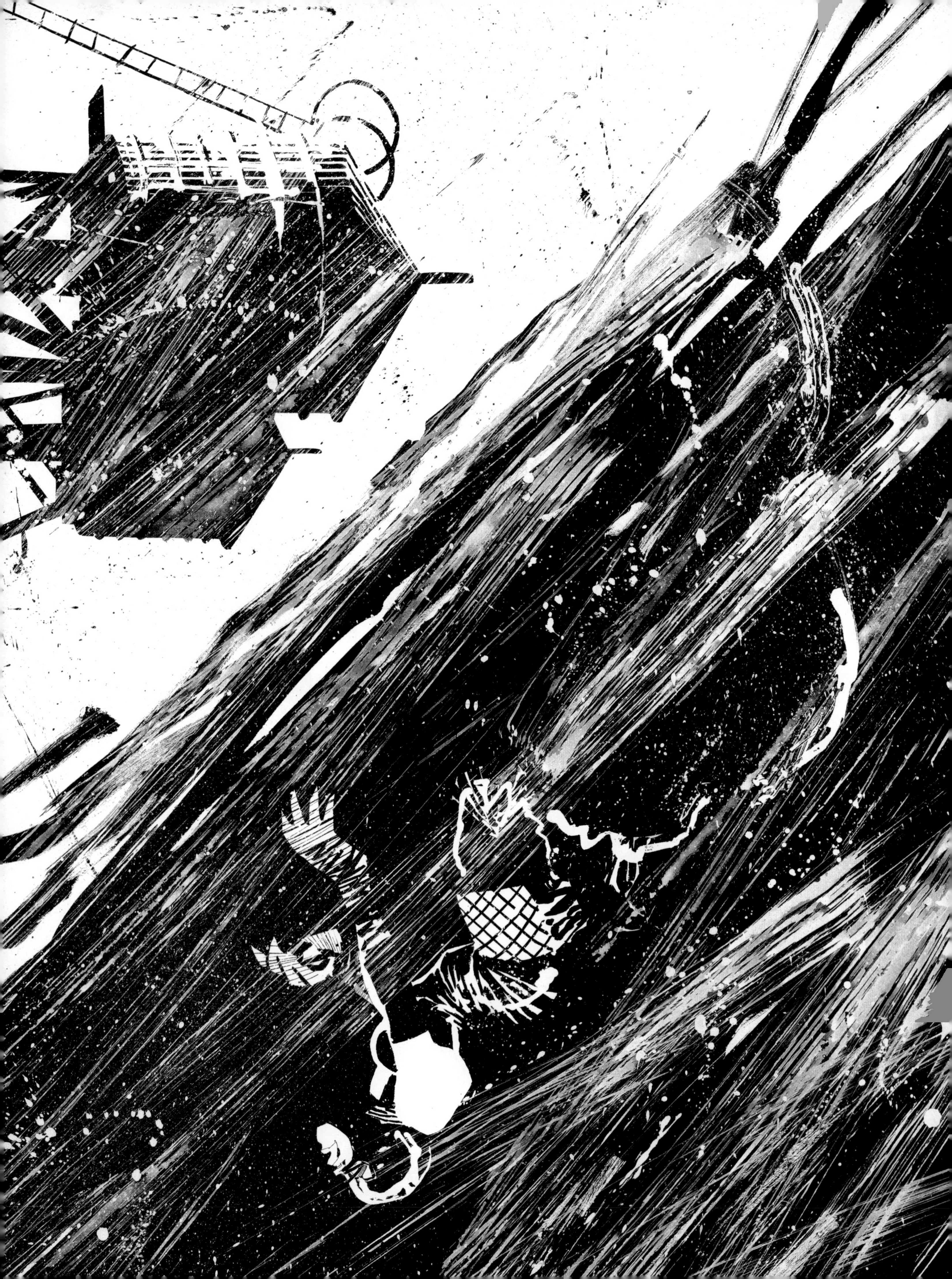

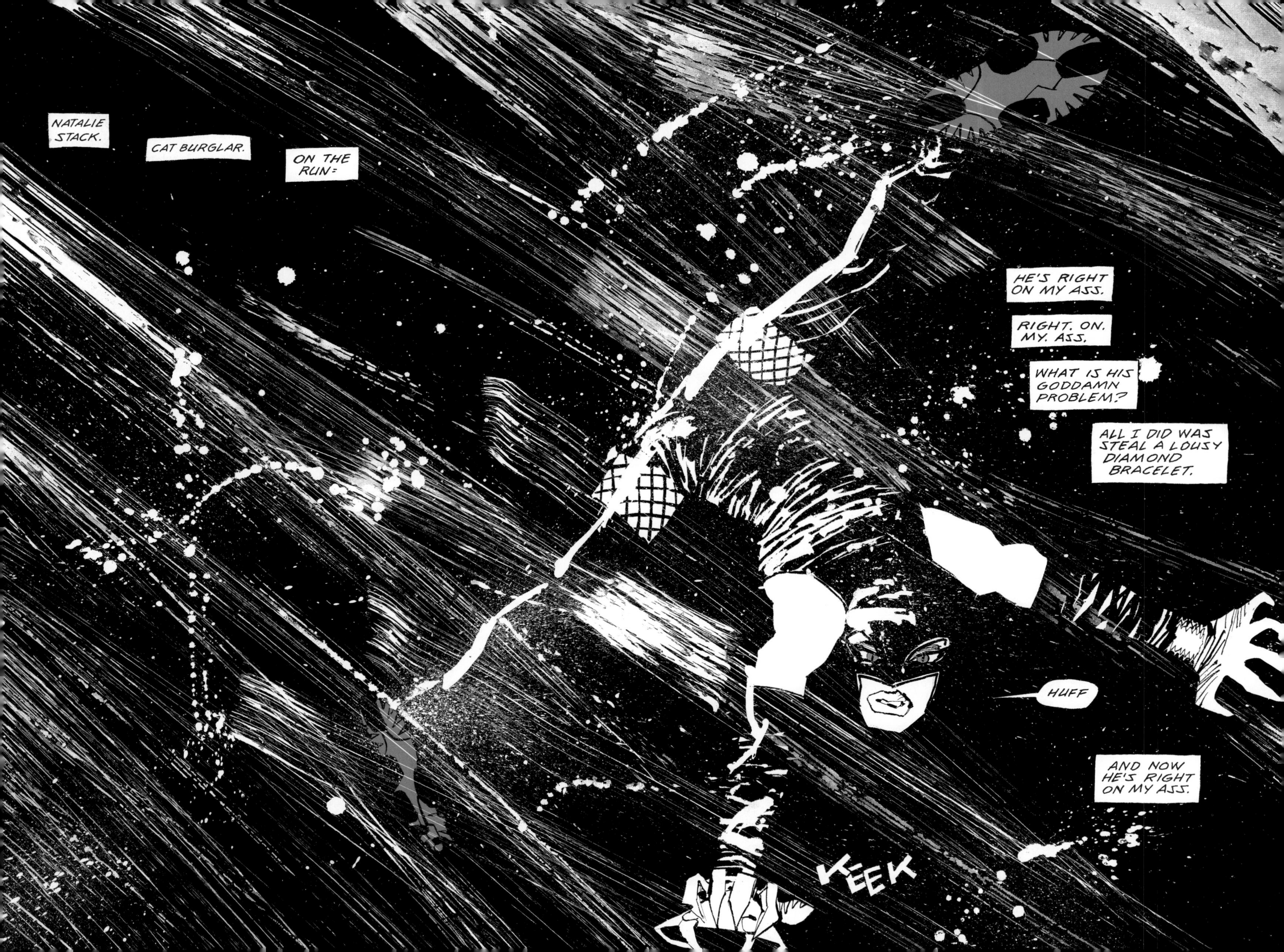
NATALIE STACK.
CAT BURGLAR.
ON THE RUN=
HE'S RIGHT ON MY ASS.
RIGHT. ON. MY. ASS.
WHAT IS HIS GODDAMN PROBLEM?
ALL I DID WAS STEAL A LOUSY DIAMOND BRACELET.
HUFF
AND NOW HE'S RIGHT ON MY ASS.
KEEK

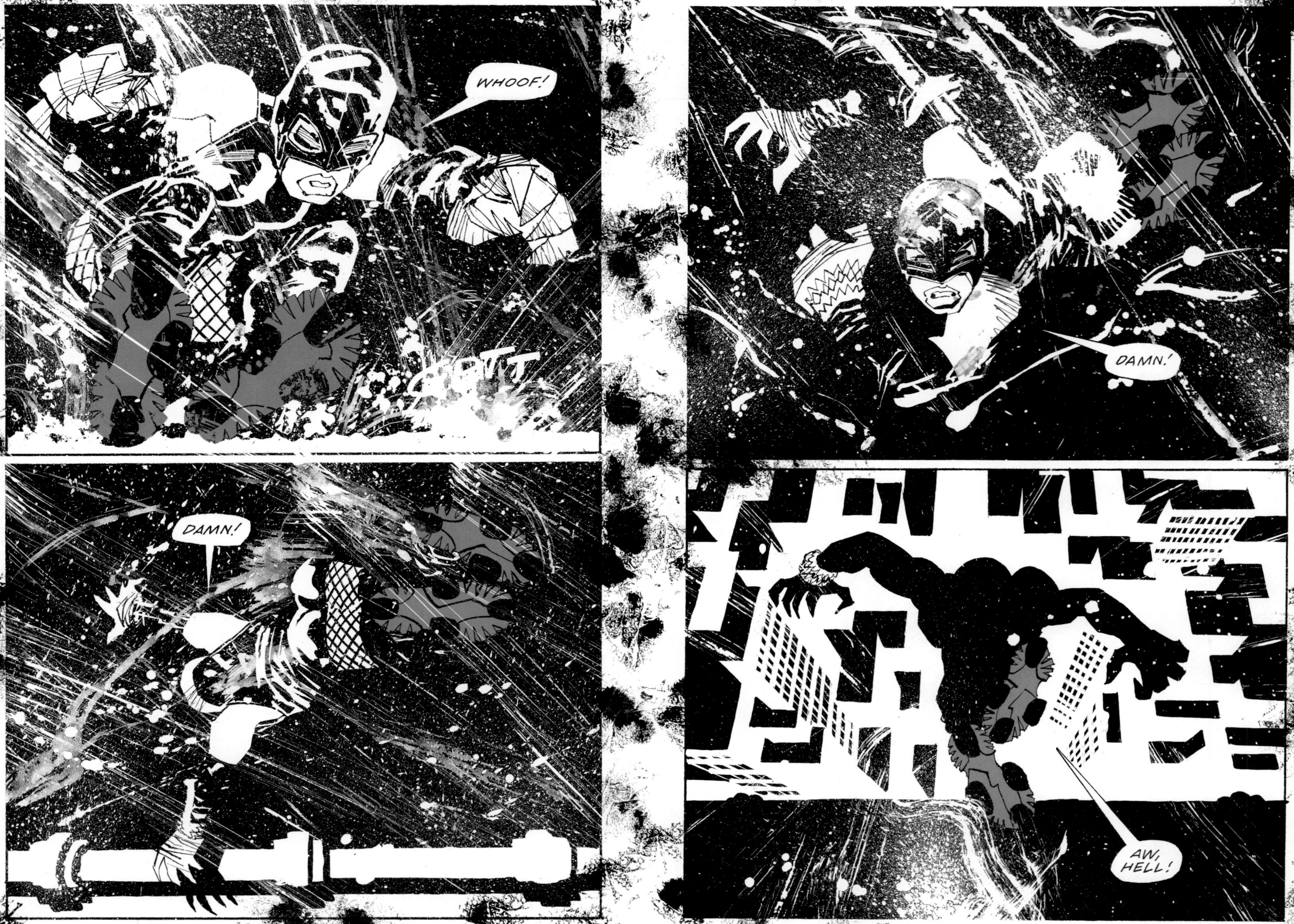
WHOOF!
DAMN!
DAMN!
AW, HELL!

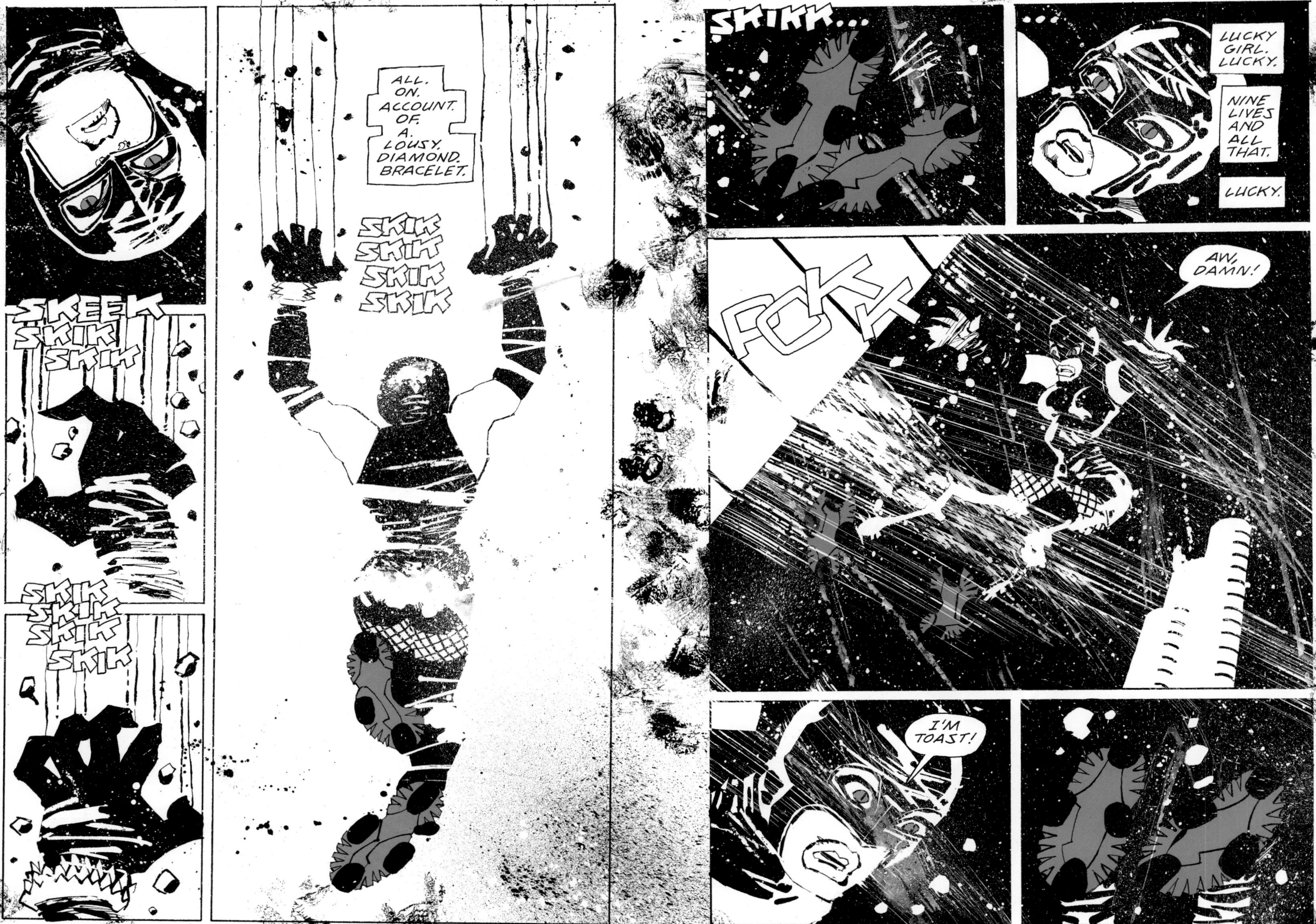
SKEEK
SKIK
SKIK
SKIK SKIK SKIK SKIK
ALL. ON. ACCOUNT. OF. A. LOUSY. DIAMOND. BRACELET.
SKIK SKIK SKIK SKIK
SKIKK...
LUCKY GIRL. LUCKY.
NINE LIVES AND ALL THAT.
LUCKY.
FOOK
AW, DAMN!
I'M TOAST!

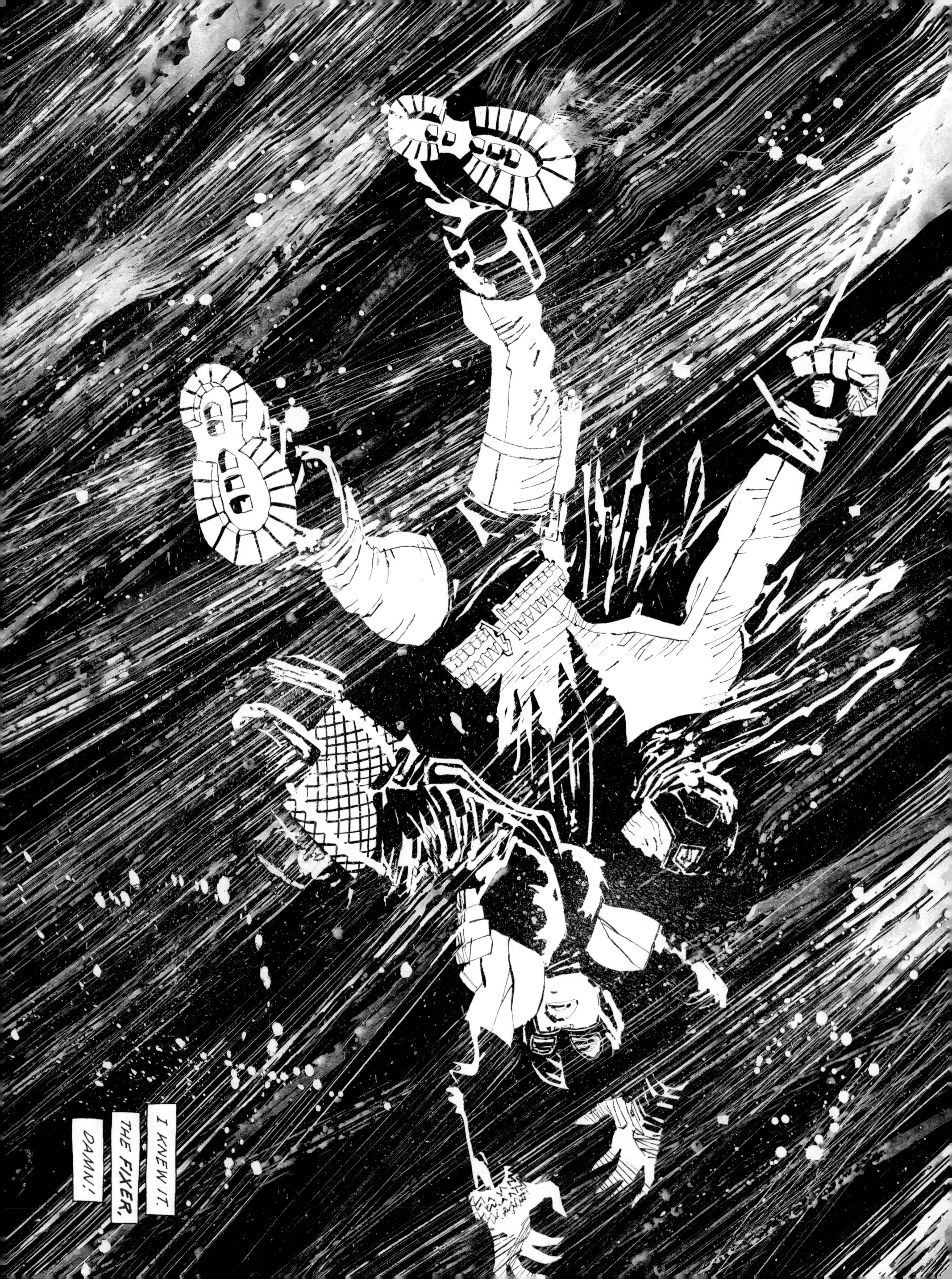
I KNEW IT.
THE FIXER.
DAMN!

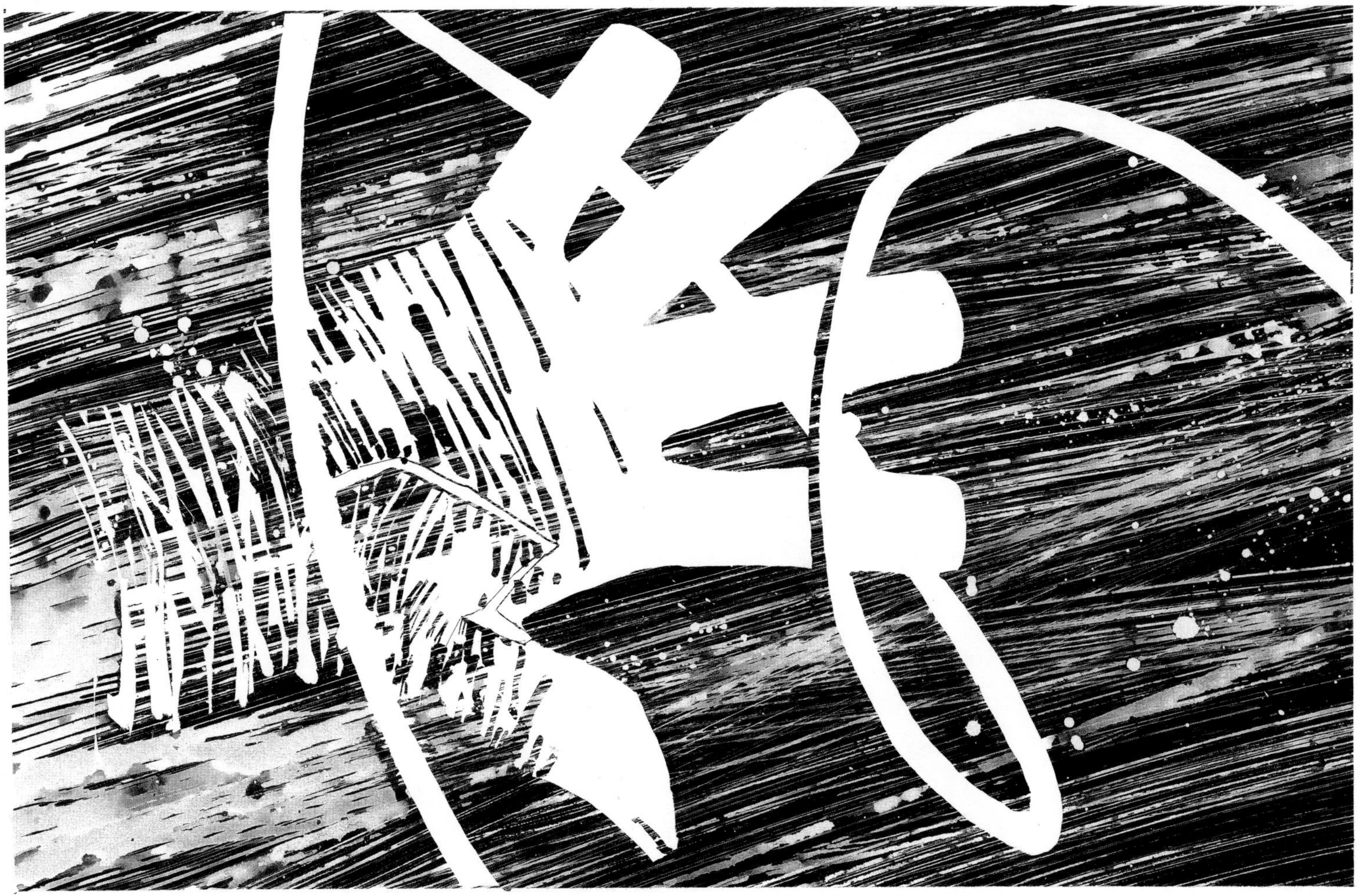

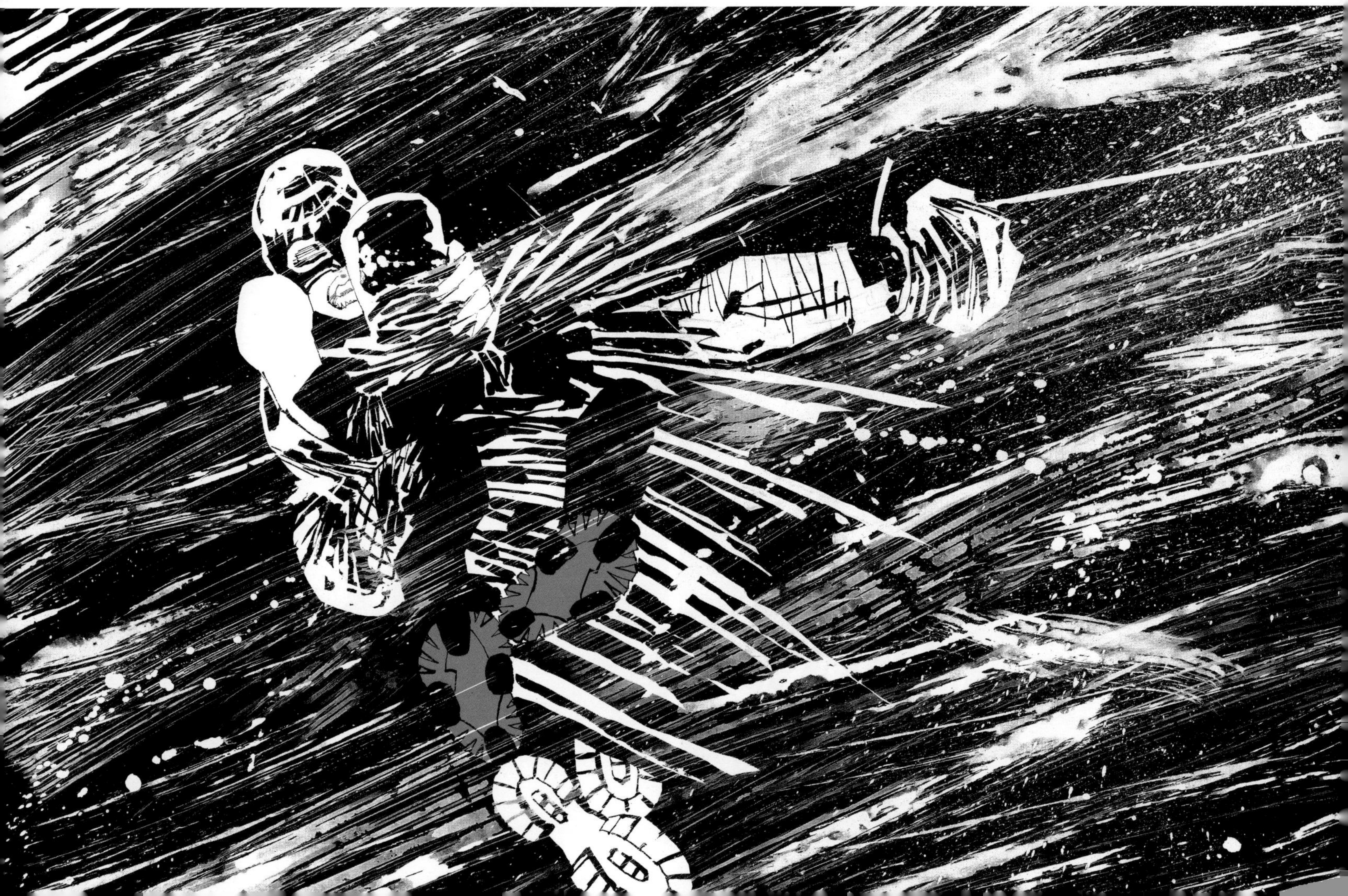

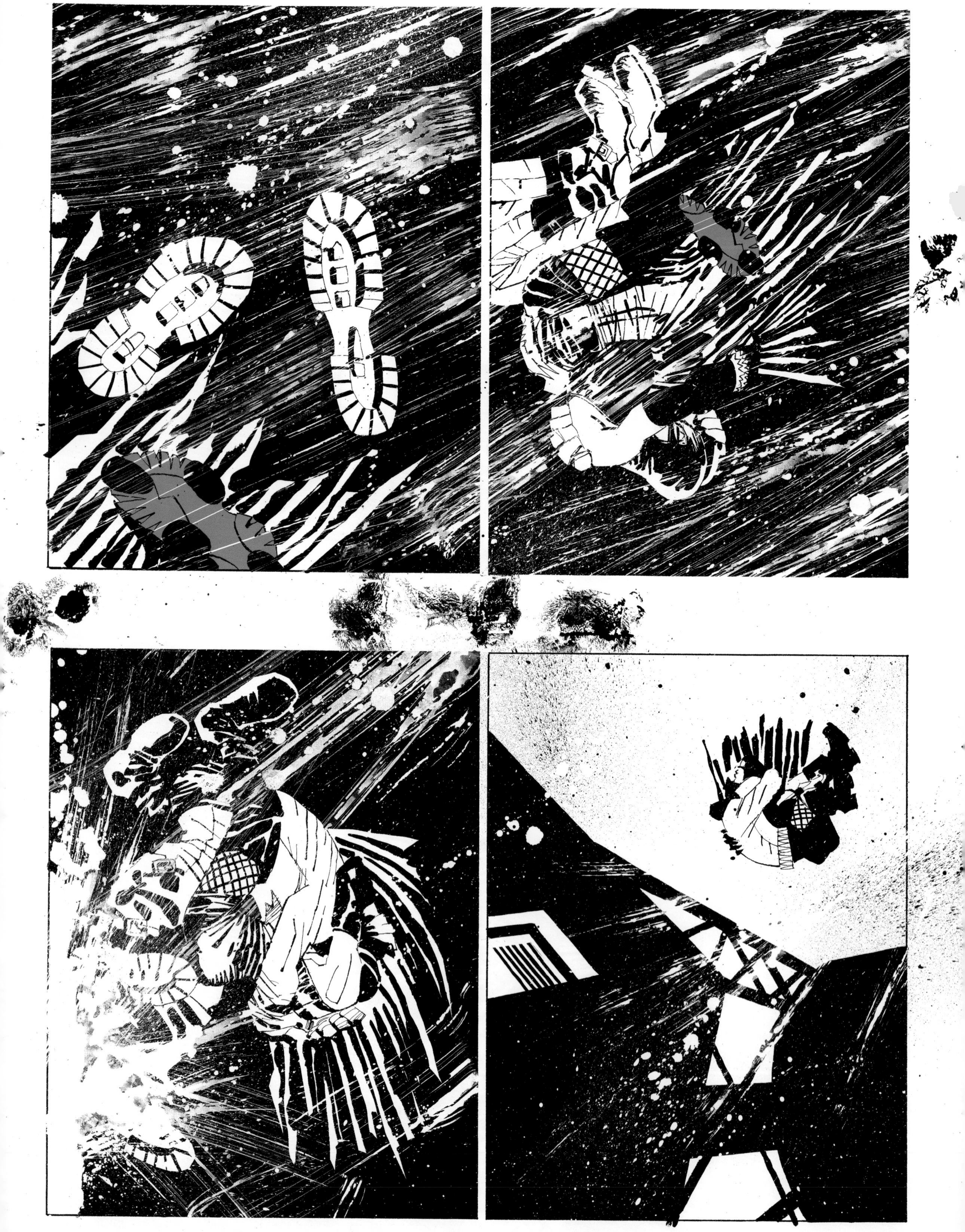

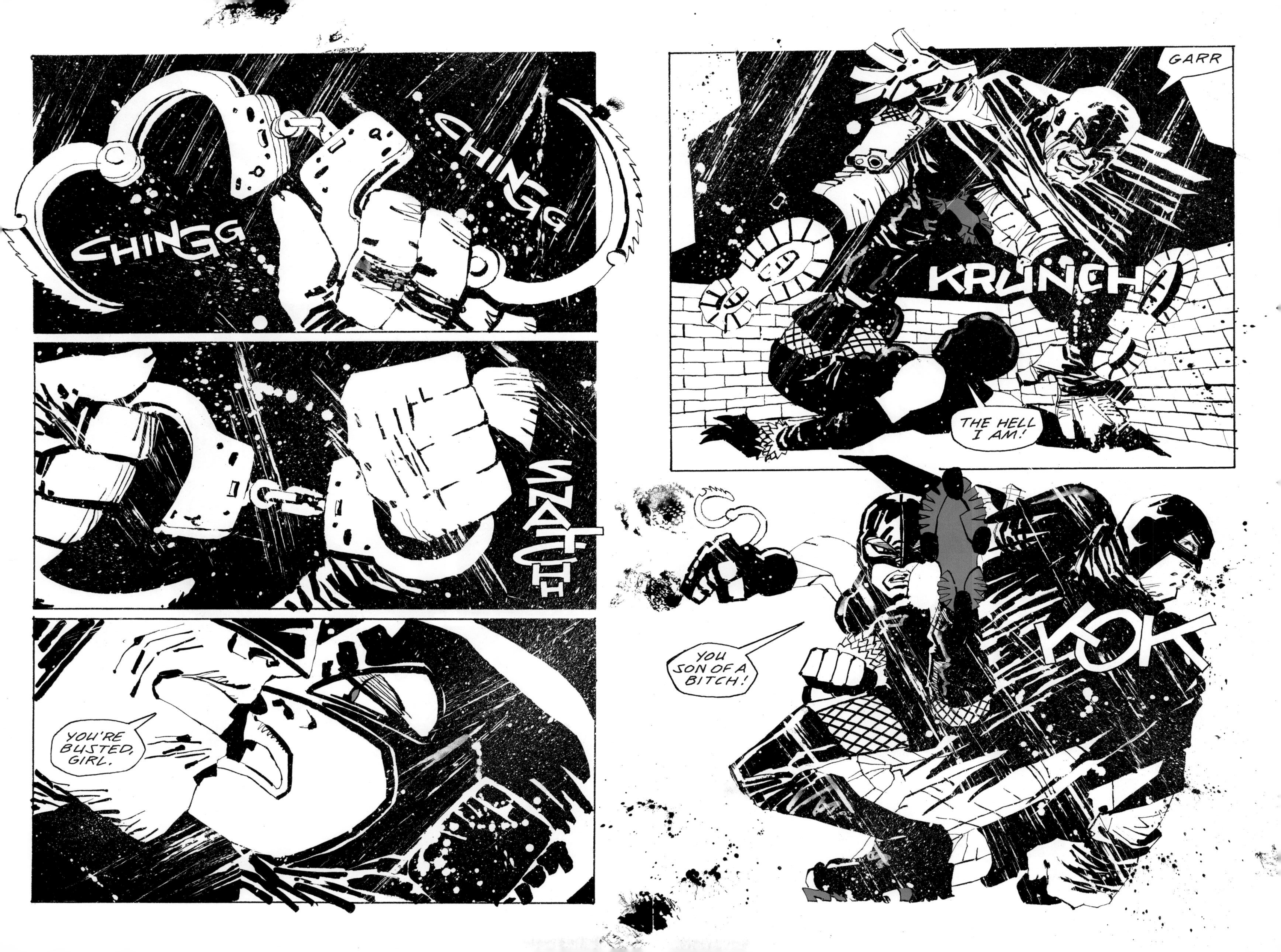
GARR
KRUNCH
THE HELL I AM!
YOU SON OF A BITCH!
KOK
CHINGG
CHINGG
SNATCHH
YOU'RE BUSTED, GIRL.

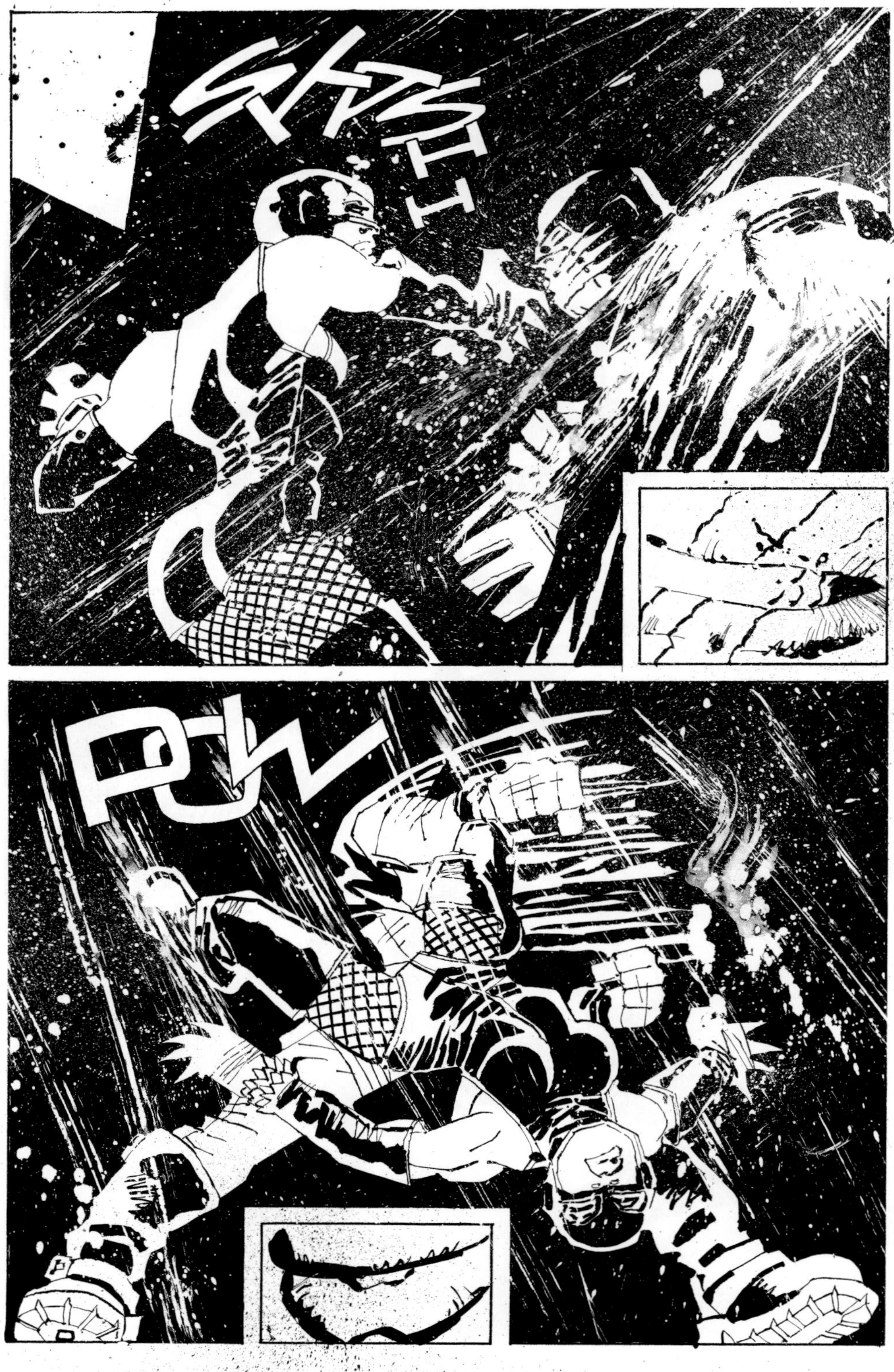
POW

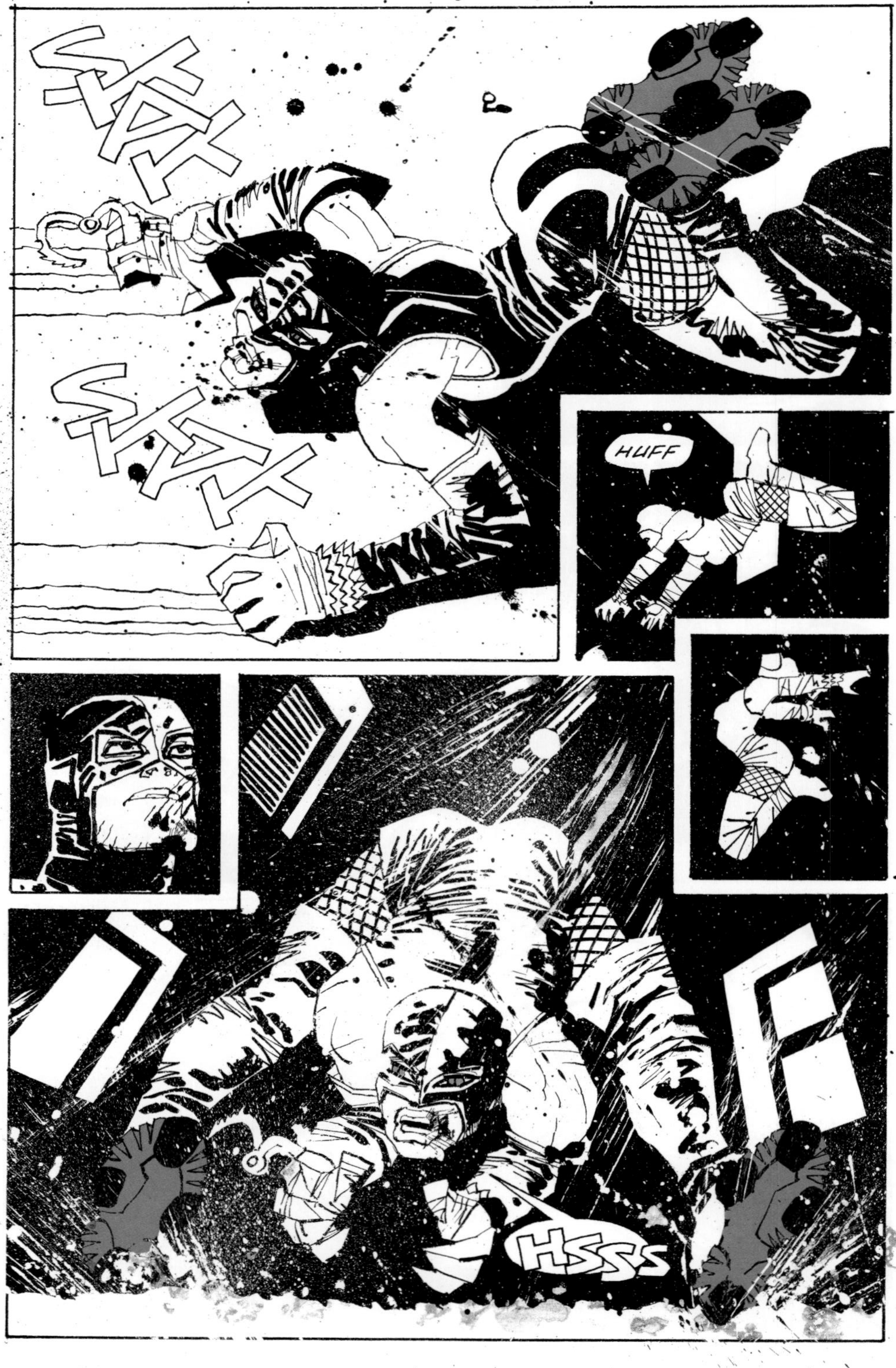
HUFF
HSSS

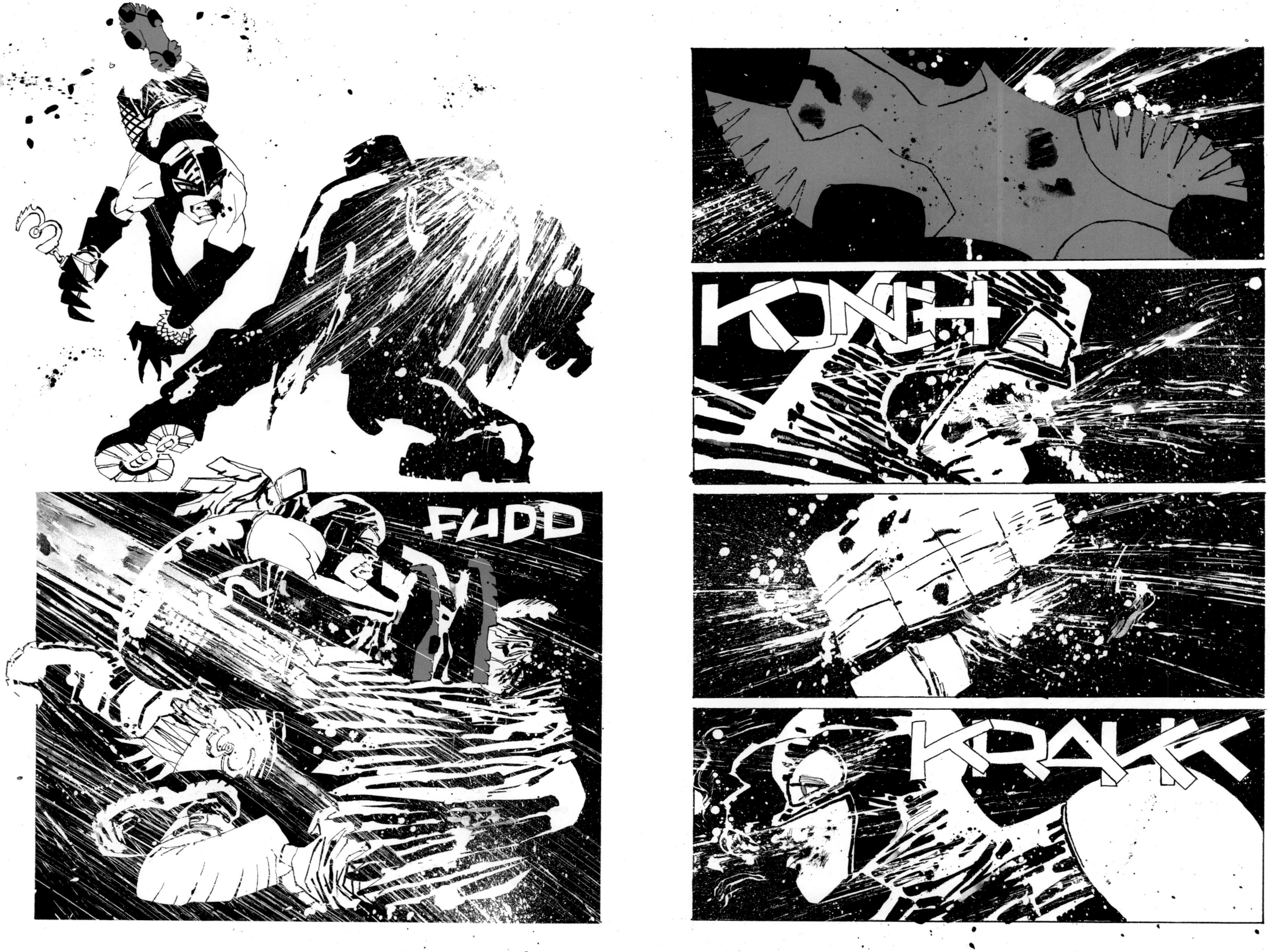
FUDD
KONCH
KRAKK

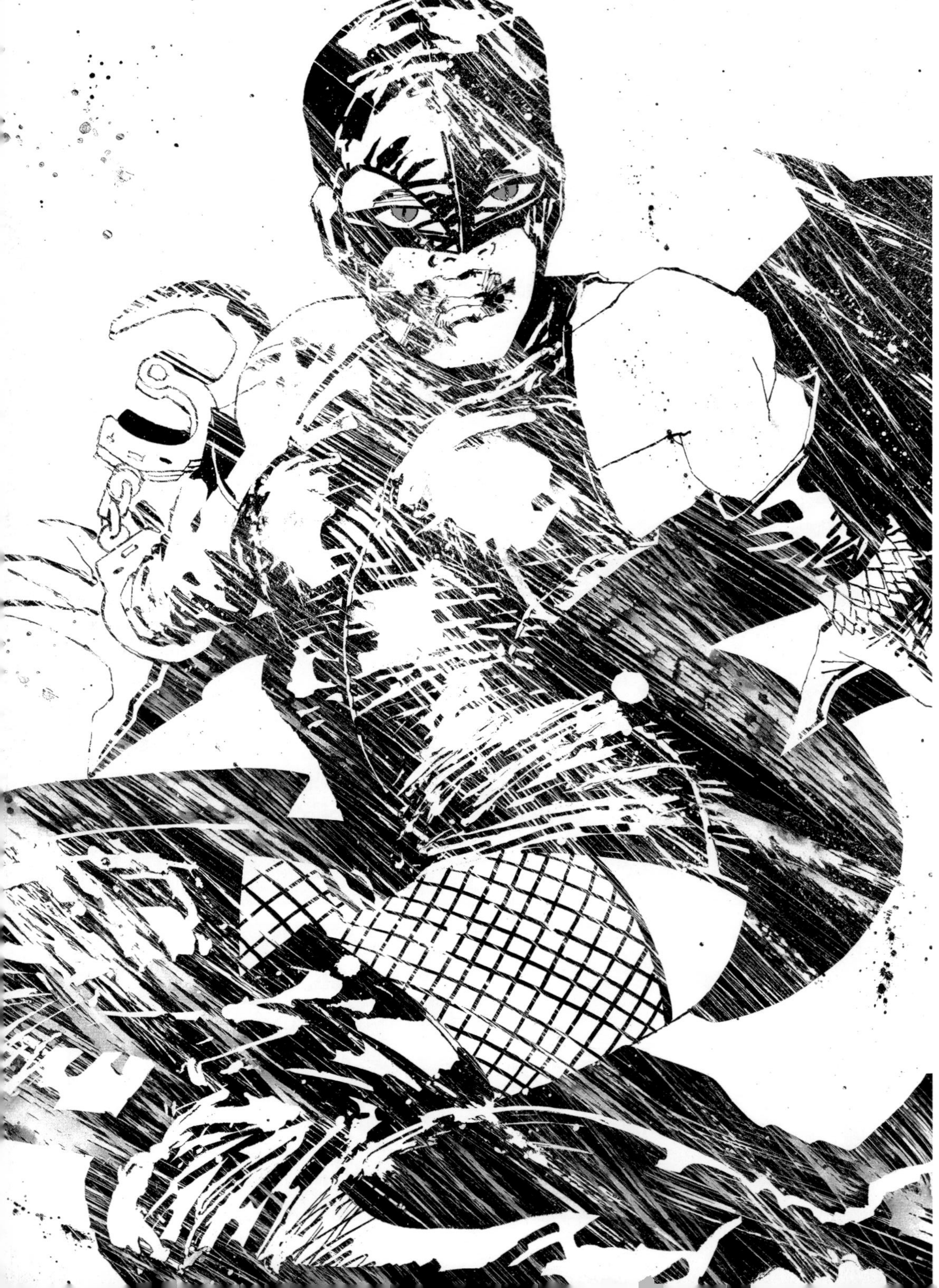

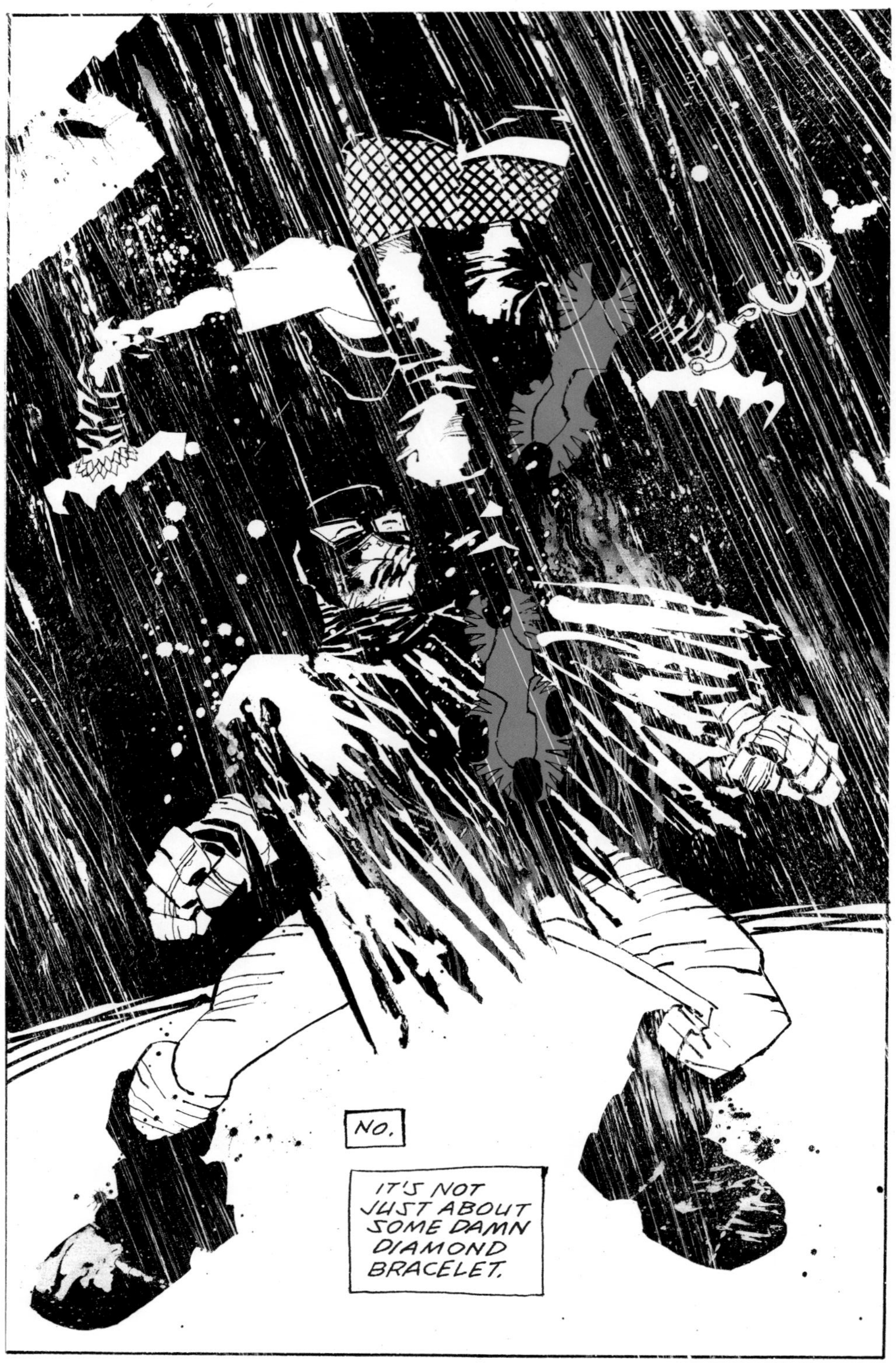
NO.
IT'S NOT JUST ABOUT SOME DAMN DIAMOND BRACELET.

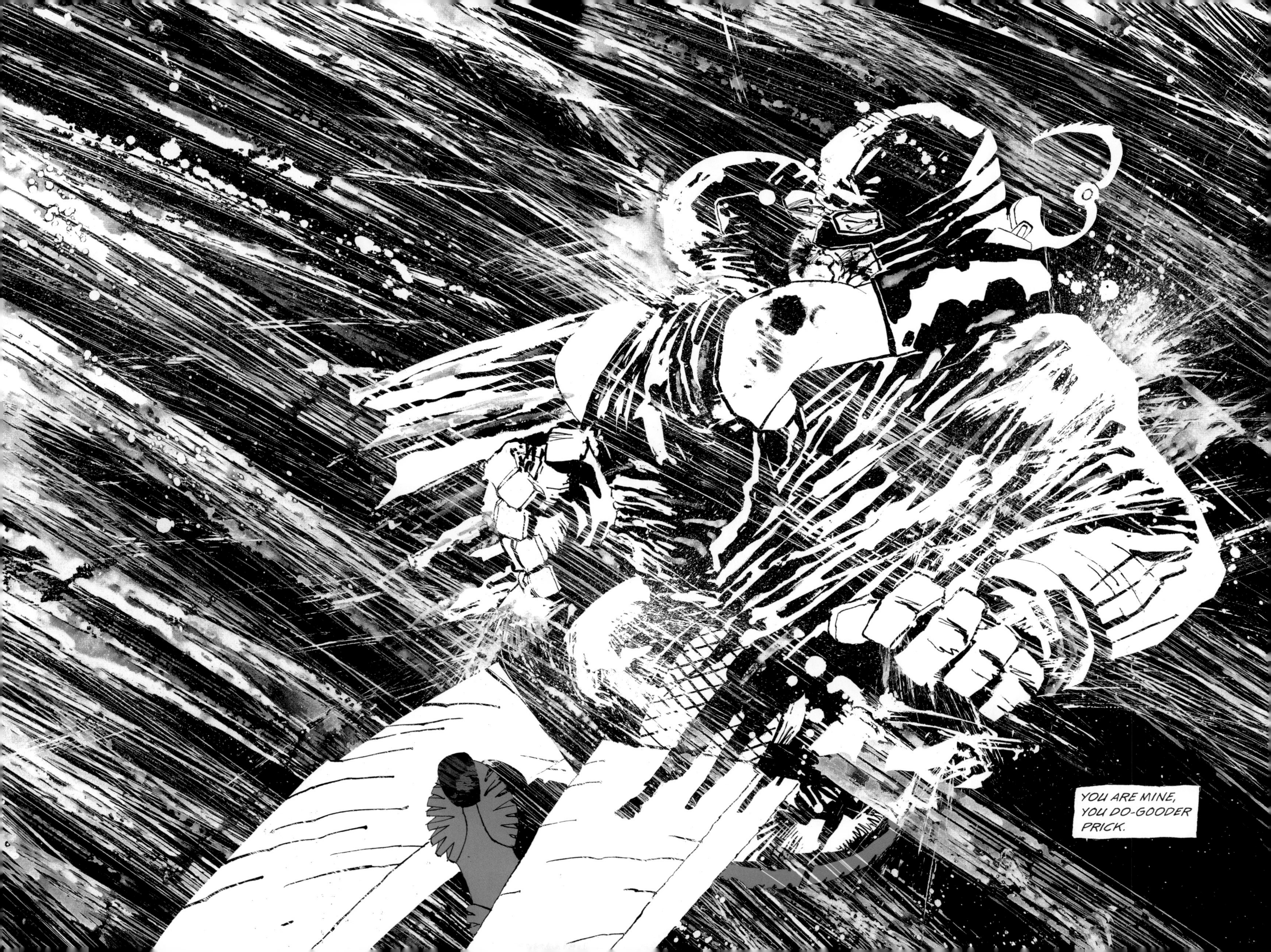
YOU ARE MINE, YOU DO-GOODER PRICK.

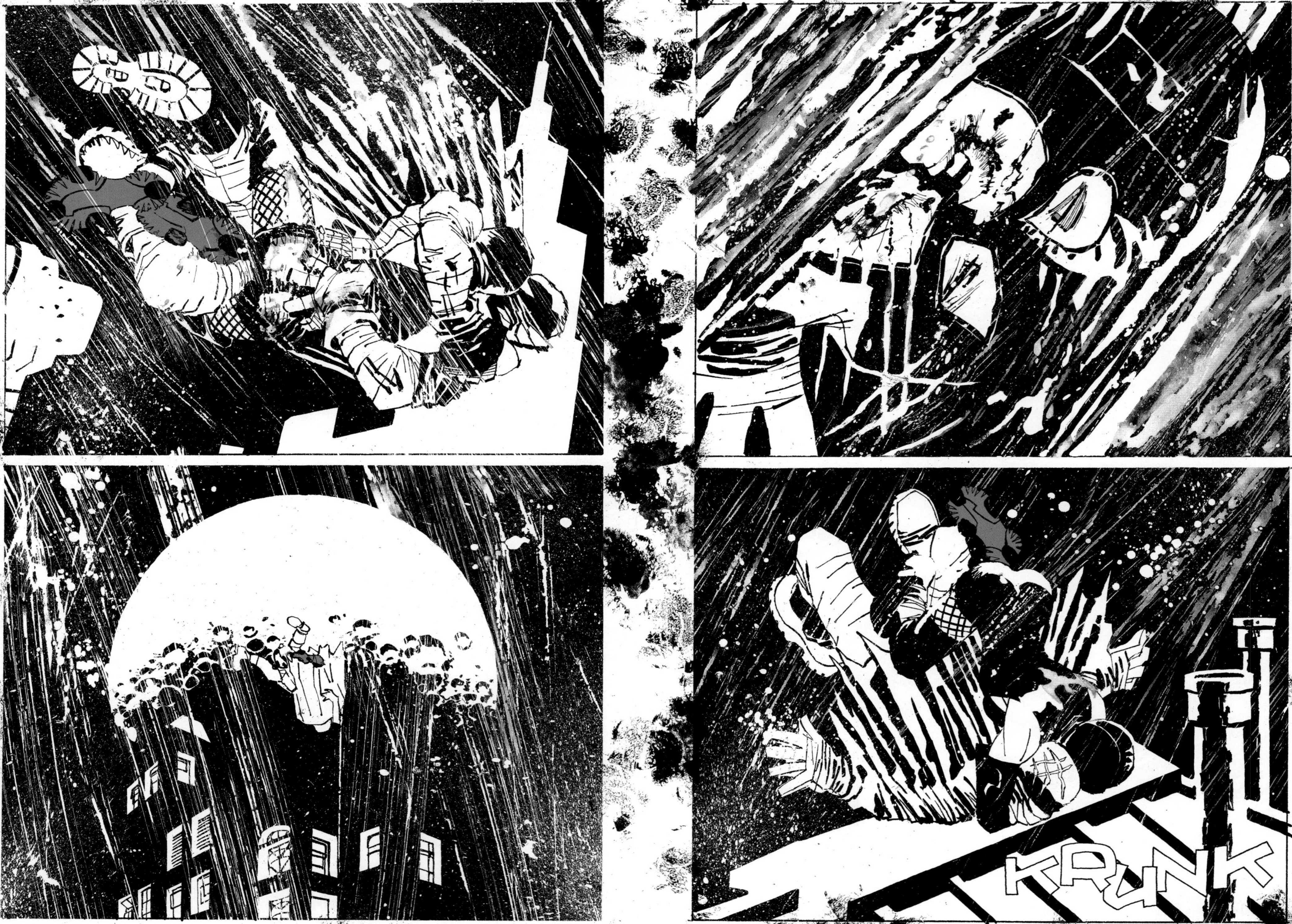
KRUNK

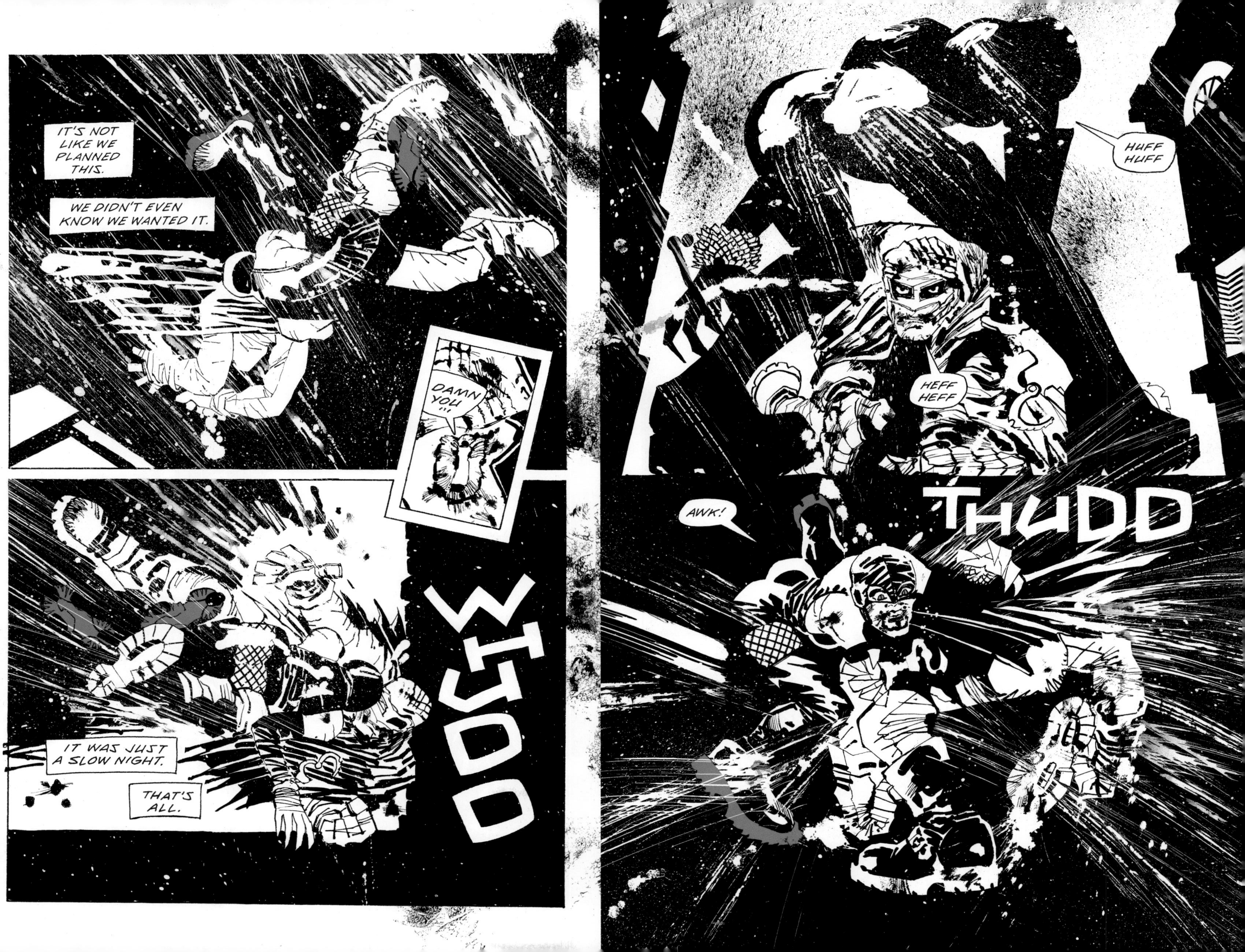
IT'S NOT LIKE WE PLANNED THIS.
WE DIDN'T EVEN KNOW WE WANTED IT.
DAMN YOU ...
WHUDD
IT WAS JUST A SLOW NIGHT.
THAT'S ALL.
HUFF HUFF
HEFF HEFF
THUDD
AWK!

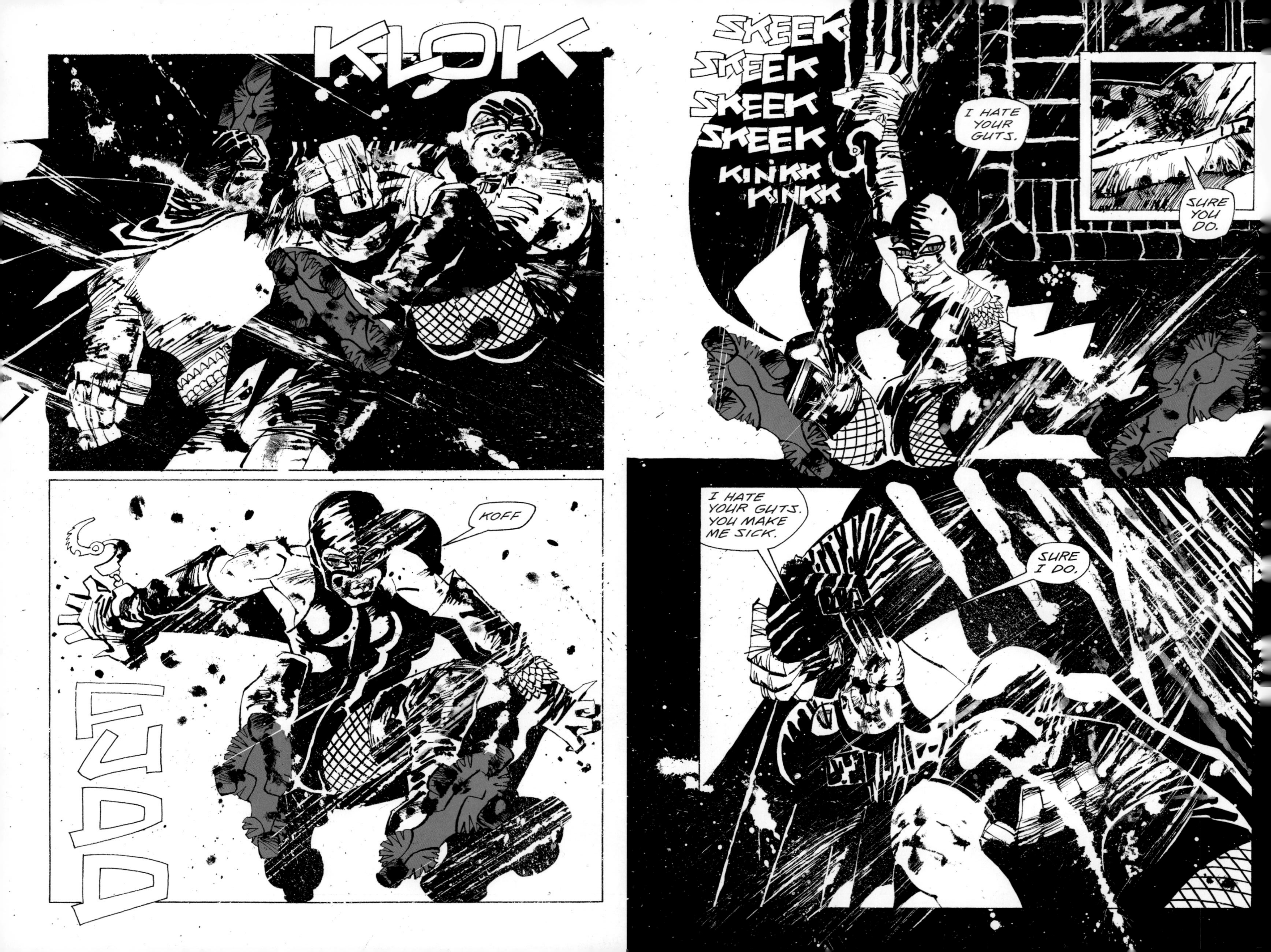
KLOK
KOFF
SKEEK
SKEEK
SKEEK
SKEEK
KINKK
KINKK
I HATE YOUR GUTS.
SURE YOU DO.
I HATE YOUR GUTS. YOU MAKE ME SICK.
SURE I DO.

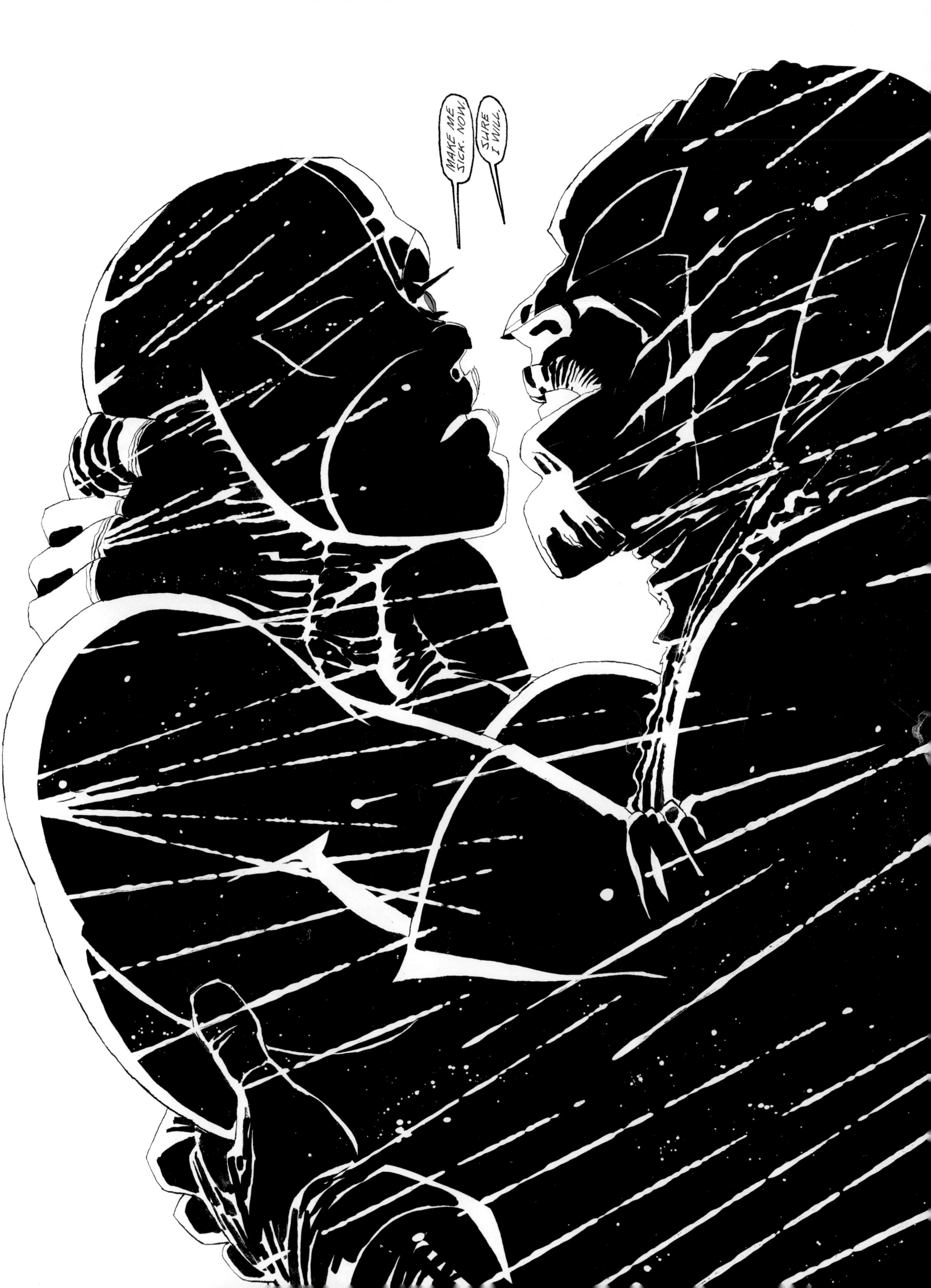
MAKE ME SICK. NOW.
SURE I WILL.

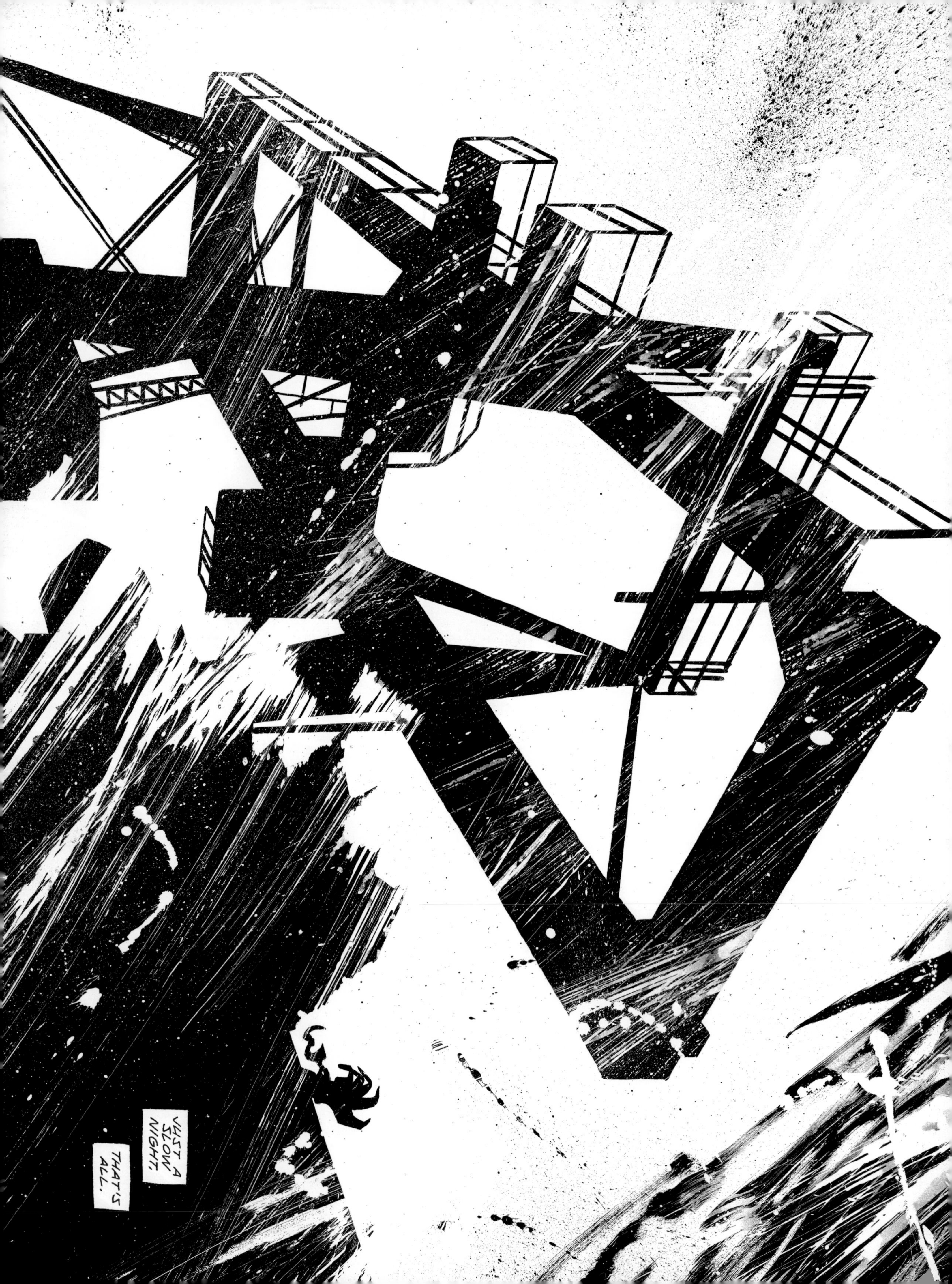
JUST A SLOW NIGHT.
THAT'S ALL.

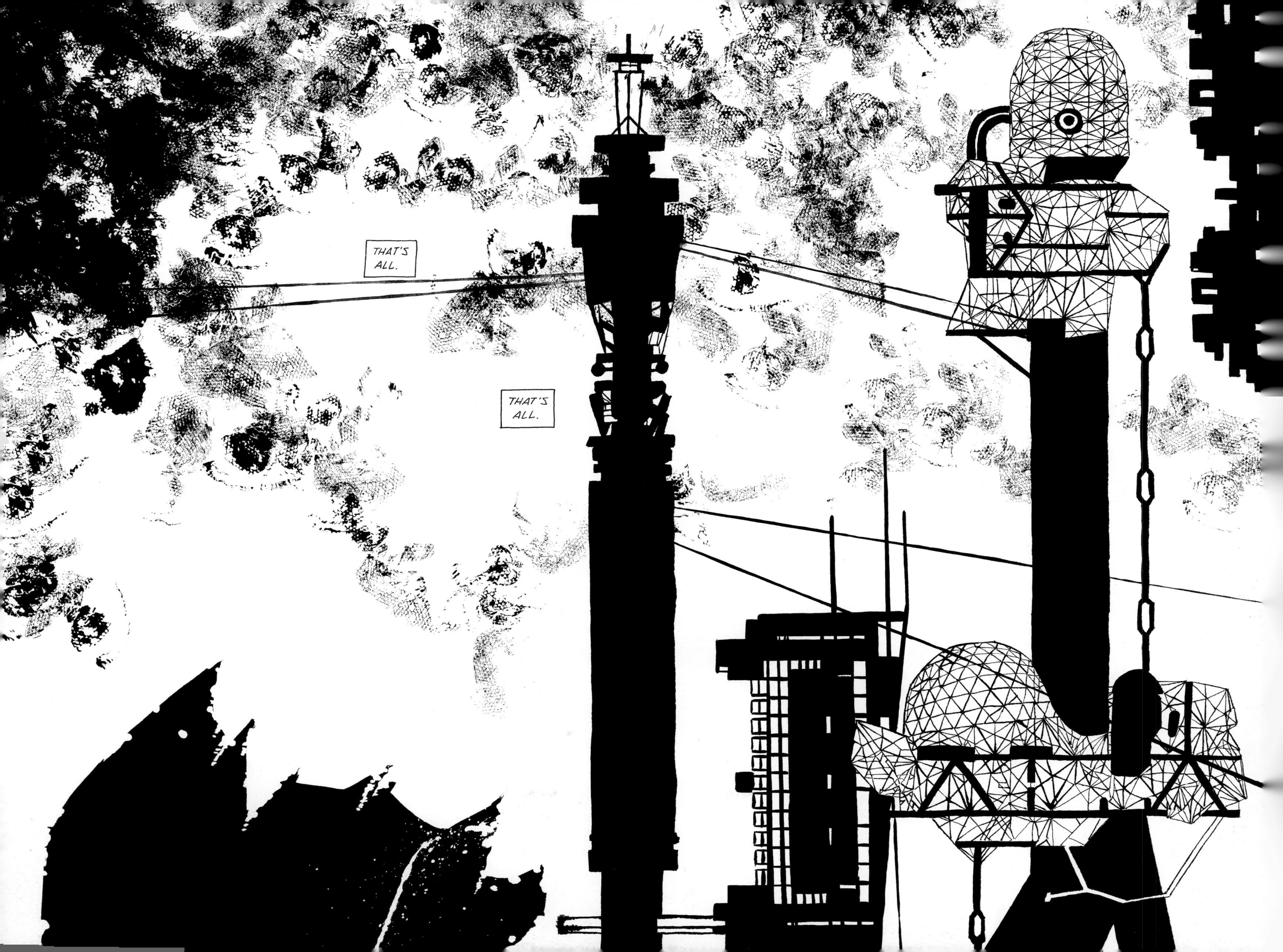
THAT'S ALL.
THAT'S ALL.

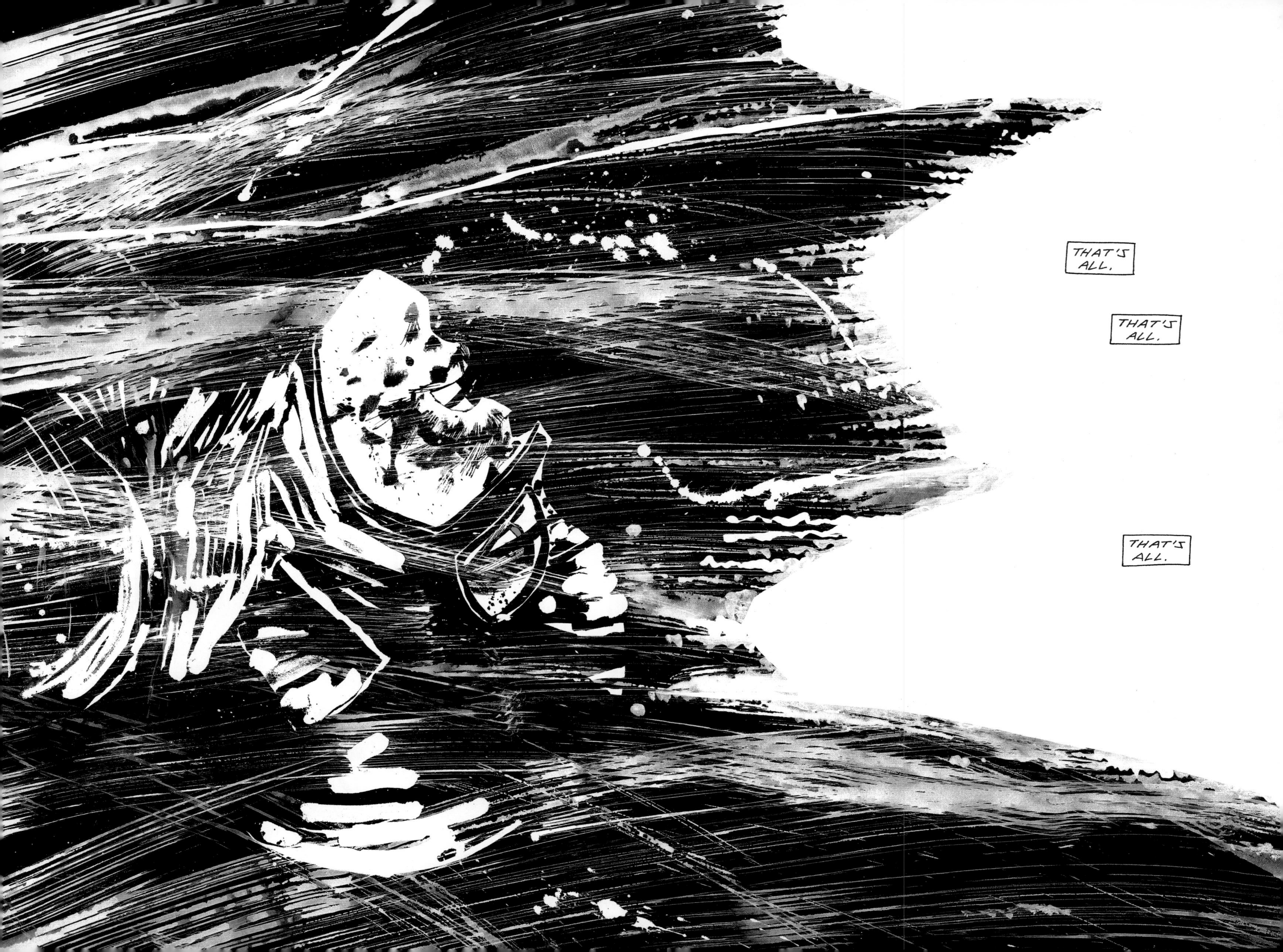
THAT'S ALL.
THAT'S ALL.
THAT'S ALL.

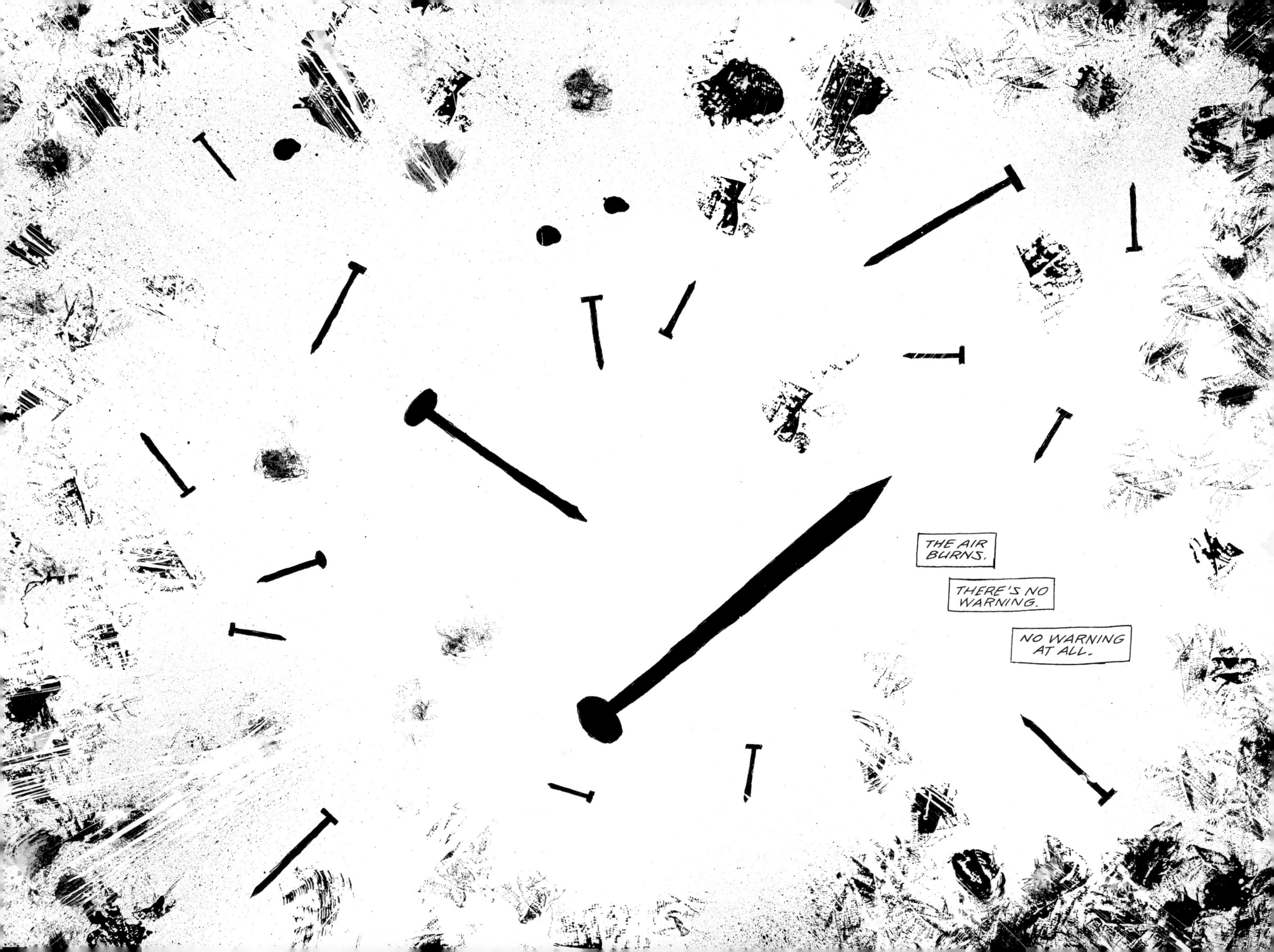
THE AIR BURNS.
THERE'S NO WARNING.
NO WARNING AT ALL.

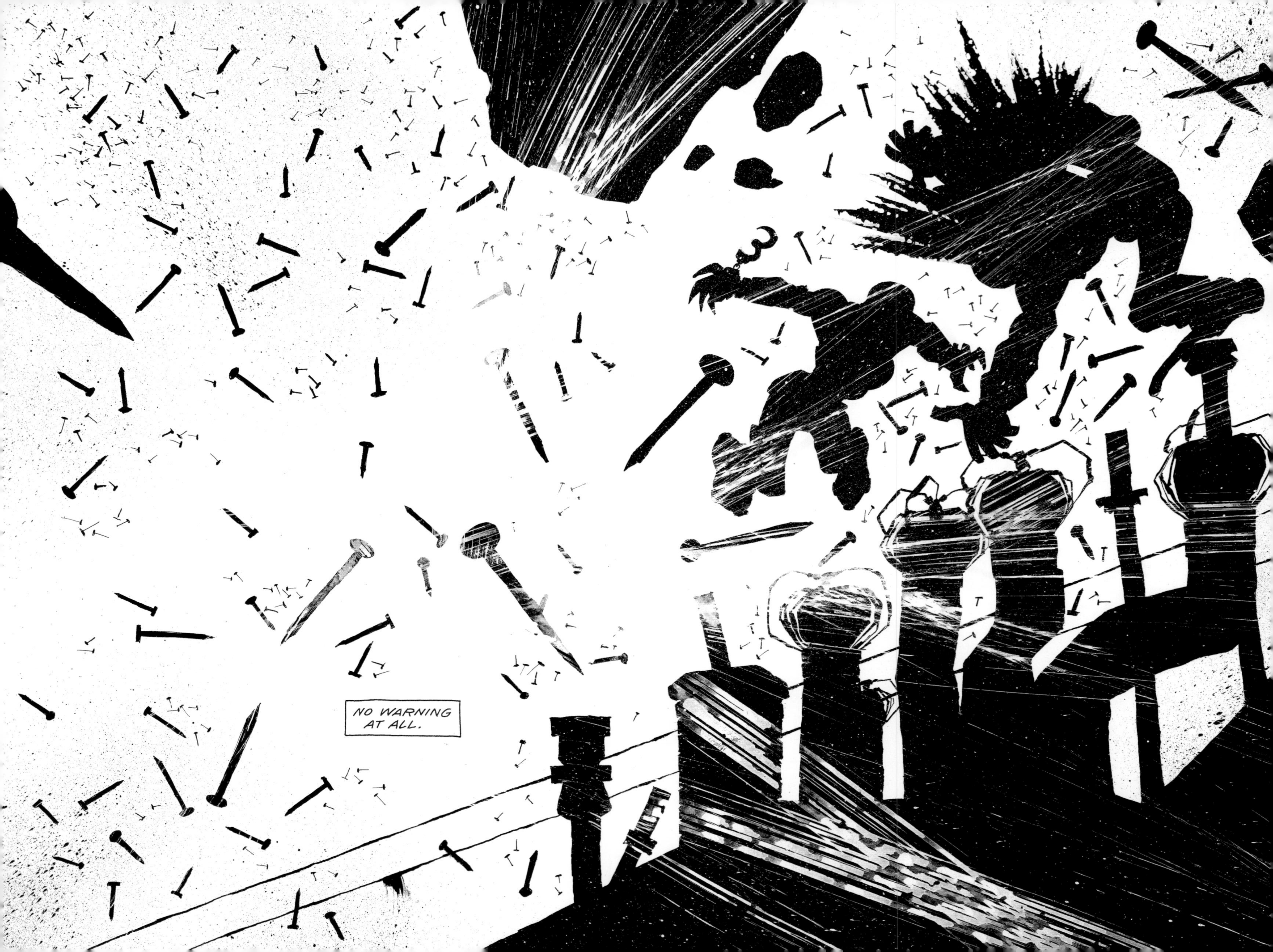
NO WARNING AT ALL.

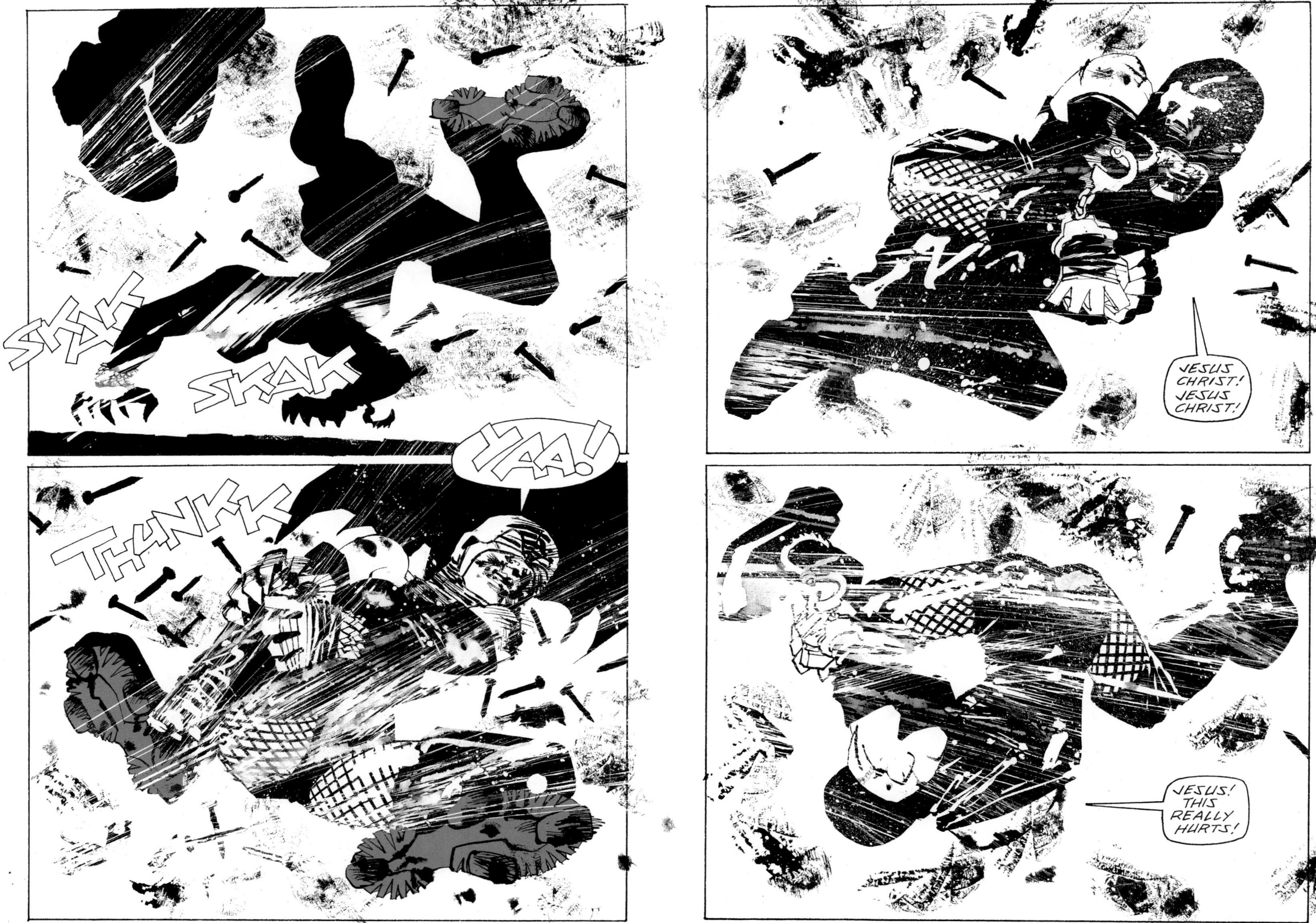
SKAK
SKAK
YAA!
THUNKK
JESUS CHRIST! JESUS CHRIST!
JESUS! THIS REALLY HURTS!

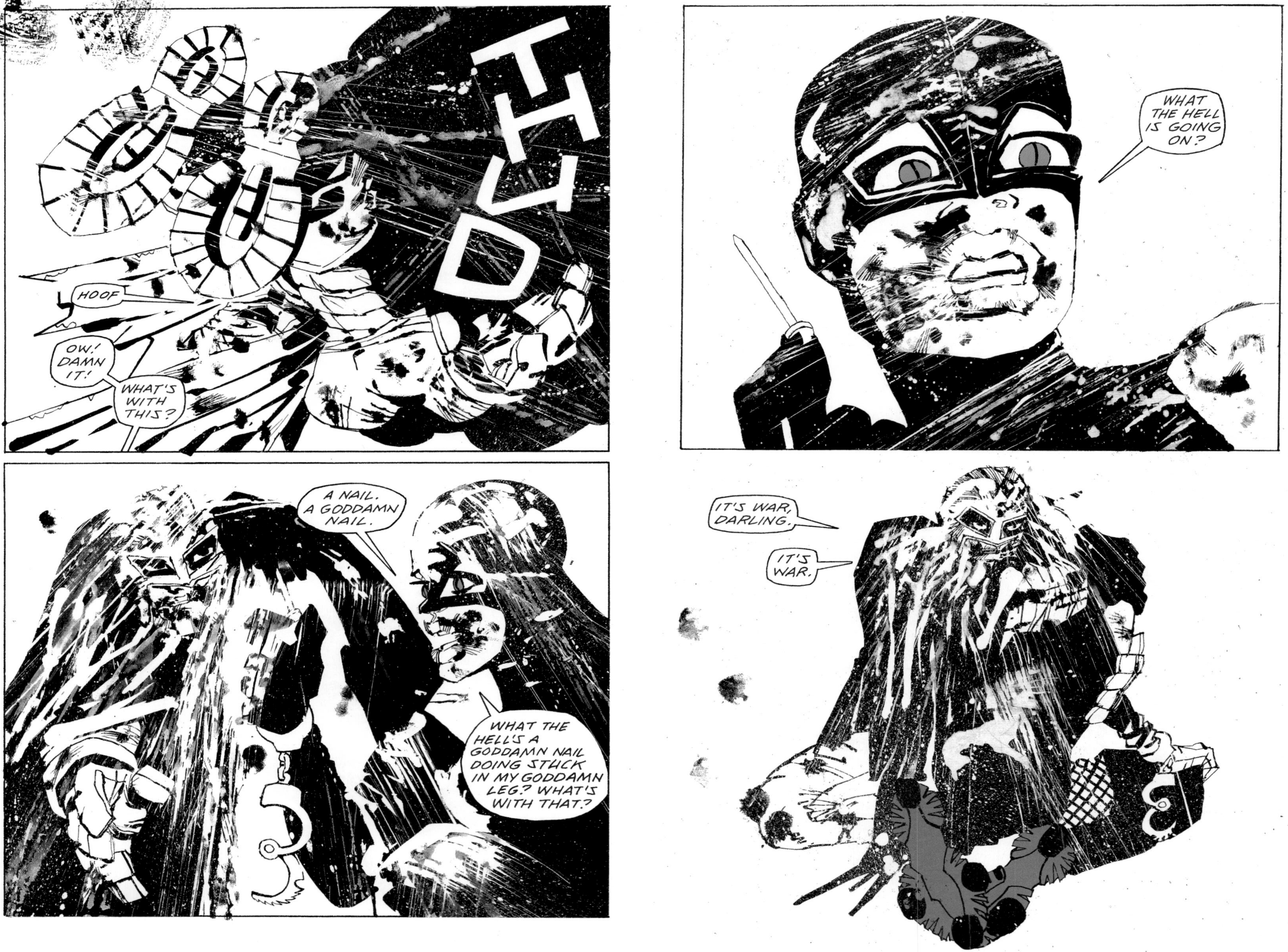
THUD
HOOF
OW! DAMN IT!
WHAT'S WITH THIS?
A NAIL. A GODDAMN NAIL.
WHAT THE HELL'S A GODDAMN NAIL DOING STUCK IN MY GODDAMN LEG? WHAT'S WITH THAT?
WHAT THE HELL IS GOING ON?
IT'S WAR, DARLING.
IT'S WAR.

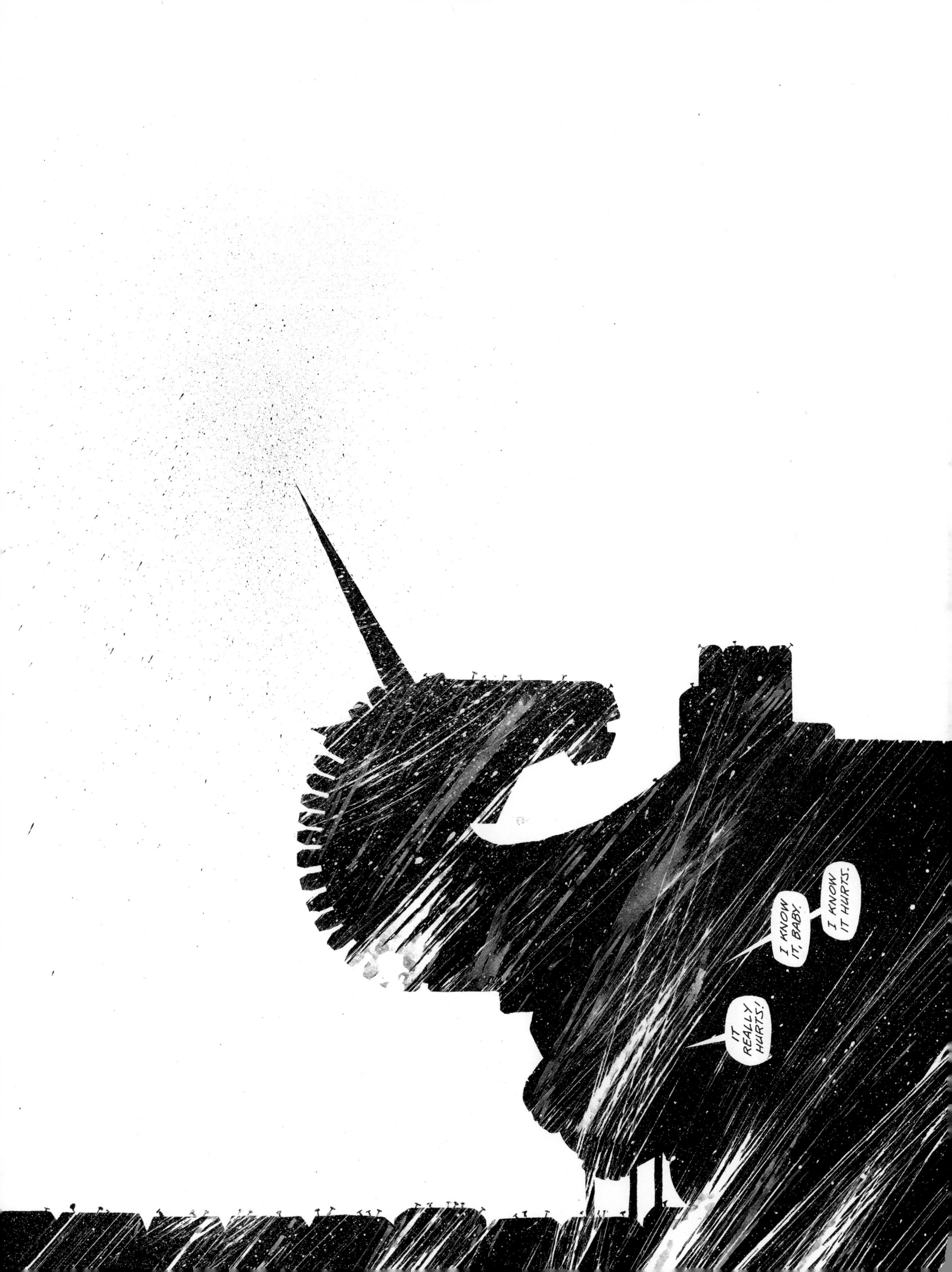
I KNOW IT, BABY.
I KNOW IT HURTS.
IT REALLY HURTS!

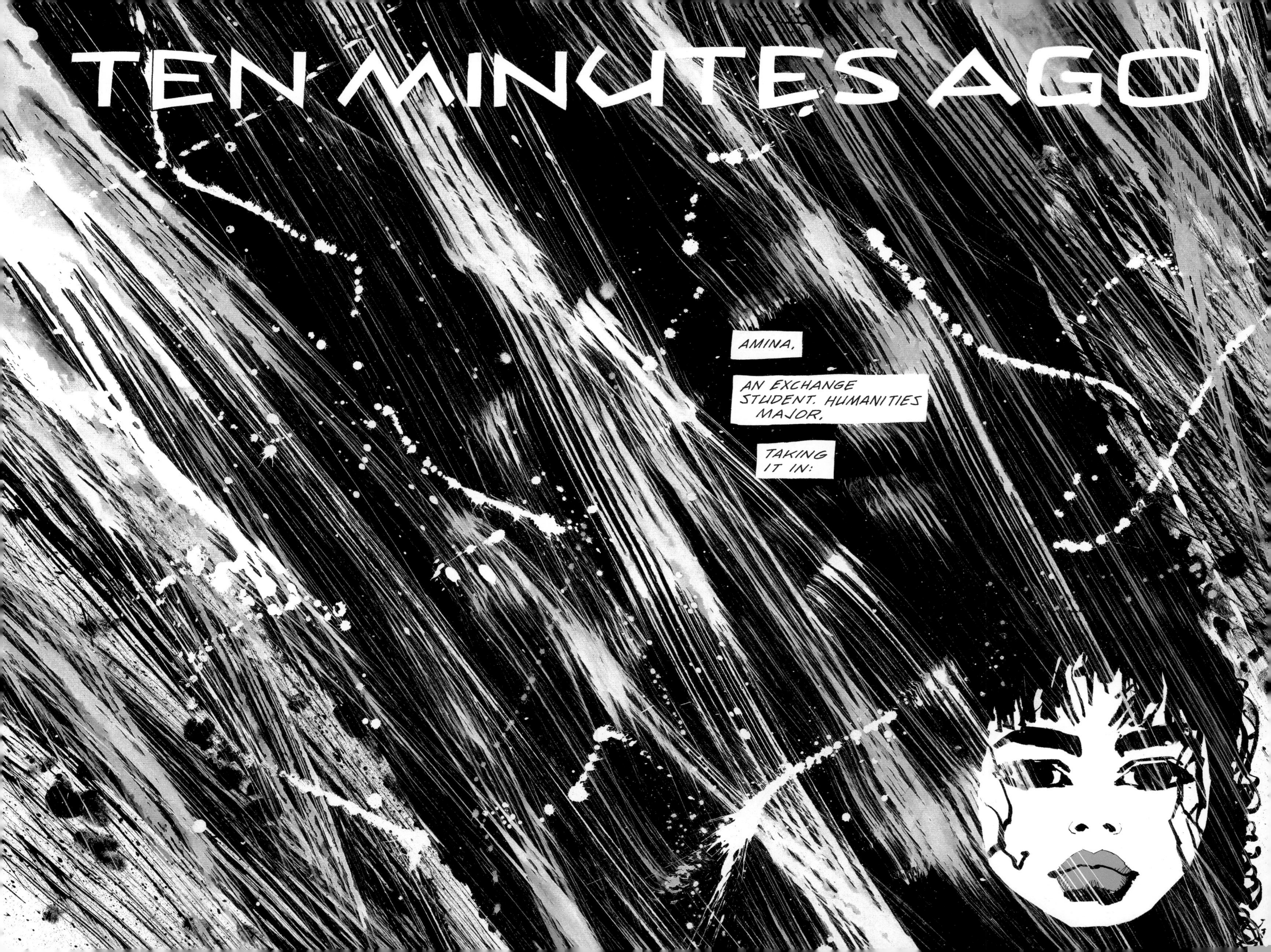
TEN MINUTES AGO
AMINA.
AN EXCHANGE STUDENT. HUMANITIES MAJOR.
TAKING IT IN:

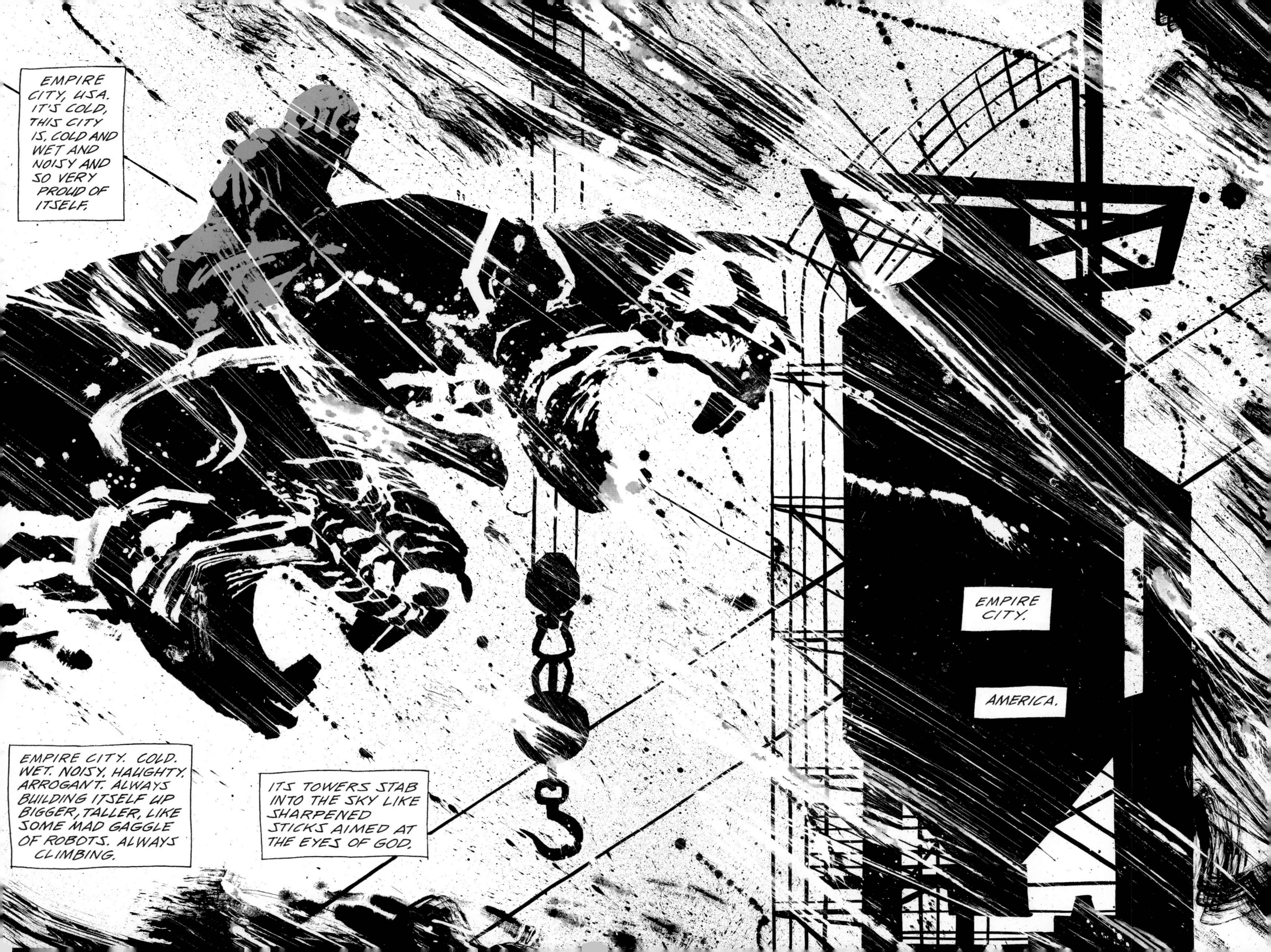
EMPIRE CITY, USA. IT'S COLD, THIS CITY IS, COLD AND WET AND NOISY AND SO VERY PROUD OF ITSELF.
EMPIRE CITY. COLD. WET. NOISY. HAUGHTY. ARROGANT. ALWAYS BUILDING ITSELF UP BIGGER, TALLER, LIKE SOME MAD GAGGLE OF ROBOTS. ALWAYS CLIMBING.
ITS TOWERS STAB INTO THE SKY LIKE SHARPENED STICKS AIMED AT THE EYES OF GOD.
EMPIRE CITY.
AMERICA.

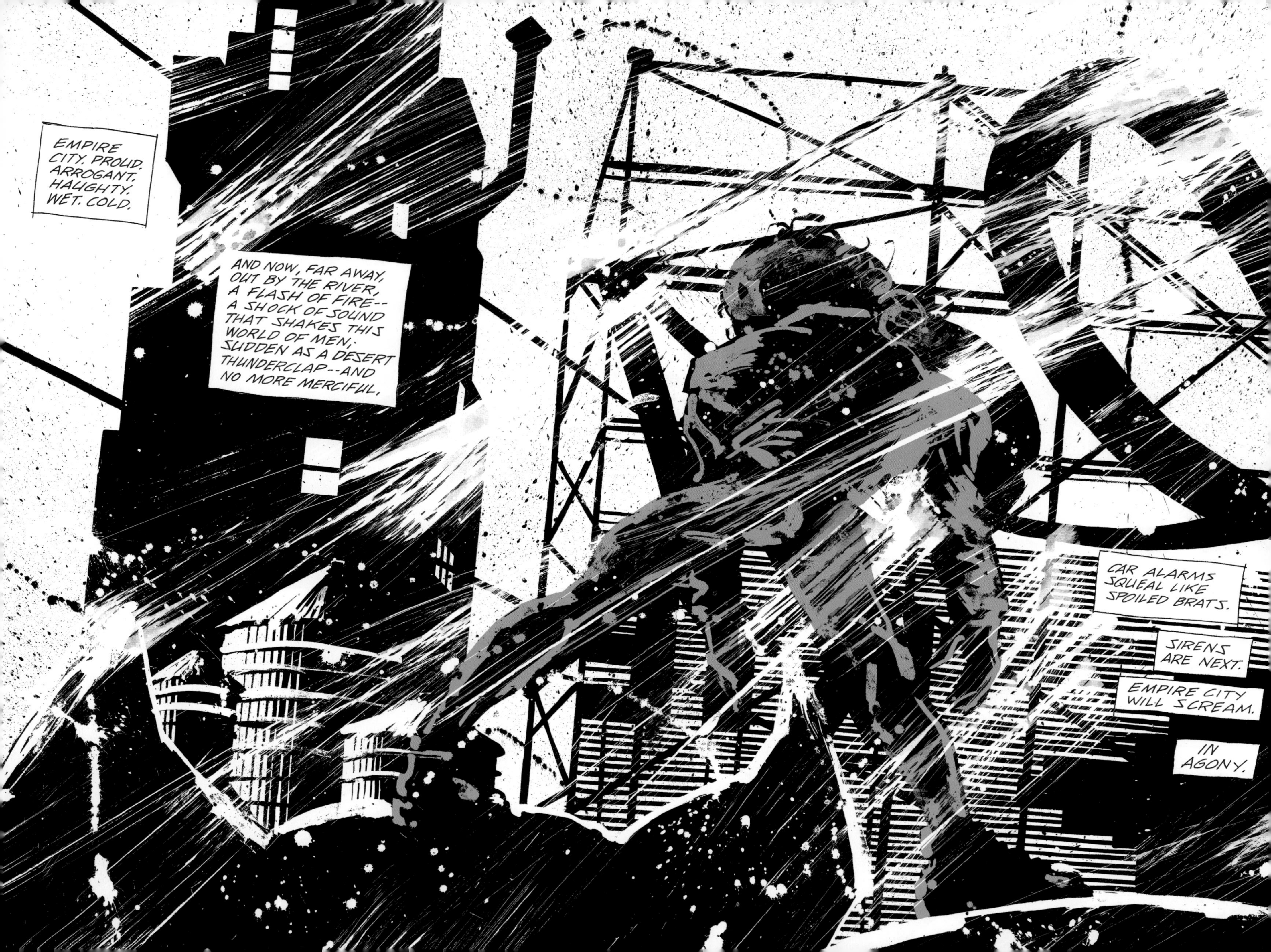
EMPIRE CITY. PROUD. ARROGANT. HAUGHTY. WET. COLD.
AND NOW, FAR AWAY, OUT BY THE RIVER, A FLASH OF FIRE-- A SHOCK OF SOUND THAT SHAKES THIS WORLD OF MEN, SUDDEN AS A DESERT THUNDERCLAP--AND NO MORE MERCIFUL.
CAR ALARMS SQUEAL LIKE SPOILED BRATS.
SIRENS ARE NEXT.
EMPIRE CITY WILL SCREAM.
IN AGONY.

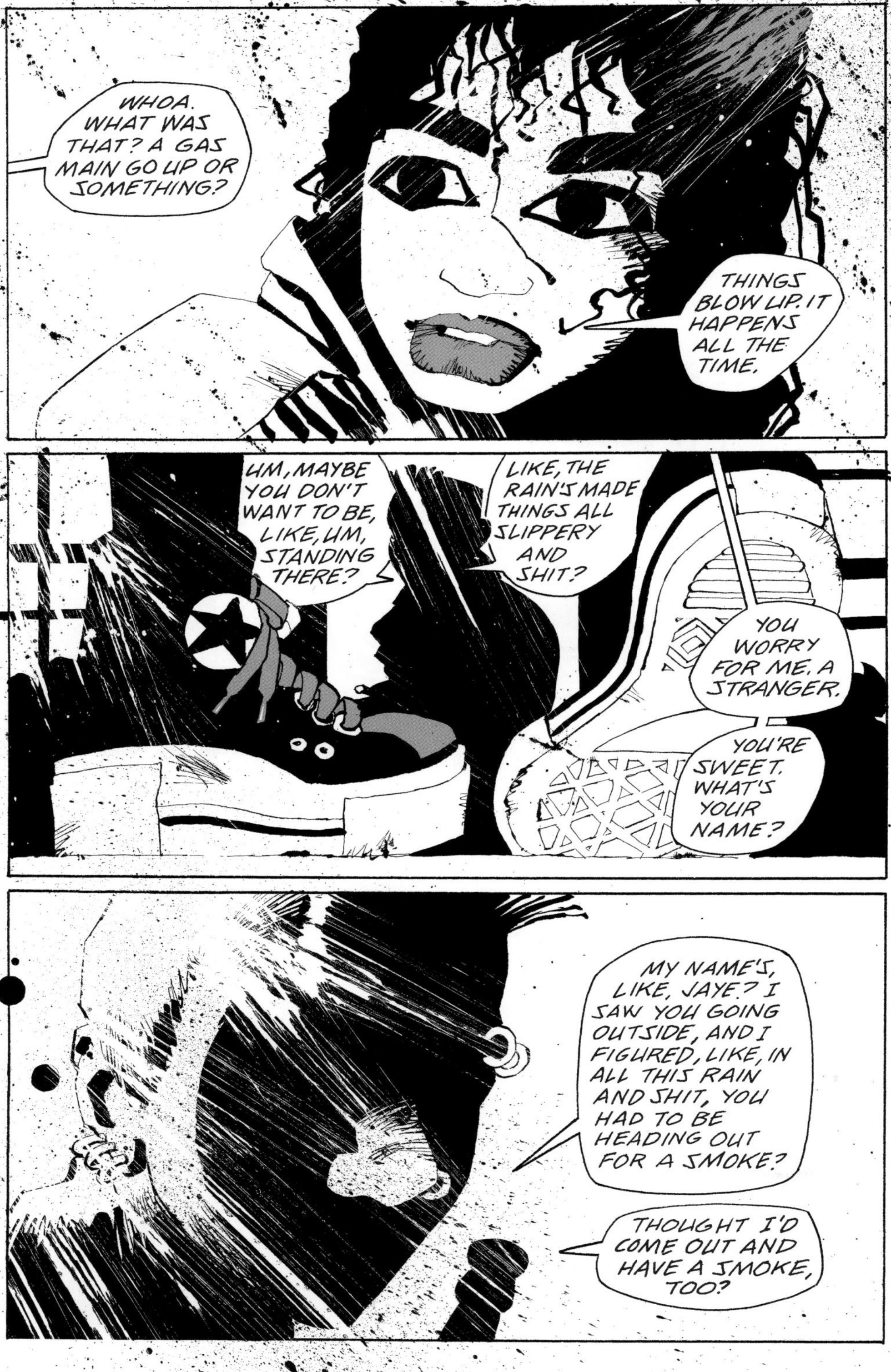
WHOA. WHAT WAS THAT? A GAS MAIN GO UP OR SOMETHING?
THINGS BLOW UP. IT HAPPENS ALL THE TIME.
UM, MAYBE YOU DON'T WANT TO BE, LIKE, UM, STANDING THERE?
LIKE, THE RAIN'S MADE THINGS ALL SLIPPERY AND SHIT?
YOU WORRY FOR ME. A STRANGER.
YOU'RE SWEET. WHAT'S YOUR NAME?
MY NAME'S, LIKE, JAYE? I SAW YOU GOING OUTSIDE, AND I FIGURED, LIKE, IN ALL THIS RAIN AND SHIT, YOU HAD TO BE HEADING OUT FOR A SMOKE?
THOUGHT I'D COME OUT AND HAVE A SMOKE, TOO?

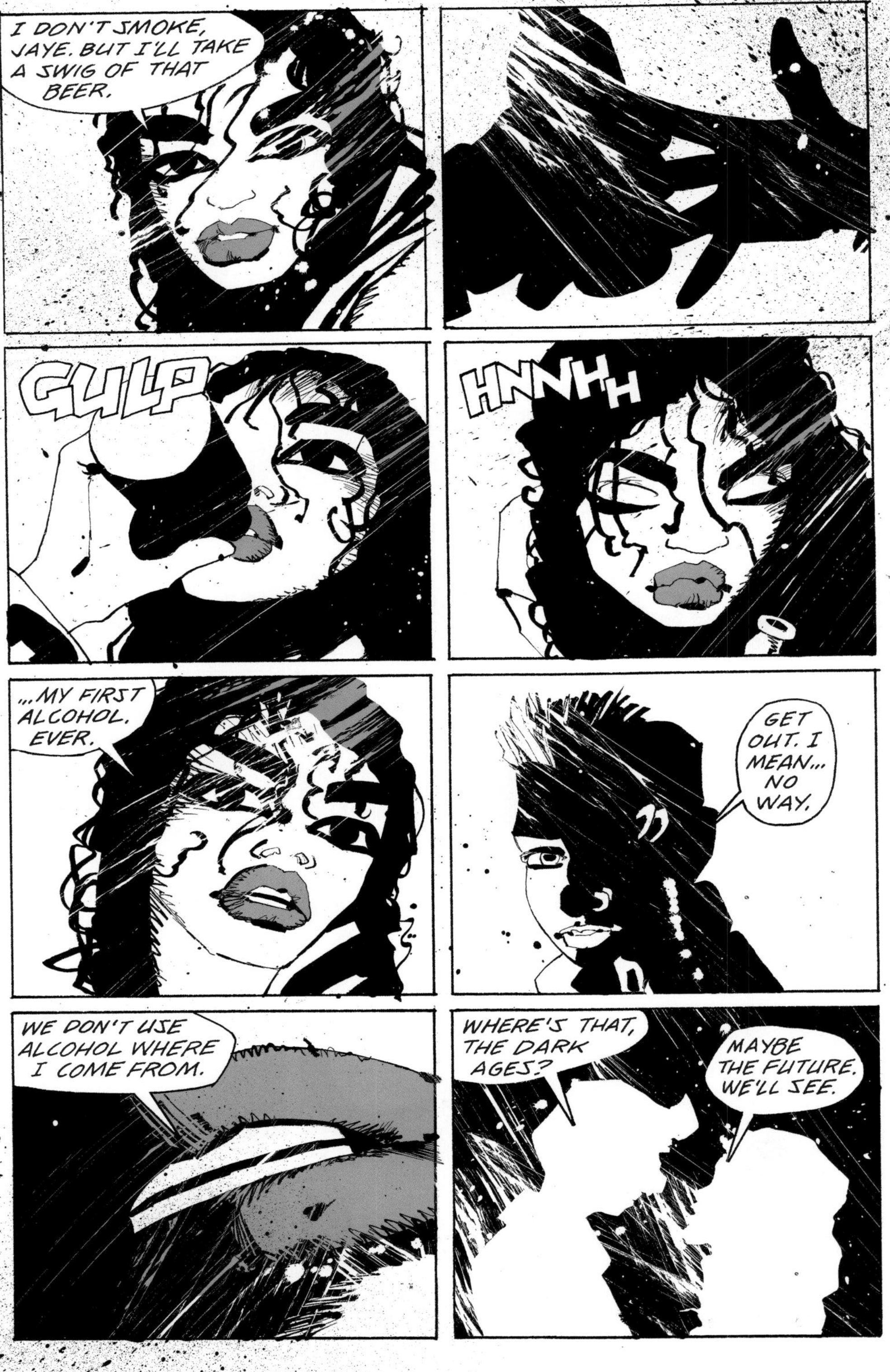
I DON'T SMOKE, JAYE. BUT I'LL TAKE A SWIG OF THAT BEER.
GULP
HNNHH
...MY FIRST ALCOHOL, EVER.
GET OUT. I MEAN... NO WAY.
WE DON'T USE ALCOHOL WHERE I COME FROM.
WHERE'S THAT, THE DARK AGES?
MAYBE THE FUTURE. WE'LL SEE.

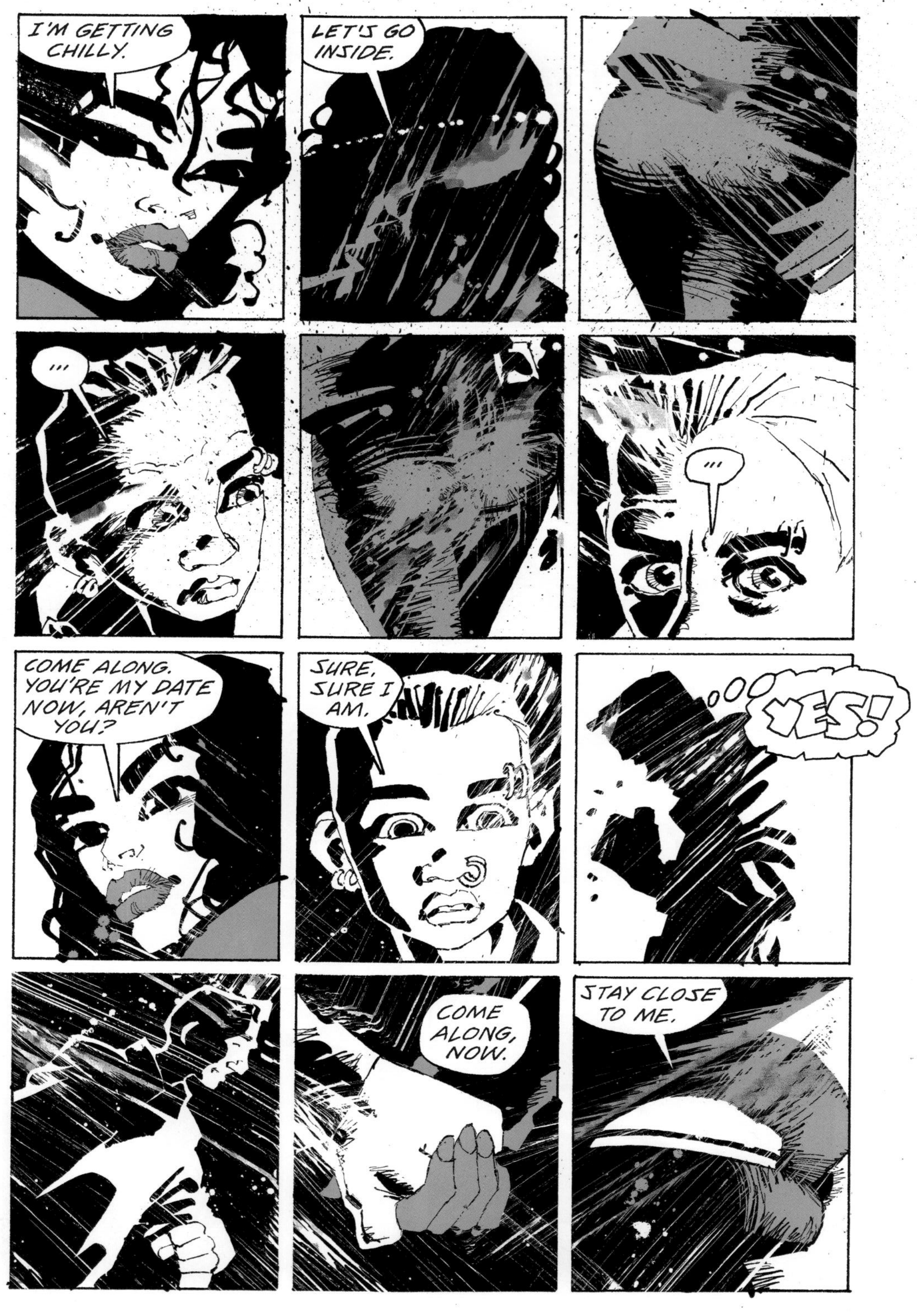
I'M GETTING CHILLY.
LET'S GO INSIDE.
...
...
COME ALONG. YOU'RE MY DATE NOW, AREN'T YOU?
SURE, SURE I AM.
OOO YES!
COME ALONG, NOW.
STAY CLOSE TO ME.

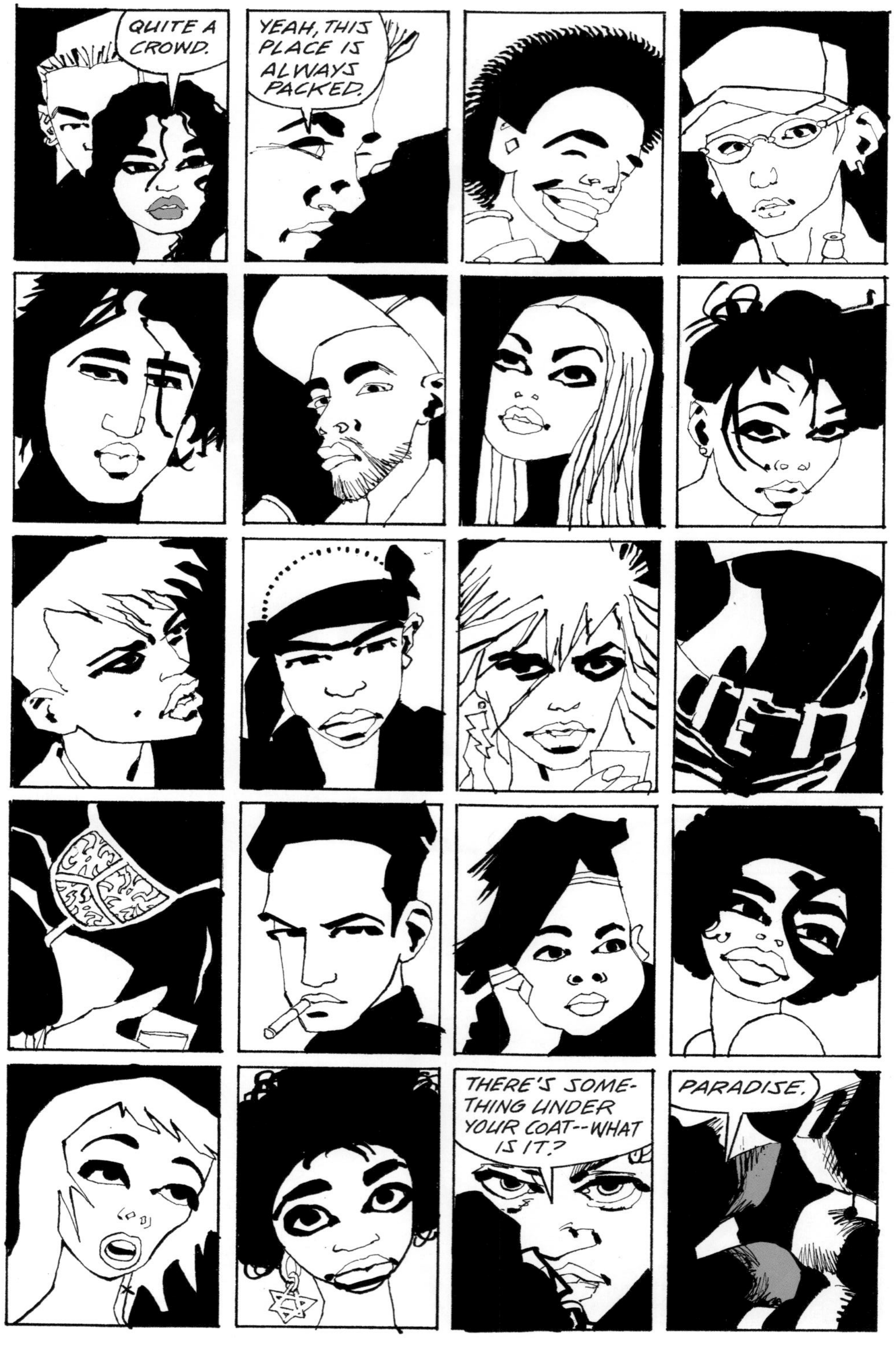
QUITE A CROWD.
YEAH, THIS PLACE IS ALWAYS PACKED.
THERE'S SOME-THING UNDER YOUR COAT--WHAT IS IT?
PARADISE.

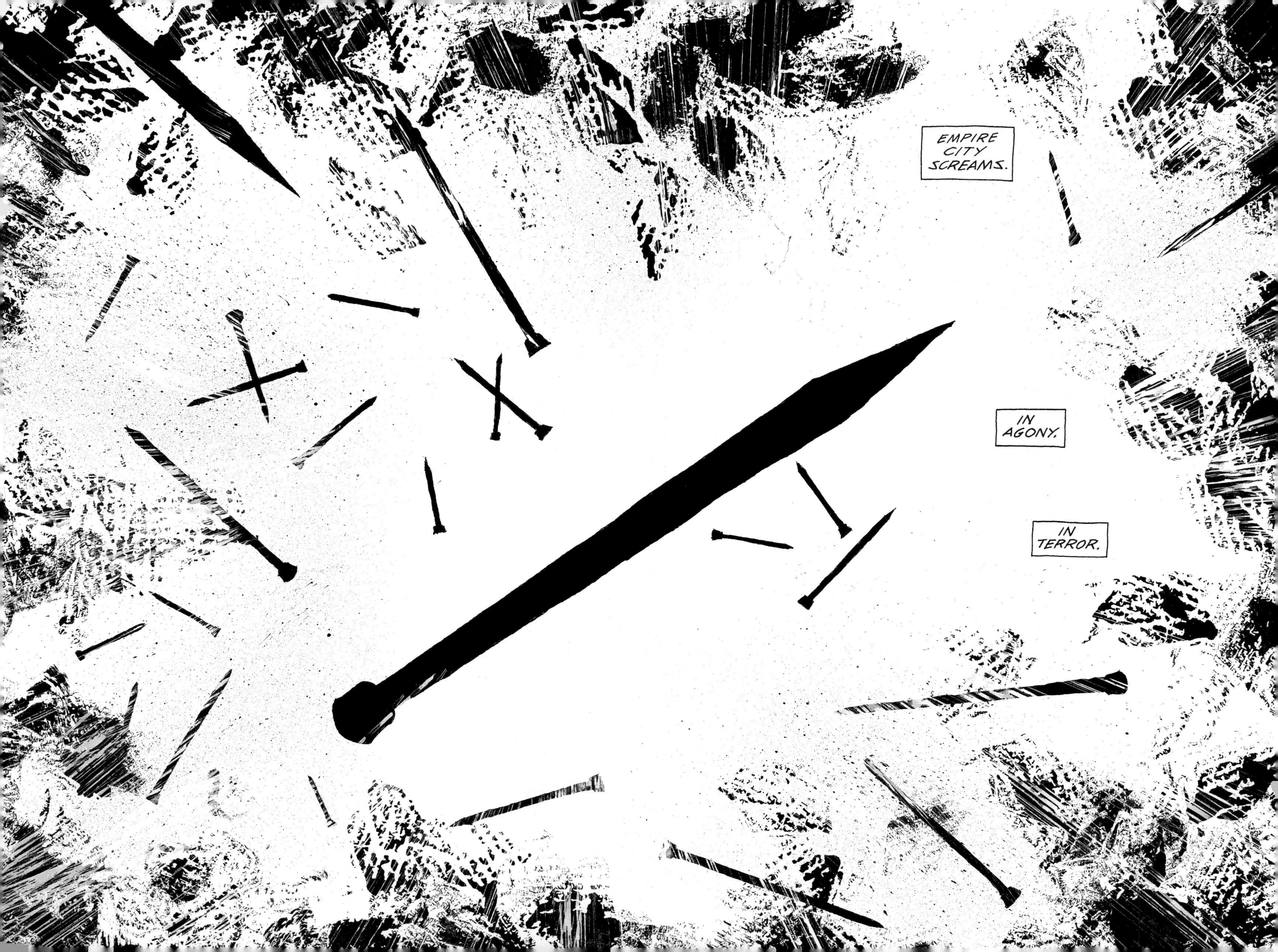
EMPIRE CITY SCREAMS.
IN AGONY.
IN TERROR.

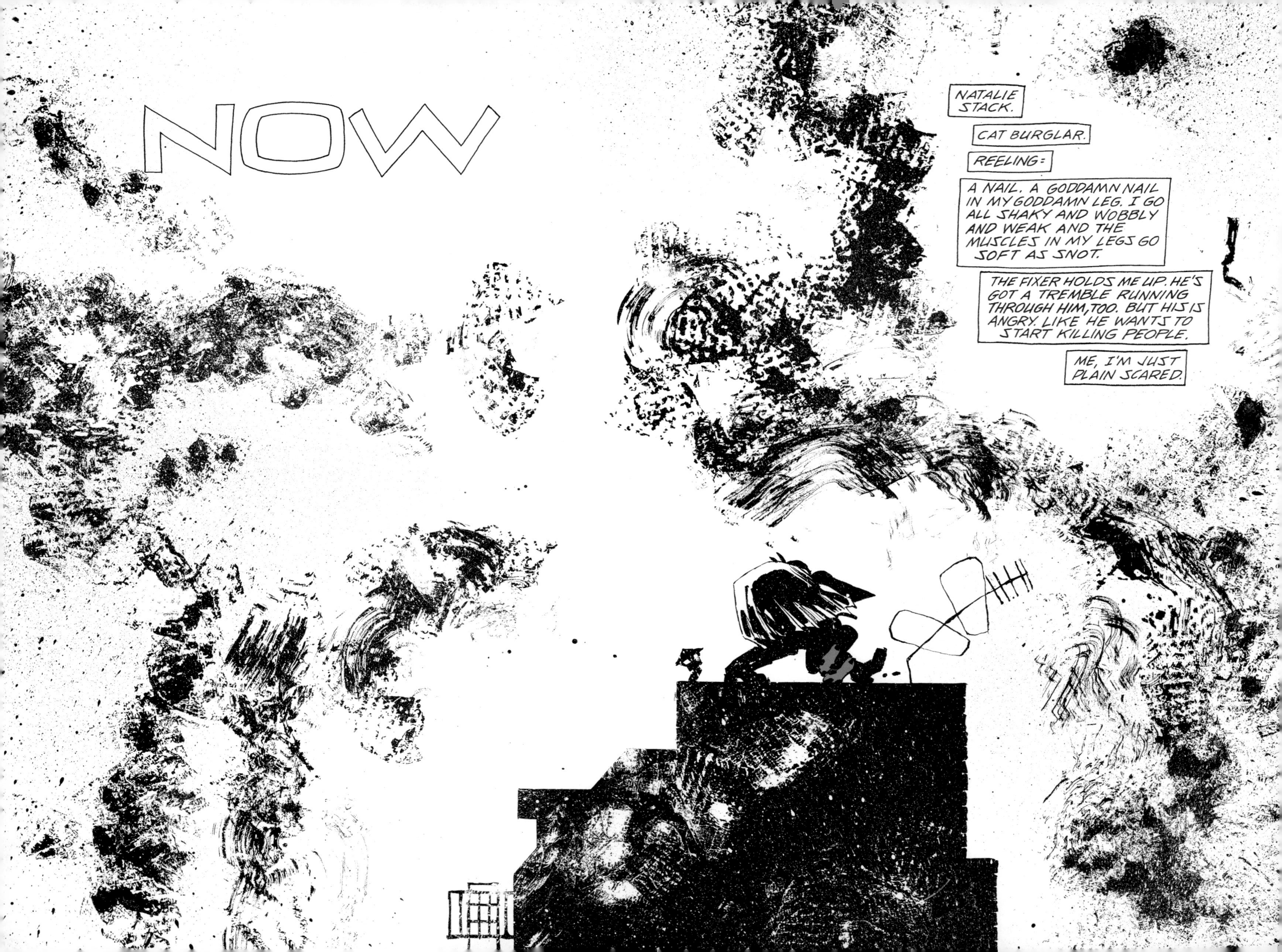
NOW
NATALIE STACK.
CAT BURGLAR.
REELING:
A NAIL. A GODDAMN NAIL IN MY GODDAMN LEG. I GO ALL SHAKY AND WOBBLY AND WEAK AND THE MUSCLES IN MY LEGS GO SOFT AS SNOT.
THE FIXER HOLDS ME UP. HE'S GOT A TREMBLE RUNNING THROUGH HIM, TOO. BUT HIS IS ANGRY. LIKE HE WANTS TO START KILLING PEOPLE.
ME, I'M JUST PLAIN SCARED.

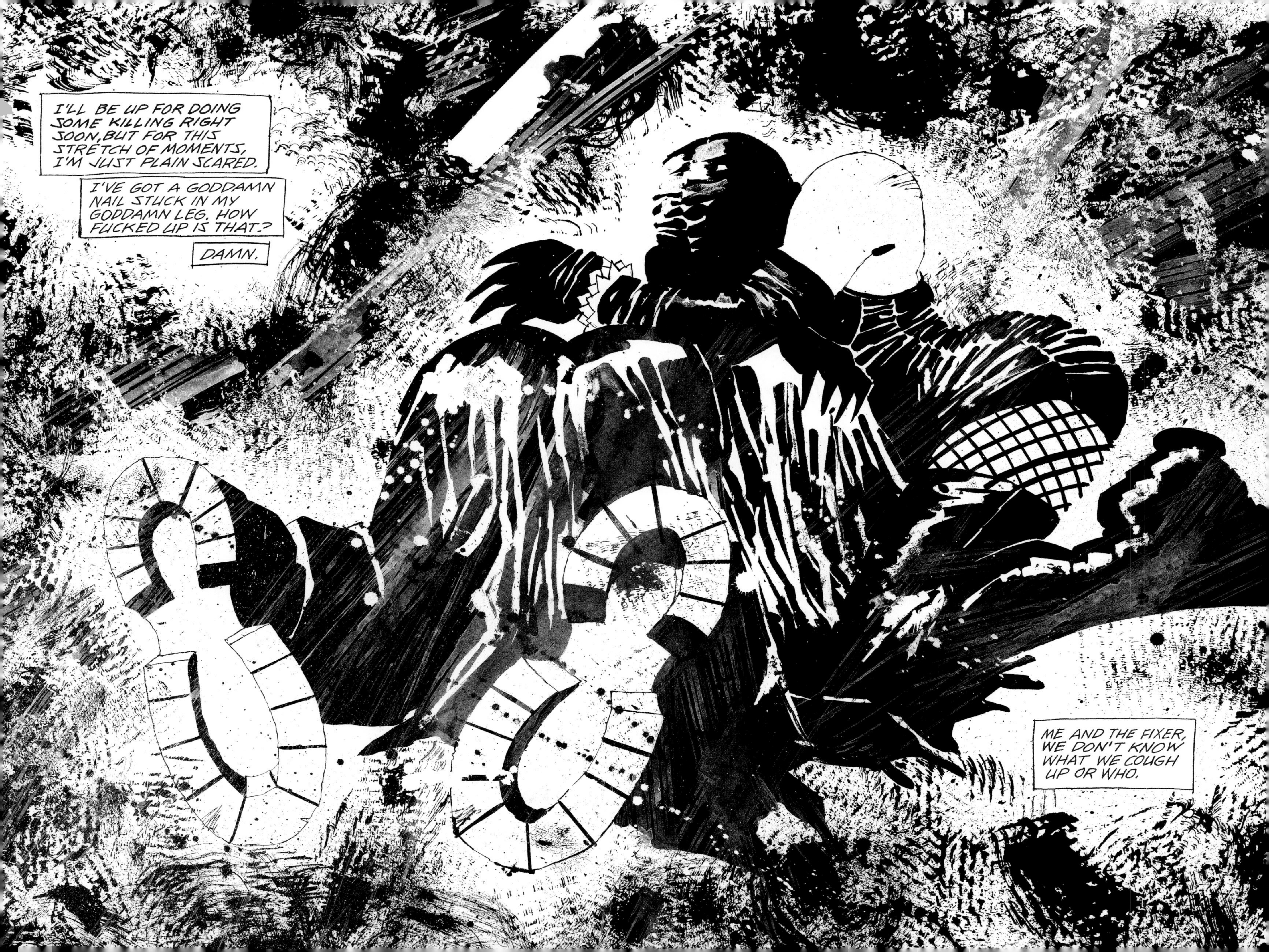
I'LL BE UP FOR DOING SOME KILLING RIGHT SOON, BUT FOR THIS STRETCH OF MOMENTS, I'M JUST PLAIN SCARED.
I'VE GOT A GODDAMN NAIL STUCK IN MY GODDAMN LEG. HOW FUCKED UP IS THAT?
DAMN.
ME AND THE FIXER, WE DON'T KNOW WHAT WE COUGH UP OR WHO.

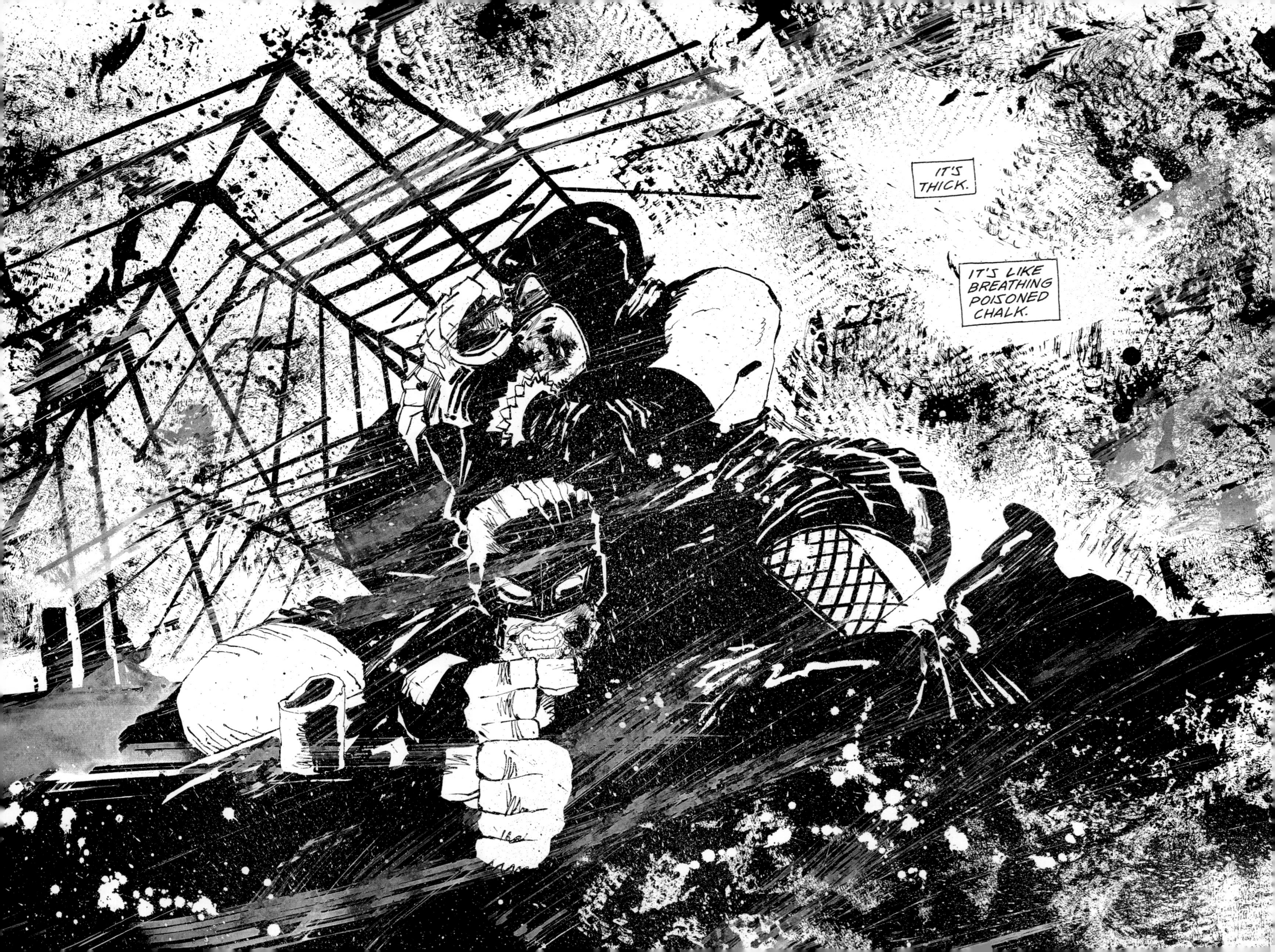
IT'S THICK.
IT'S LIKE BREATHING POISONED CHALK.

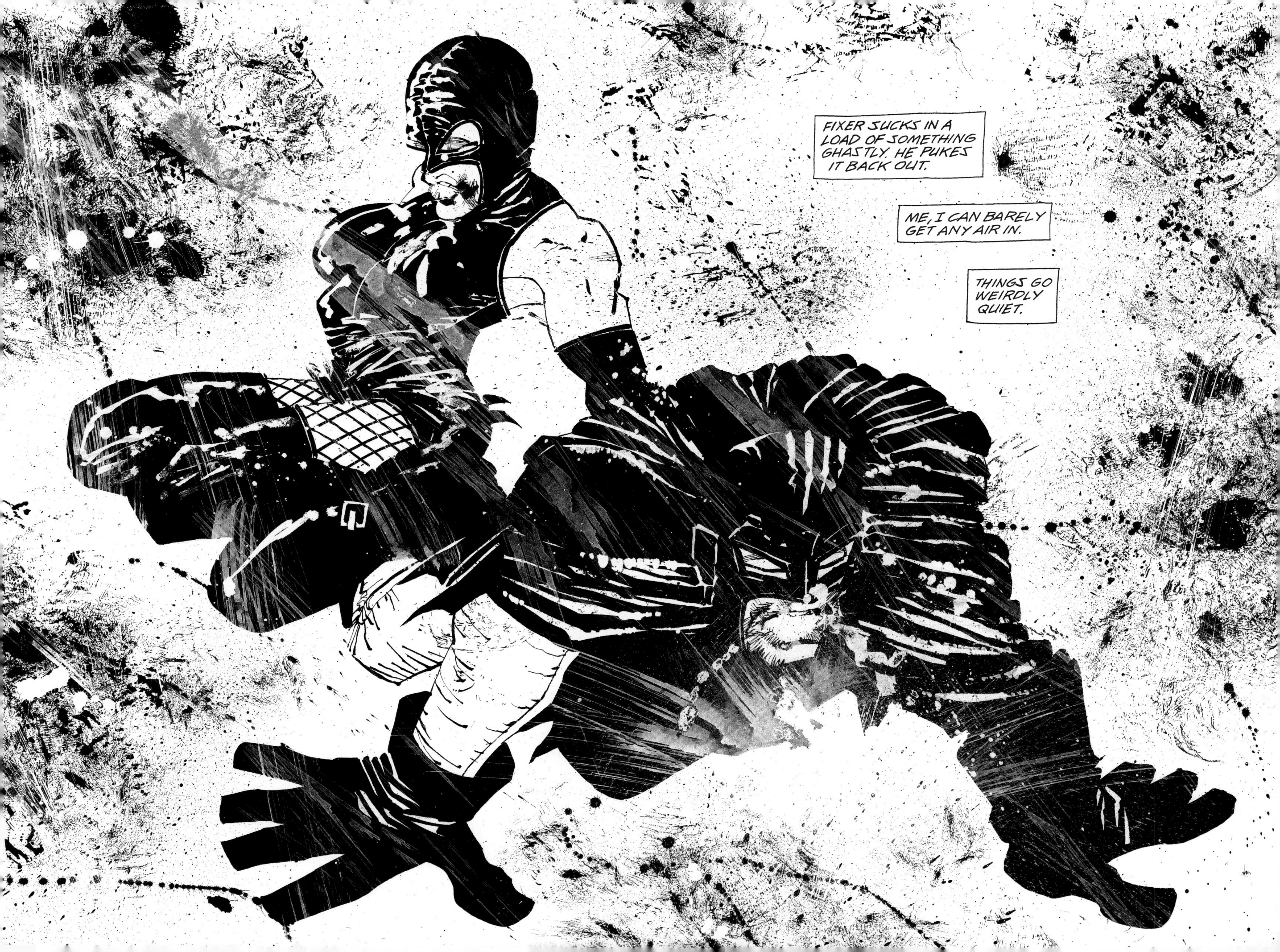
FIXER SUCKS IN A LOAD OF SOMETHING GHASTLY. HE PUKES IT BACK OUT.
ME, I CAN BARELY GET ANY AIR IN.
THINGS GO WEIRDLY QUIET.

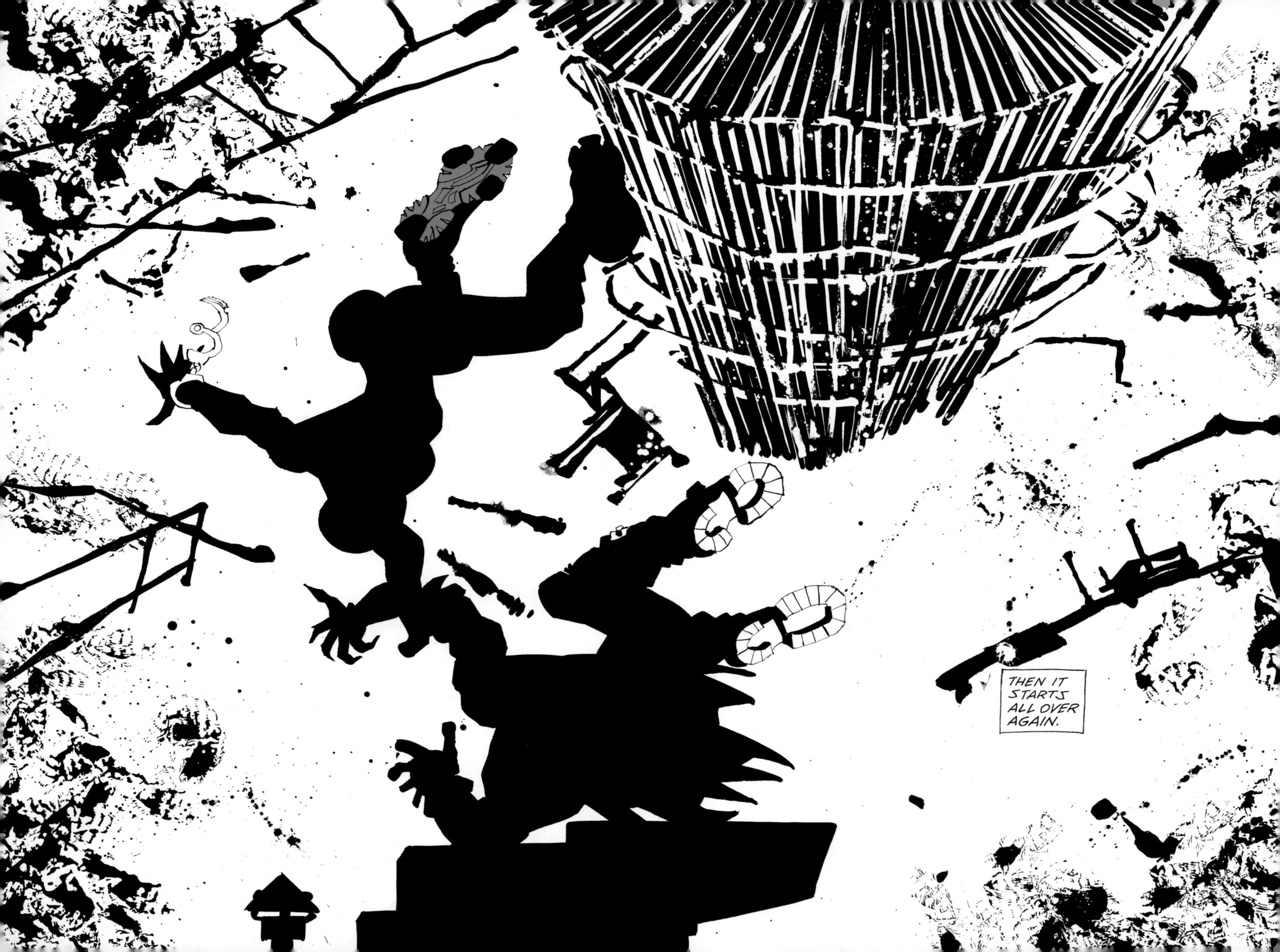
THEN IT STARTS ALL OVER AGAIN.

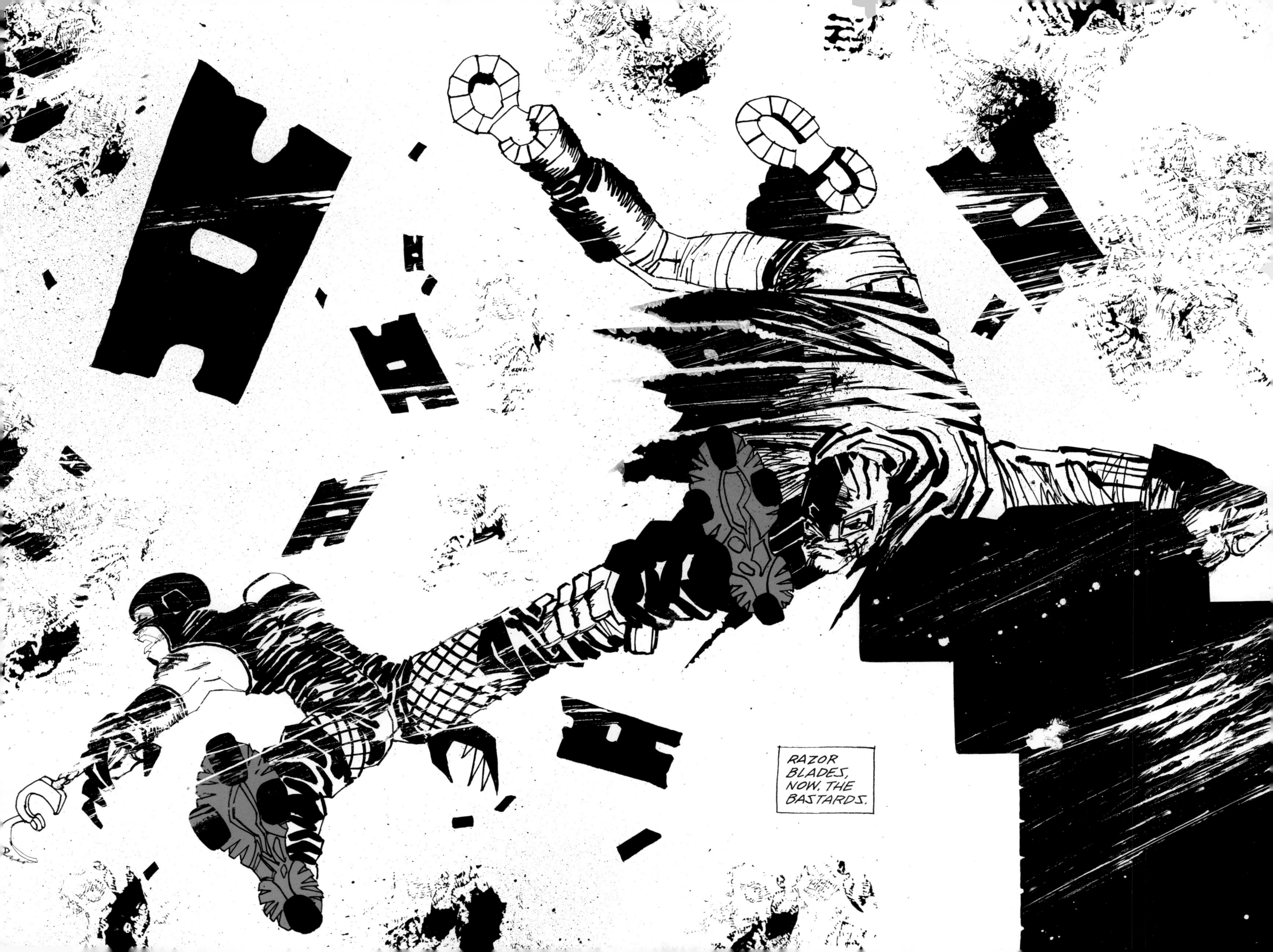
RAZOR BLADES, NOW. THE BASTARDS.

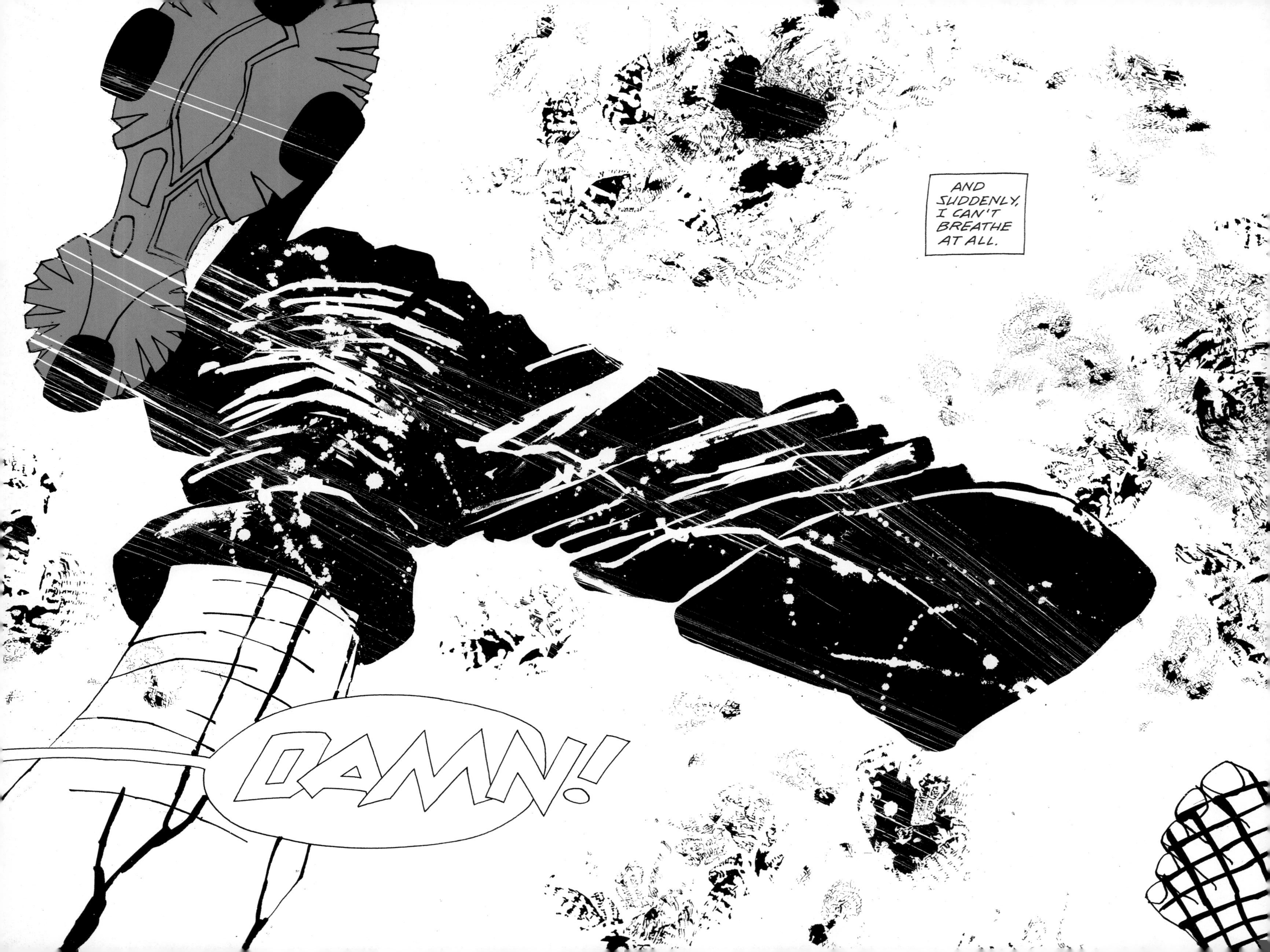
AND SUDDENLY, I CAN'T BREATHE AT ALL.
DAMN!

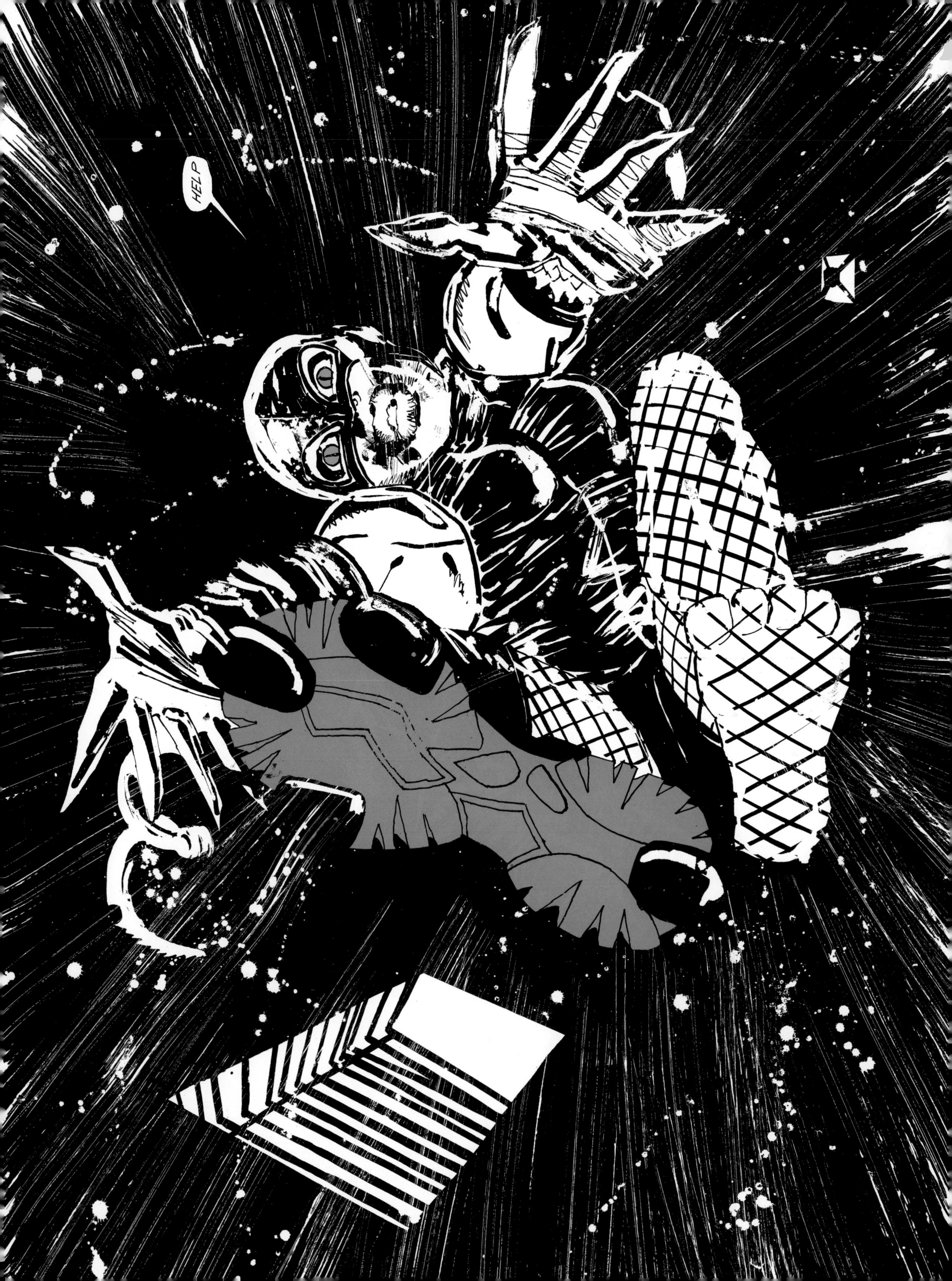
HELP

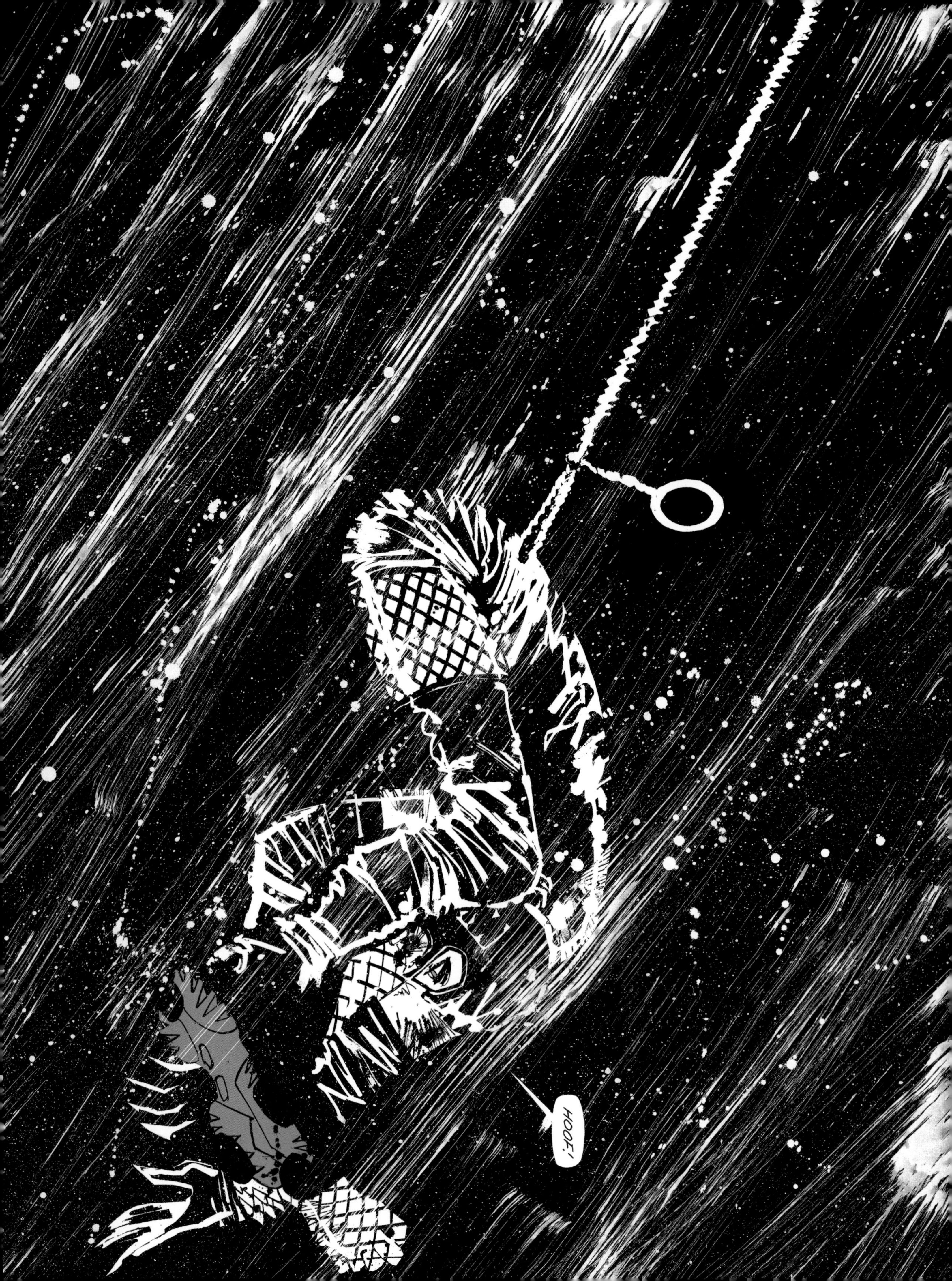
HOOF!

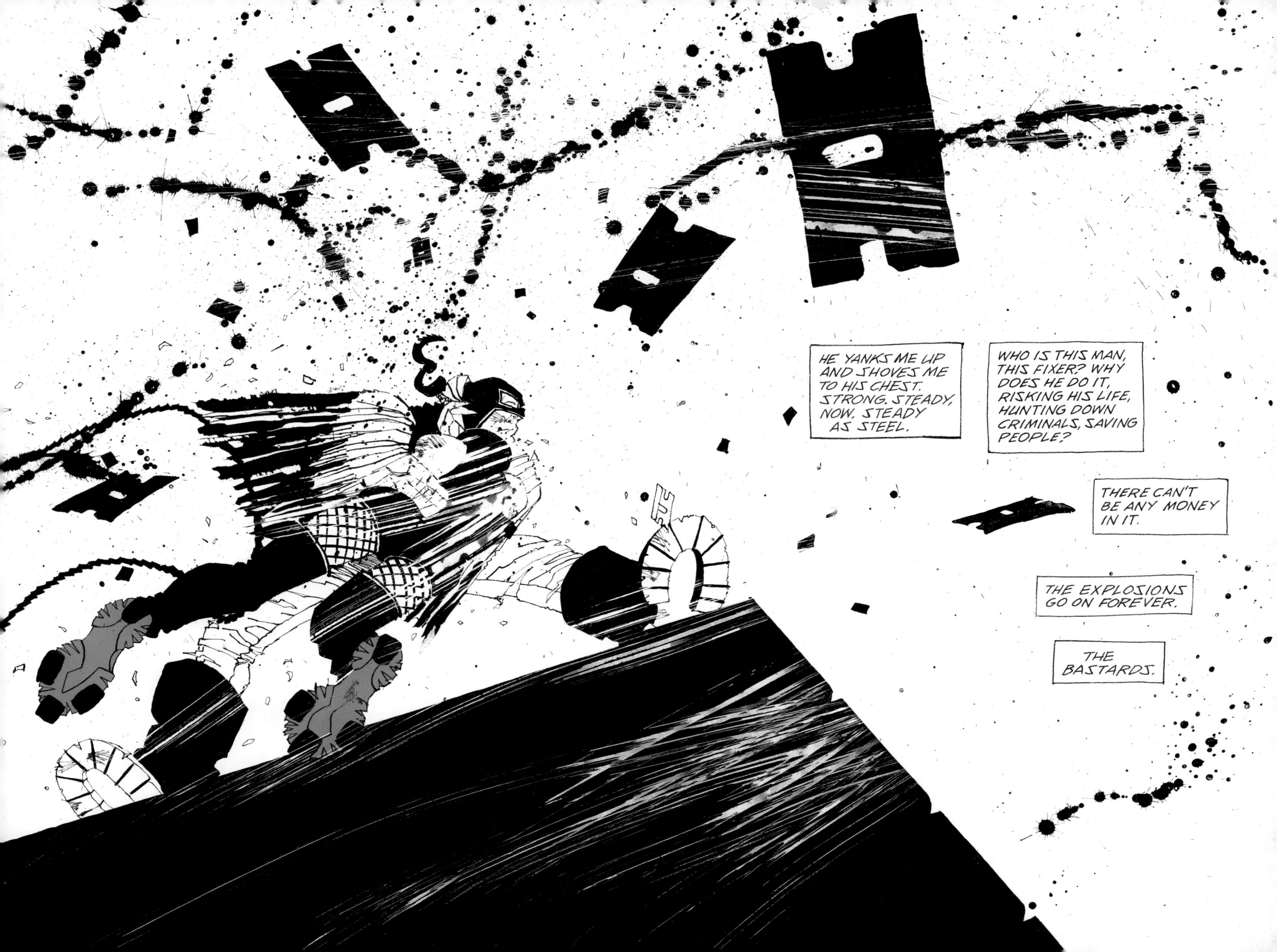
HE YANKS ME UP AND SHOVES ME TO HIS CHEST. STRONG. STEADY, NOW. STEADY AS STEEL.
WHO IS THIS MAN, THIS FIXER? WHY DOES HE DO IT, RISKING HIS LIFE, HUNTING DOWN CRIMINALS, SAVING PEOPLE?
THERE CAN'T BE ANY MONEY IN IT.
THE EXPLOSIONS GO ON FOREVER.
THE BASTARDS.

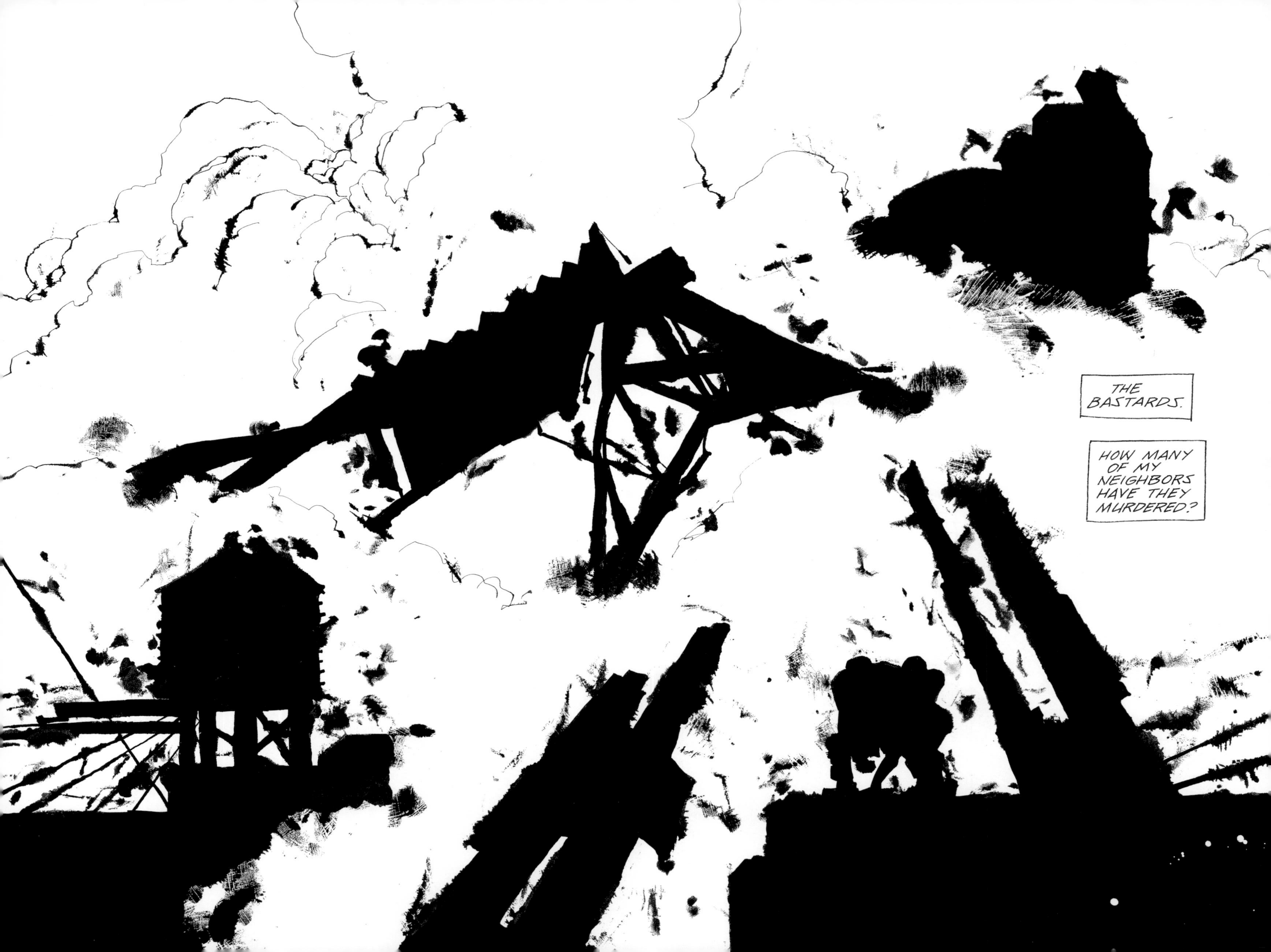
THE BASTARDS.
HOW MANY OF MY NEIGHBORS HAVE THEY MURDERED?

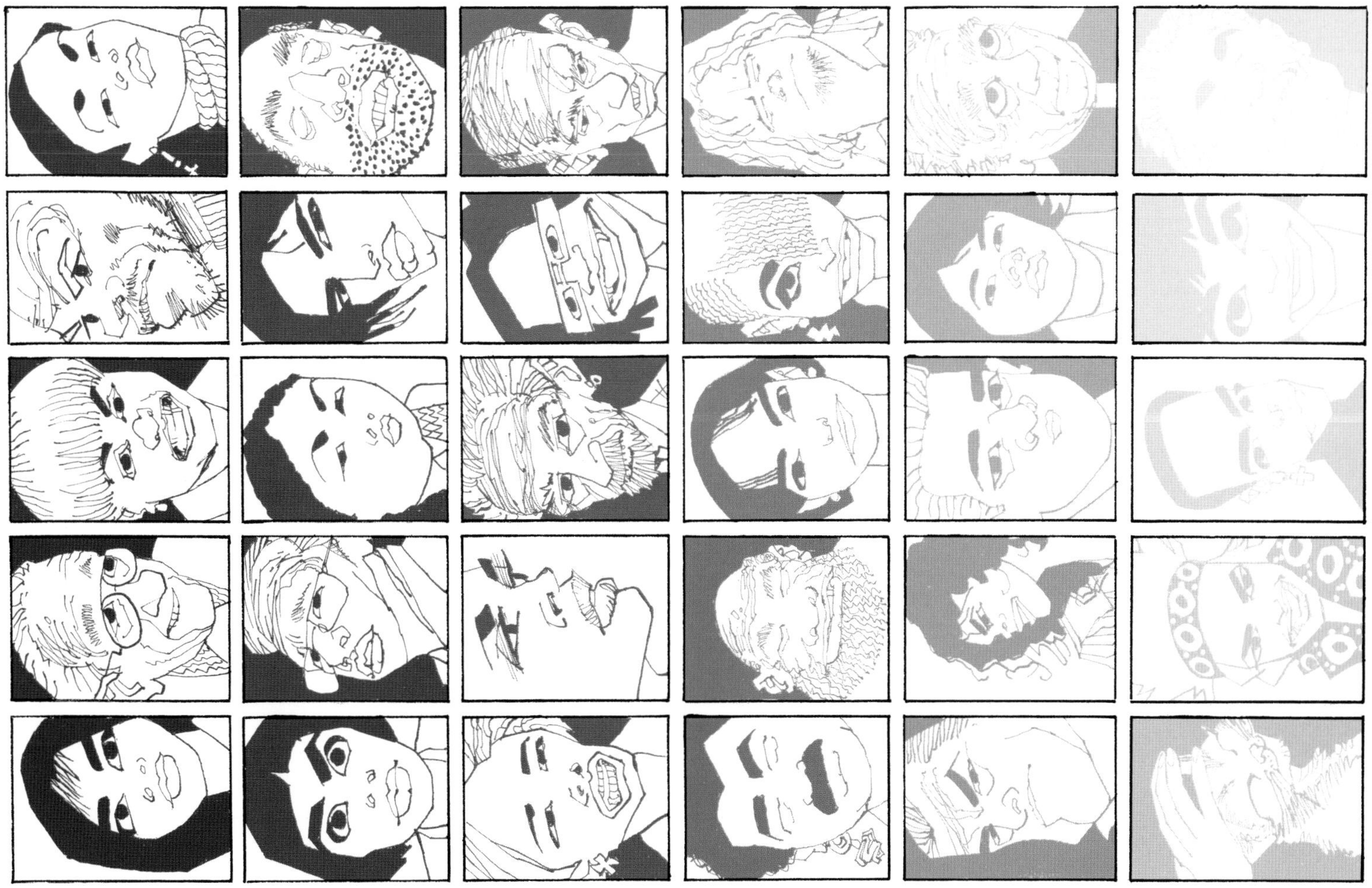

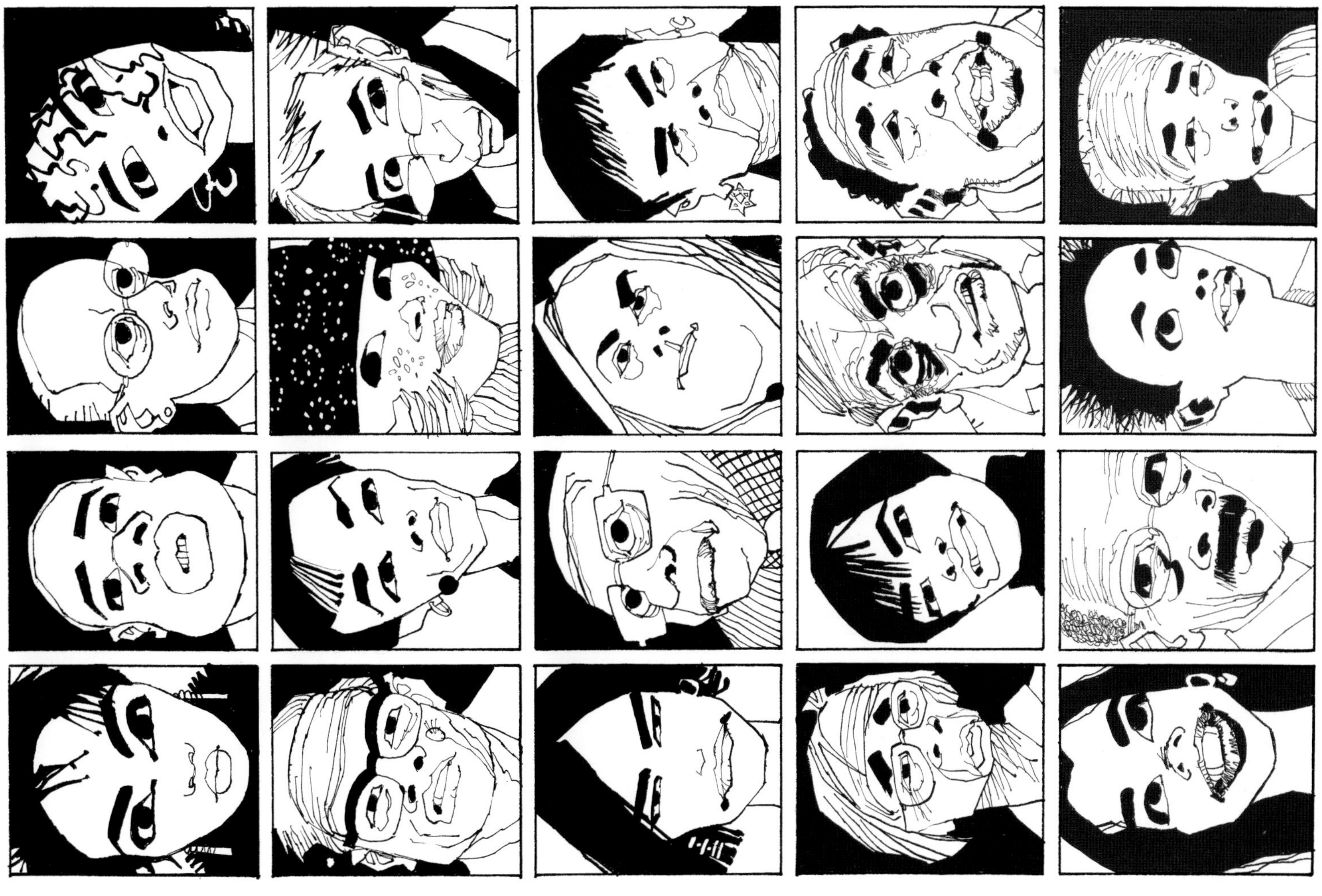

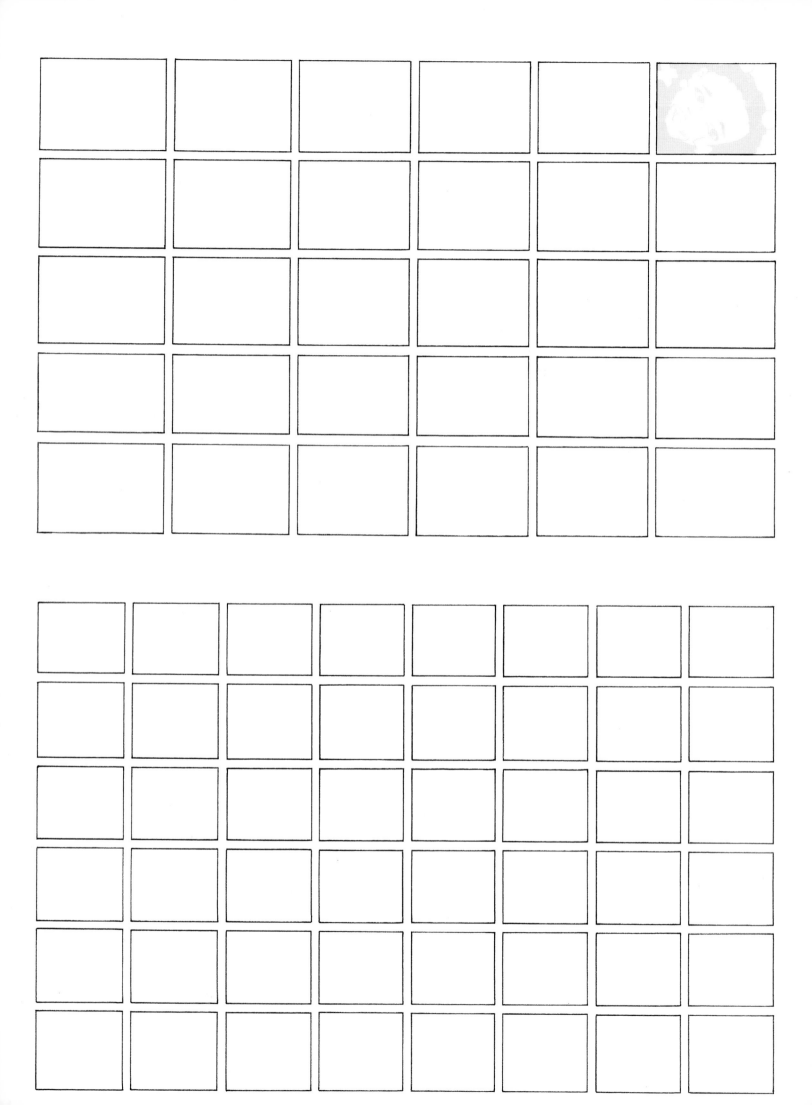

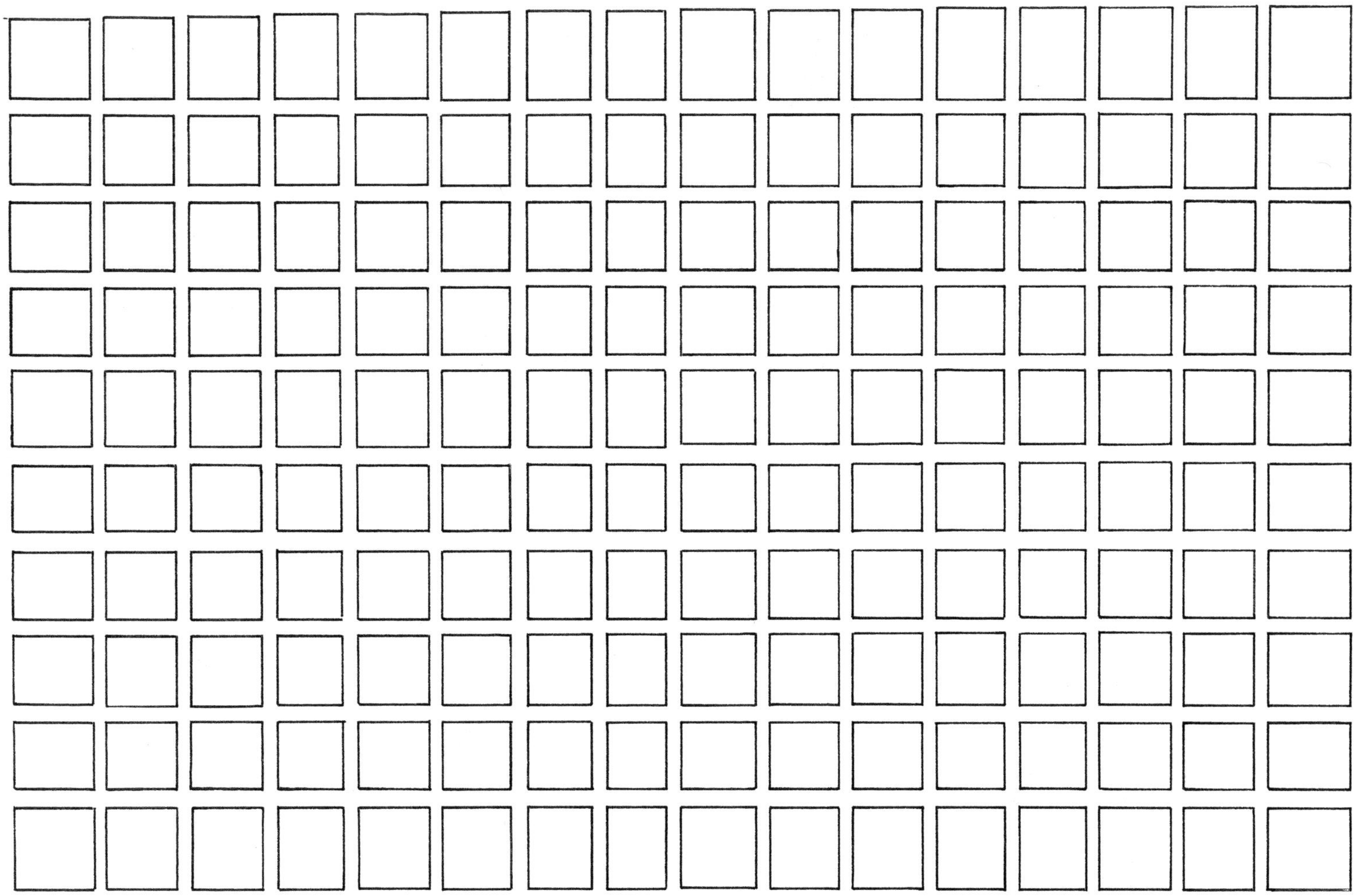

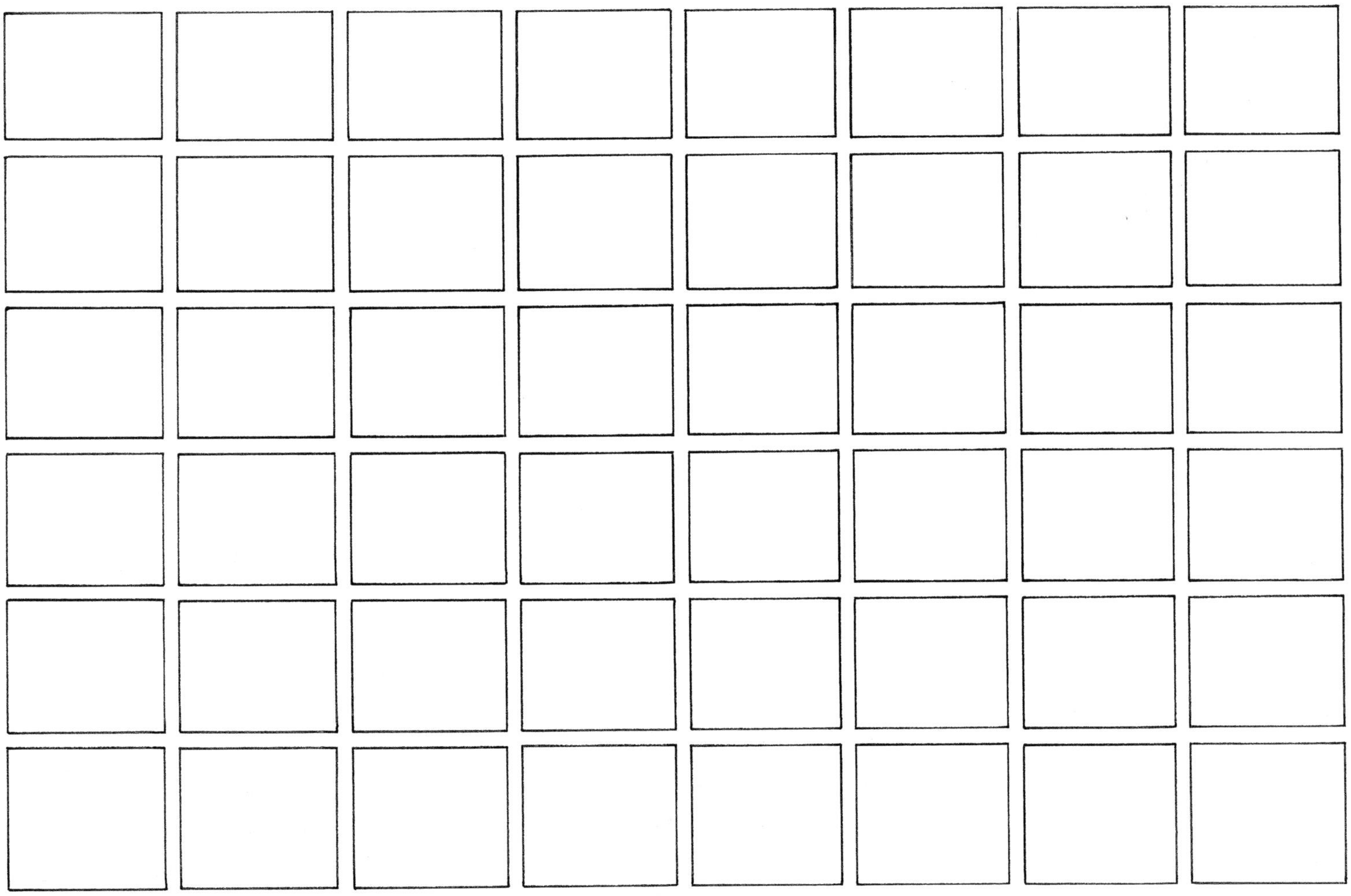

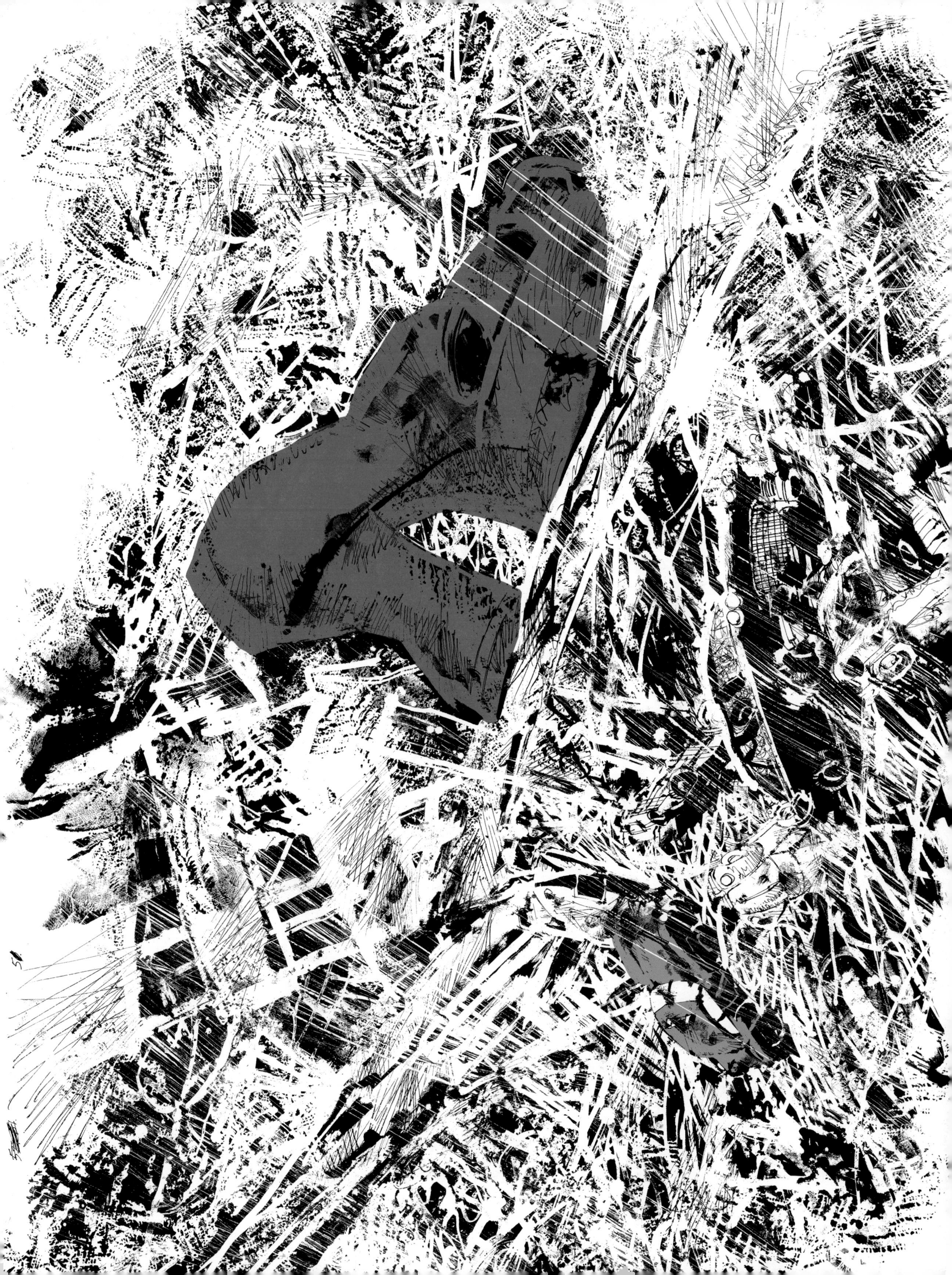

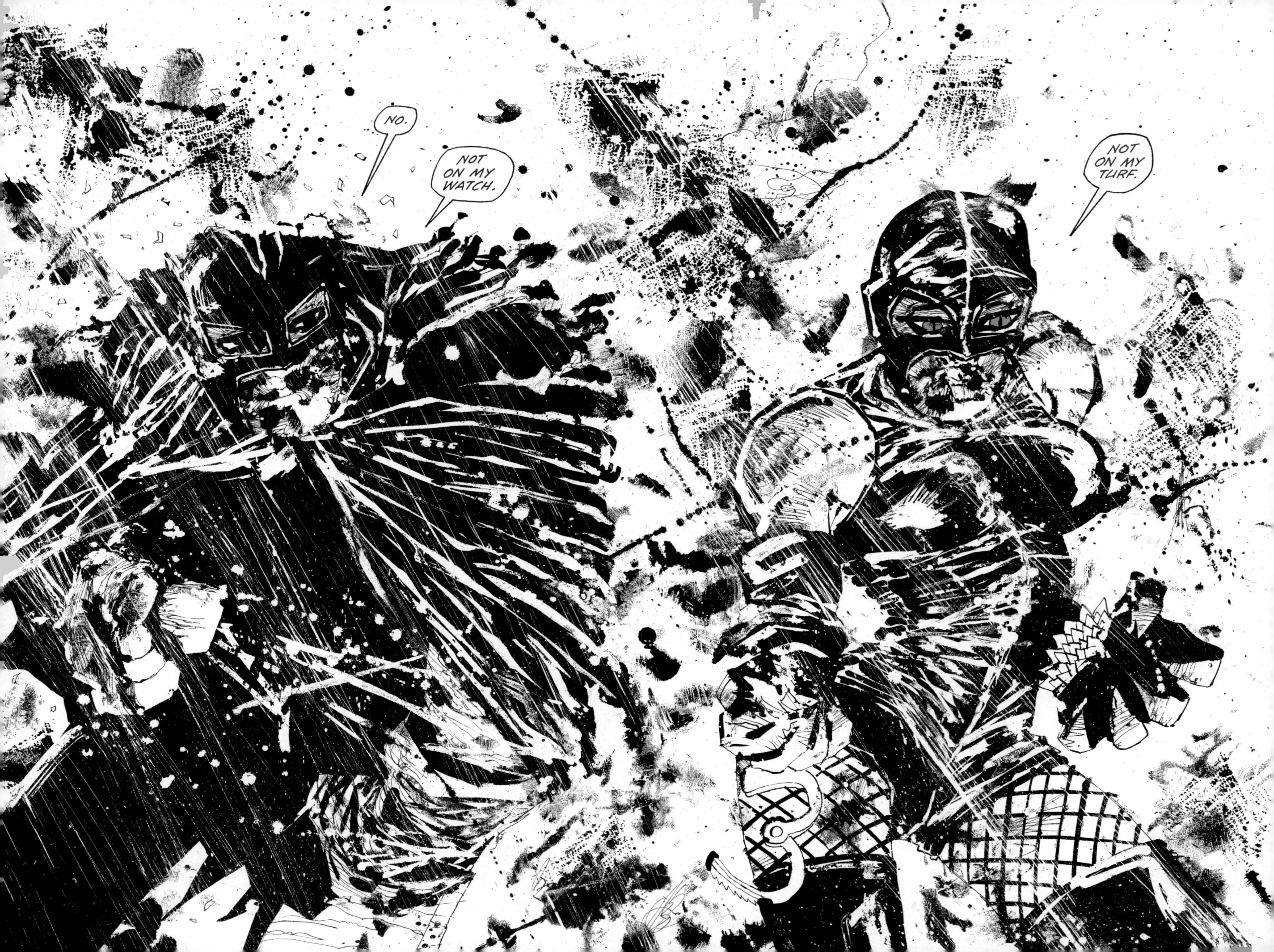
NO.
NOT ON MY WATCH.
NOT ON MY TURF.

NO... OH, BABY, NO-- NOT CARLA...
NOT CARLA.
NOT IN MY TOWN, DAMN IT!
STERNUM! SCRAMBLE THAT MANIAC STEIGER TO ROBINSON PARK! TELL HIM IT'S IN LOCKDOWN! LOCKDOWN, YOU HEAR ME?
YES, SIR. LOUD AND CLEAR.
...YES, MA'AM. I'LL TELL HIM JUST AS SOON AS HE TAKES A BREATH...
JESUS CHRIST!
WHERE?
OH, JESUS! JESUS CHRIST!

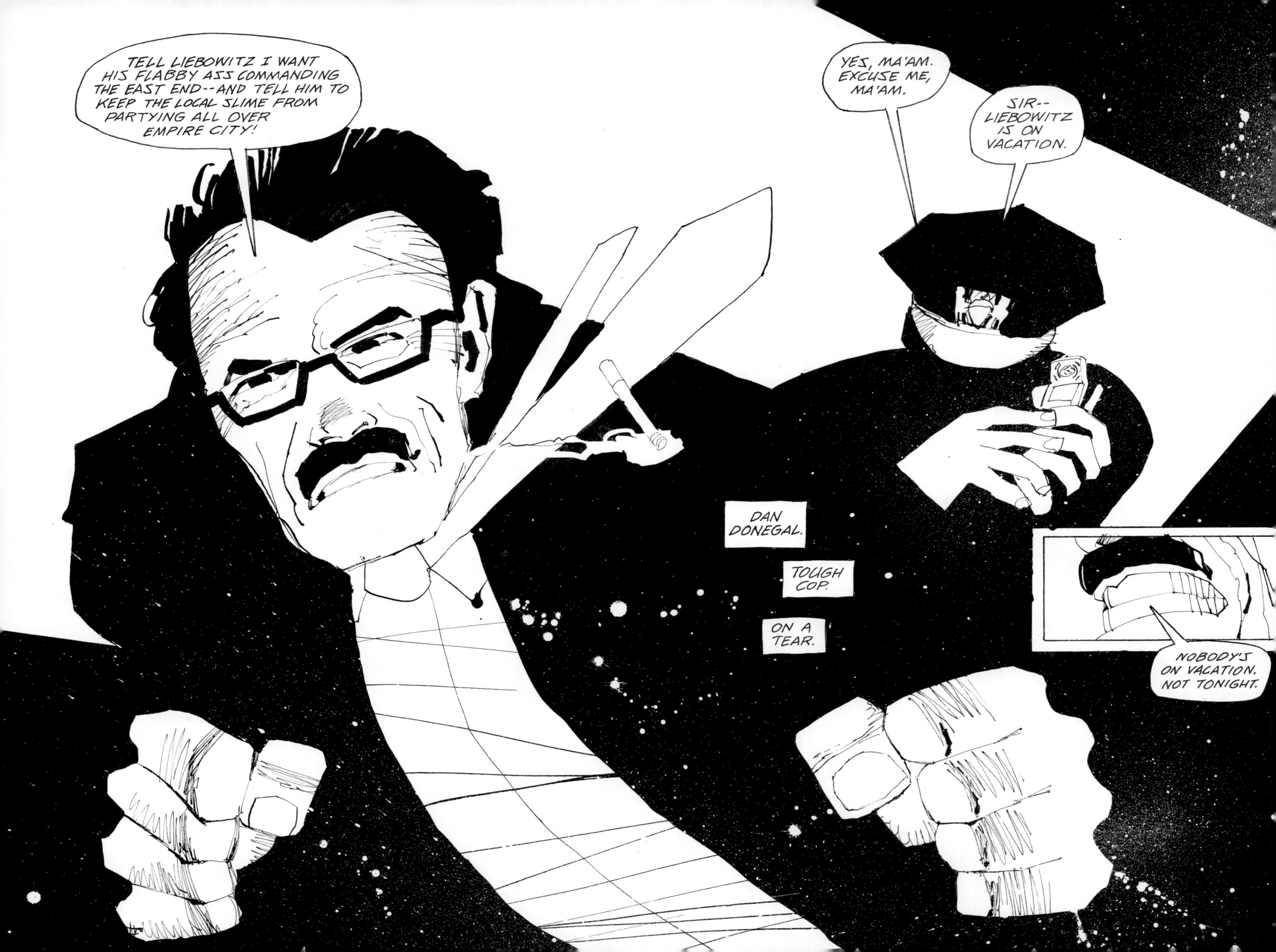
TELL LIEBOWITZ I WANT HIS FLABBY ASS COMMANDING THE EAST END--AND TELL HIM TO KEEP THE LOCAL SLIME FROM PARTYING ALL OVER EMPIRE CITY!
YES, MA'AM. EXCUSE ME, MA'AM.
SIR--LIEBOWITZ IS ON VACATION.
DAN DONEGAL.
TOUGH COP.
ON A TEAR.
NOBODY'S ON VACATION. NOT TONIGHT.

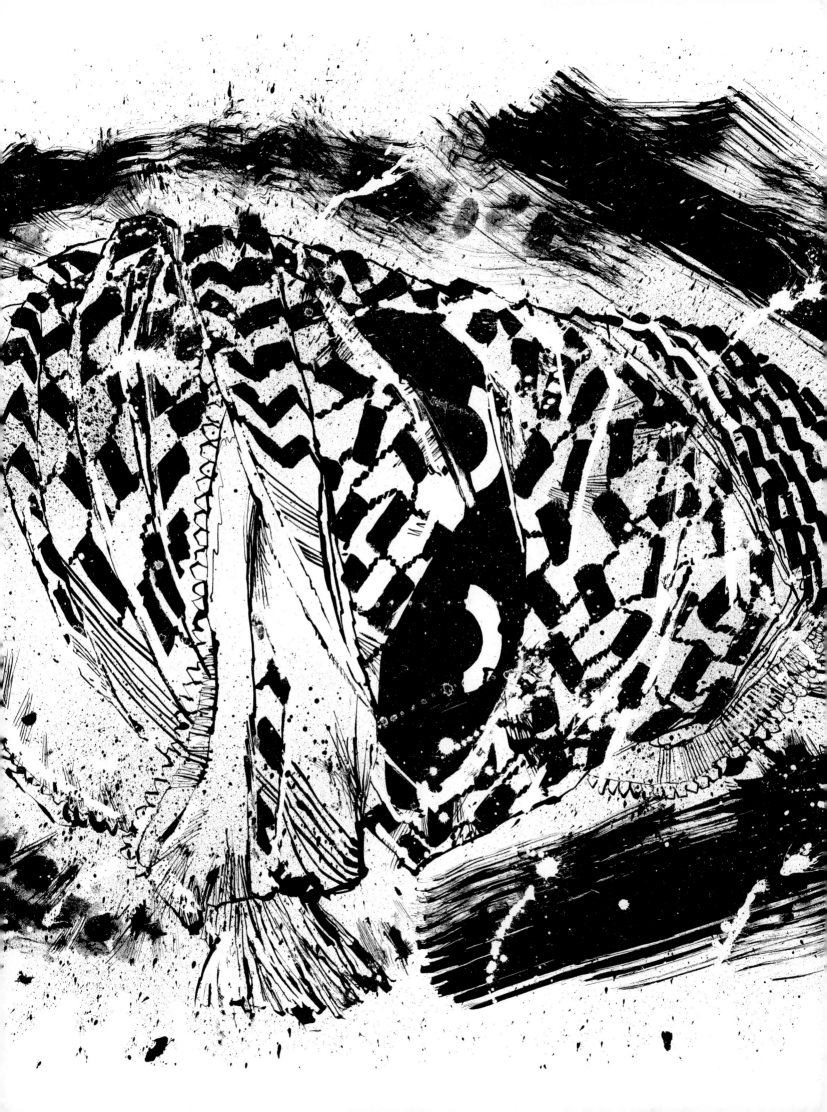

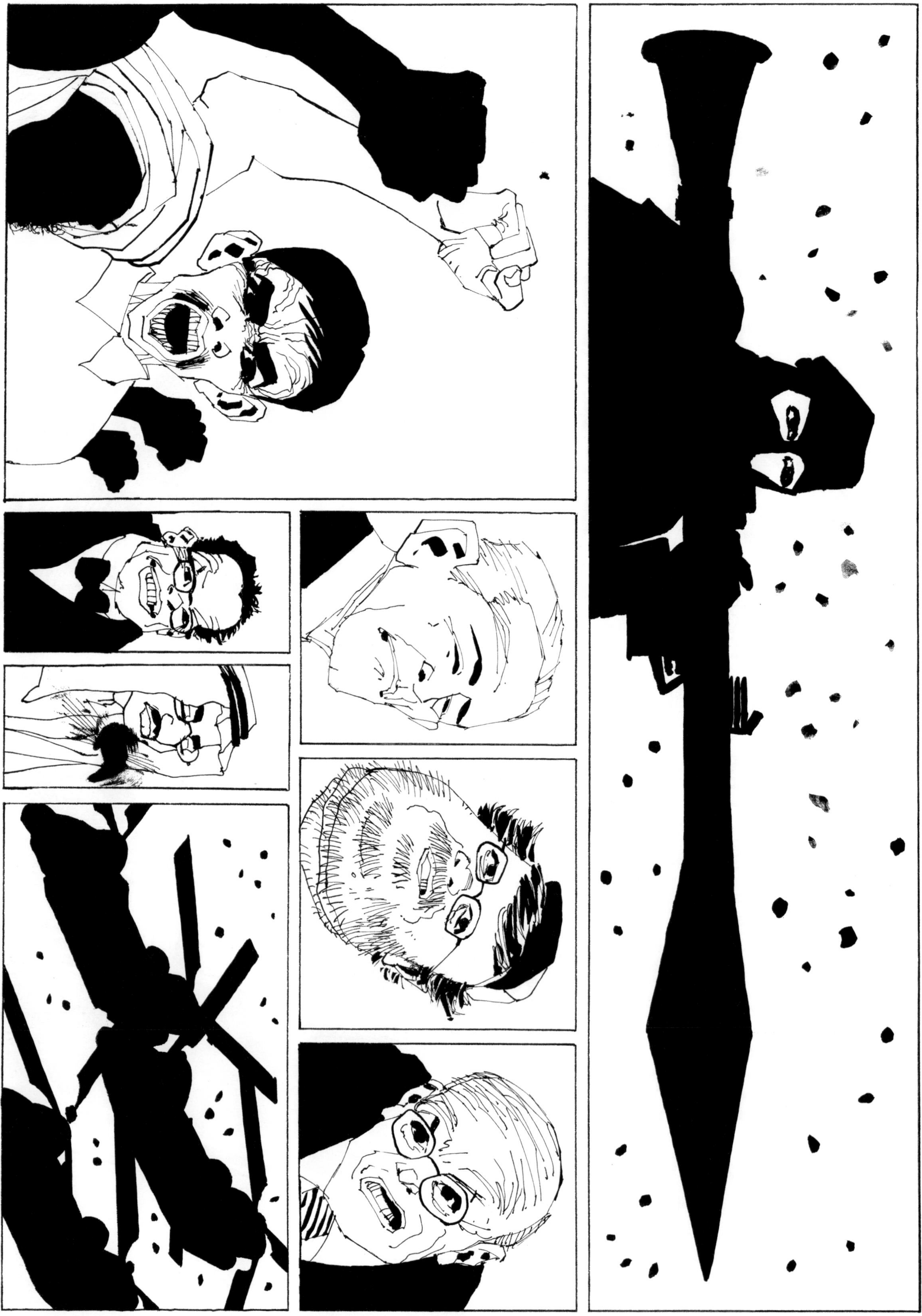

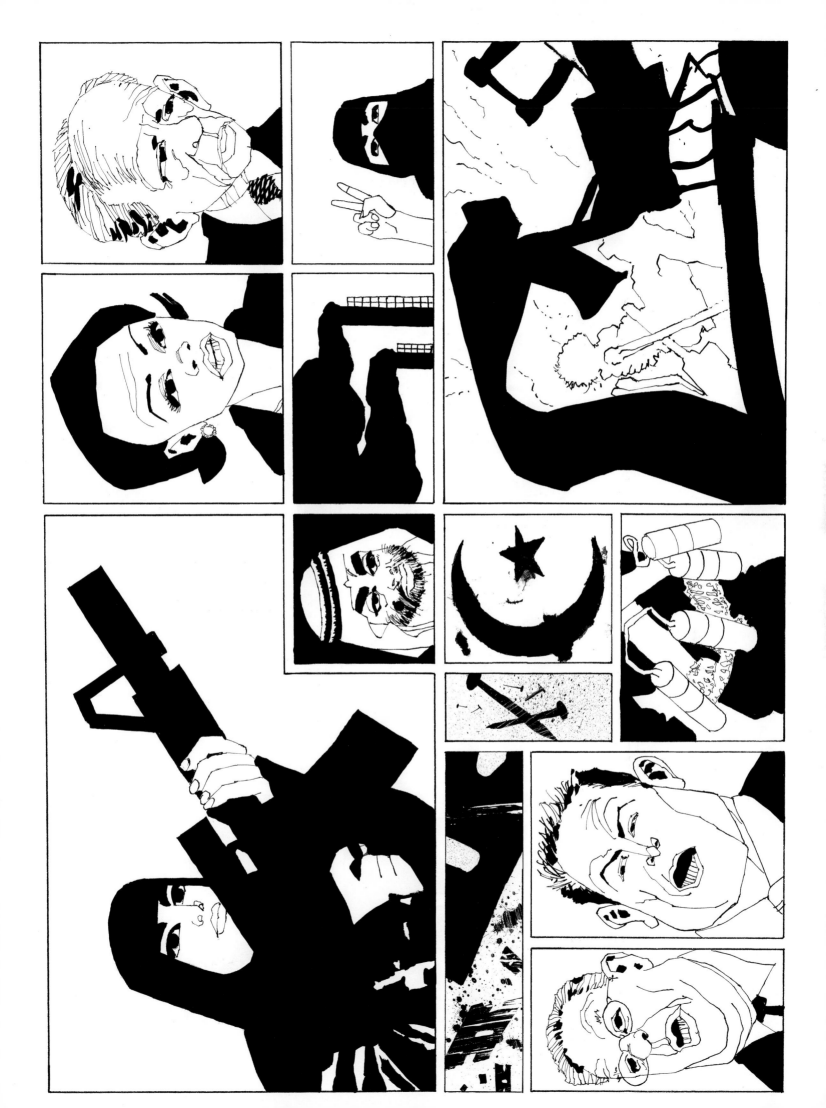

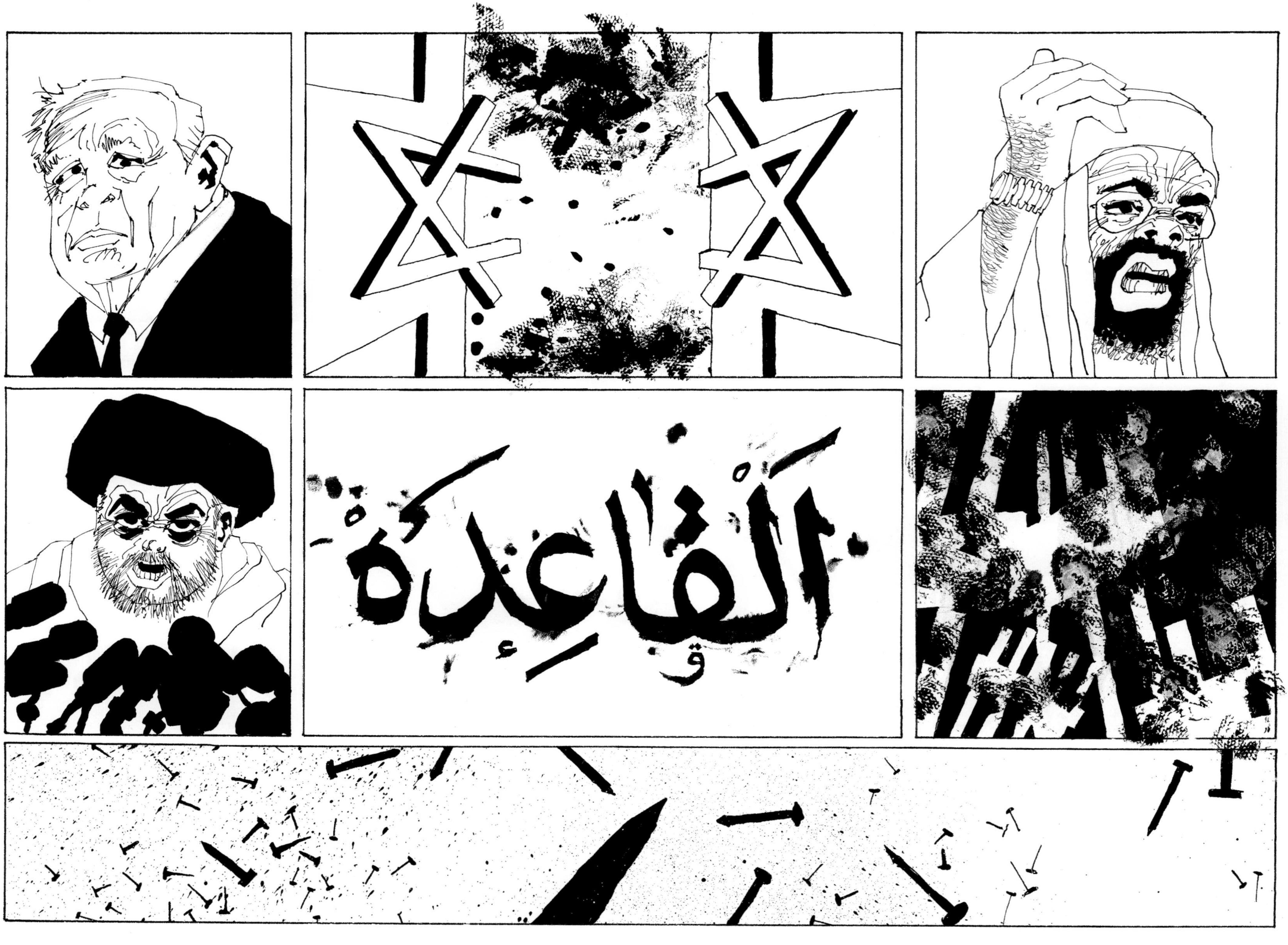
القاعدة

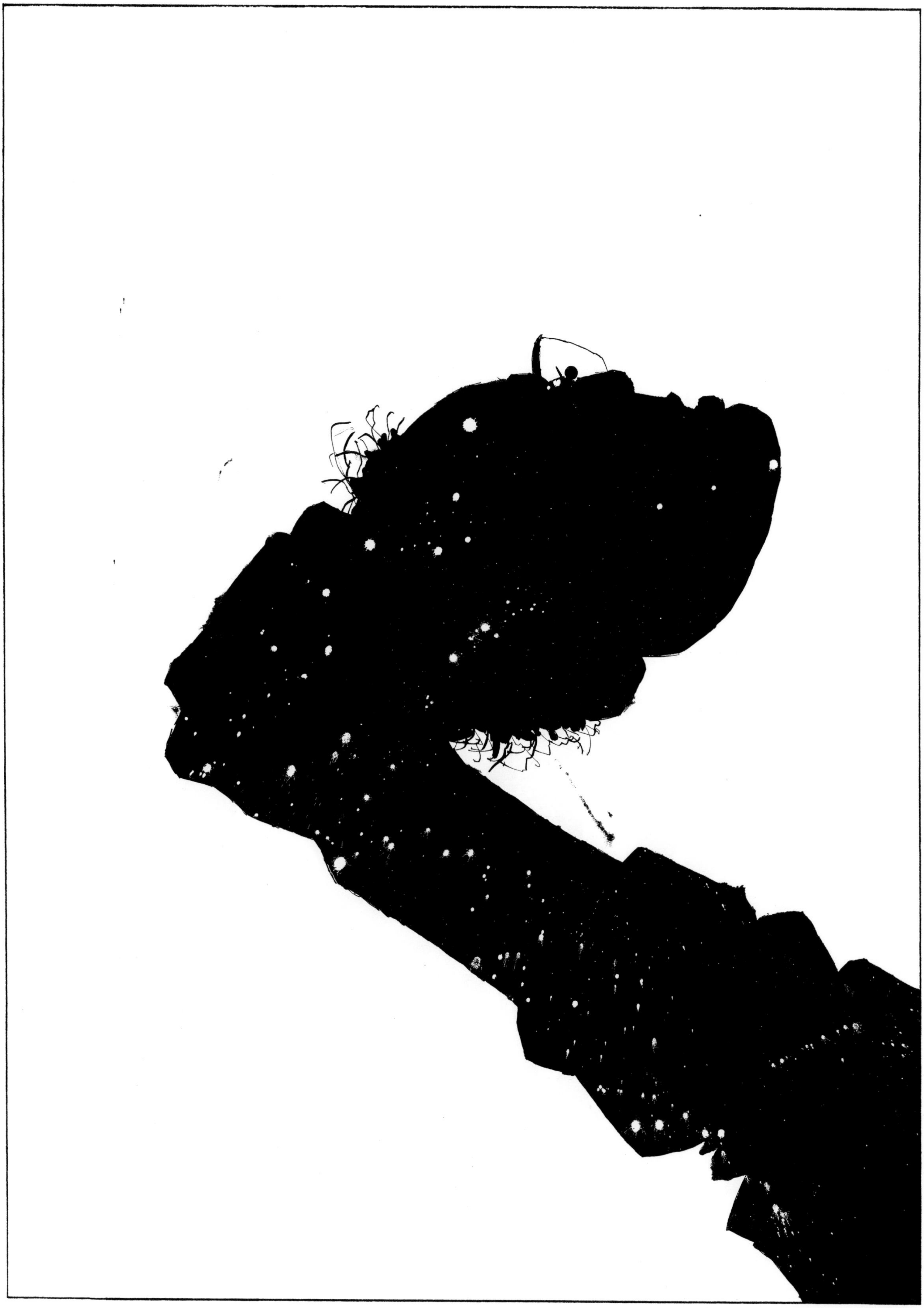

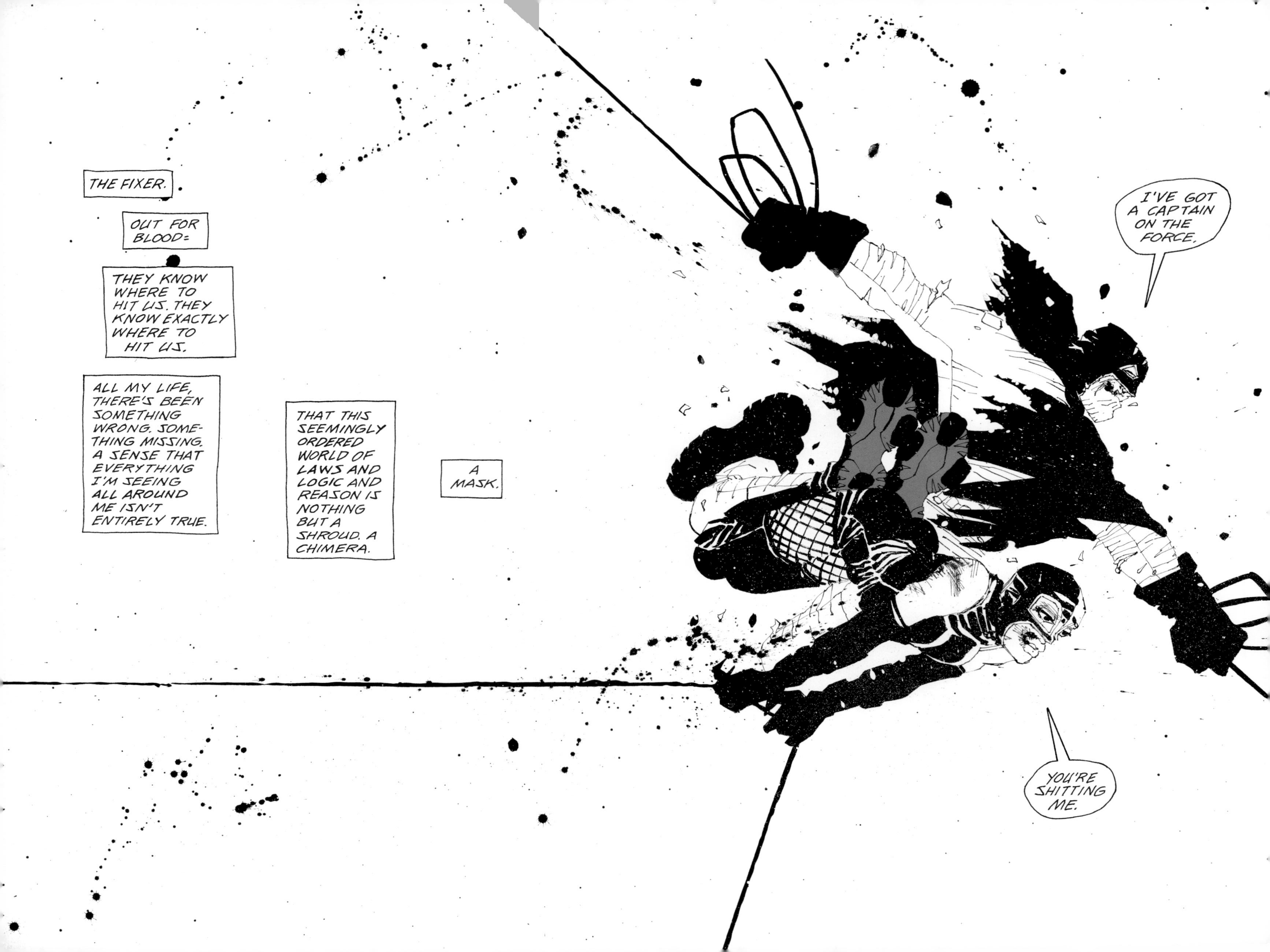
THE FIXER.
OUT FOR BLOOD=
THEY KNOW WHERE TO HIT US. THEY KNOW EXACTLY WHERE TO HIT US.
ALL MY LIFE, THERE'S BEEN SOMETHING WRONG. SOME-THING MISSING. A SENSE THAT EVERYTHING I'M SEEING ALL AROUND ME ISN'T ENTIRELY TRUE.
THAT THIS SEEMINGLY ORDERED WORLD OF LAWS AND LOGIC AND REASON IS NOTHING BUT A SHROUD. A CHIMERA.
A MASK.
I'VE GOT A CAPTAIN ON THE FORCE.
YOU'RE SHITTING ME.

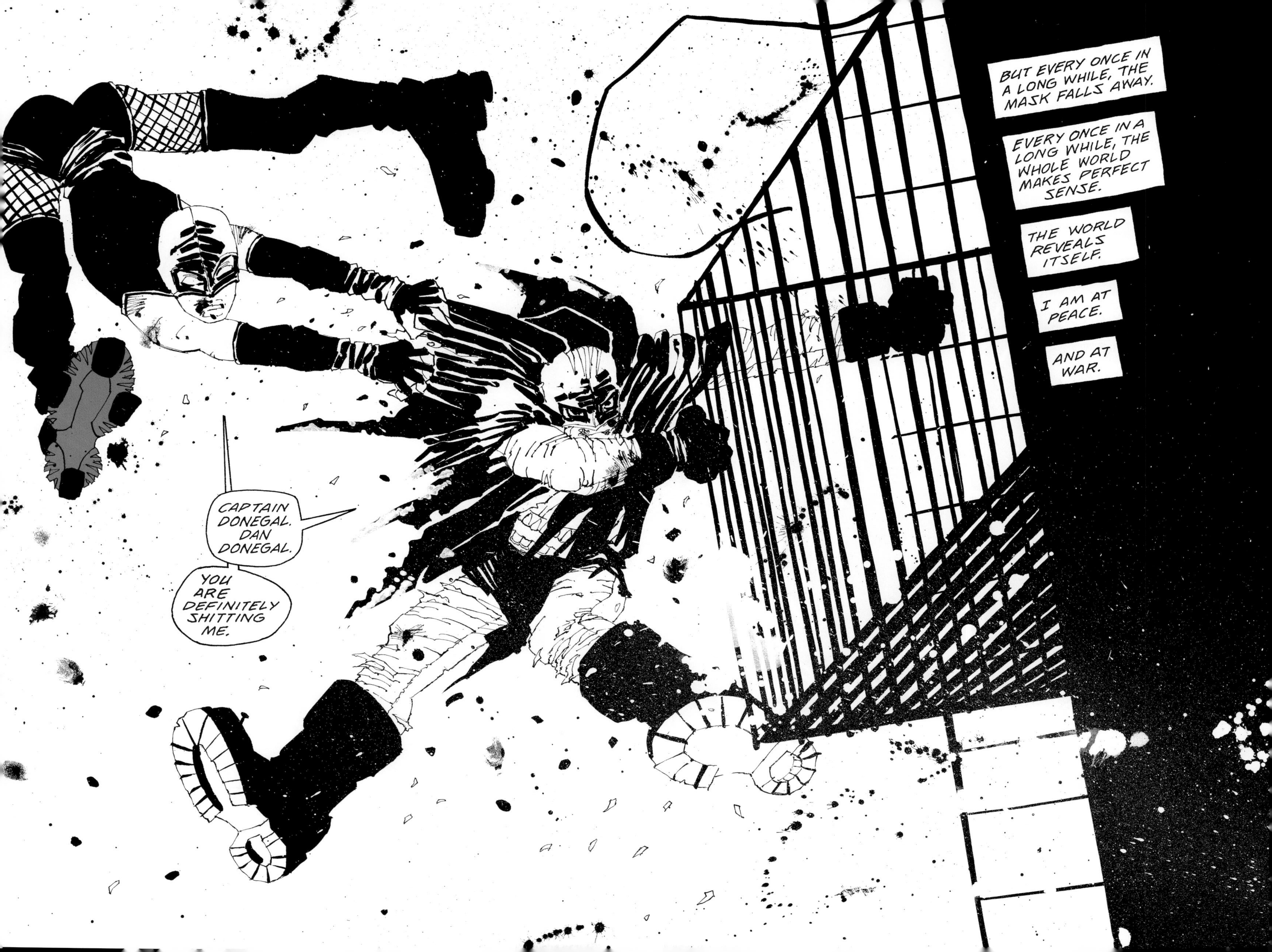
BUT EVERY ONCE IN A LONG WHILE, THE MASK FALLS AWAY.
EVERY ONCE IN A LONG WHILE, THE WHOLE WORLD MAKES PERFECT SENSE.
THE WORLD REVEALS ITSELF.
I AM AT PEACE.
AND AT WAR.
CAPTAIN DONEGAL. DAN DONEGAL.
YOU ARE DEFINITELY SHITTING ME.

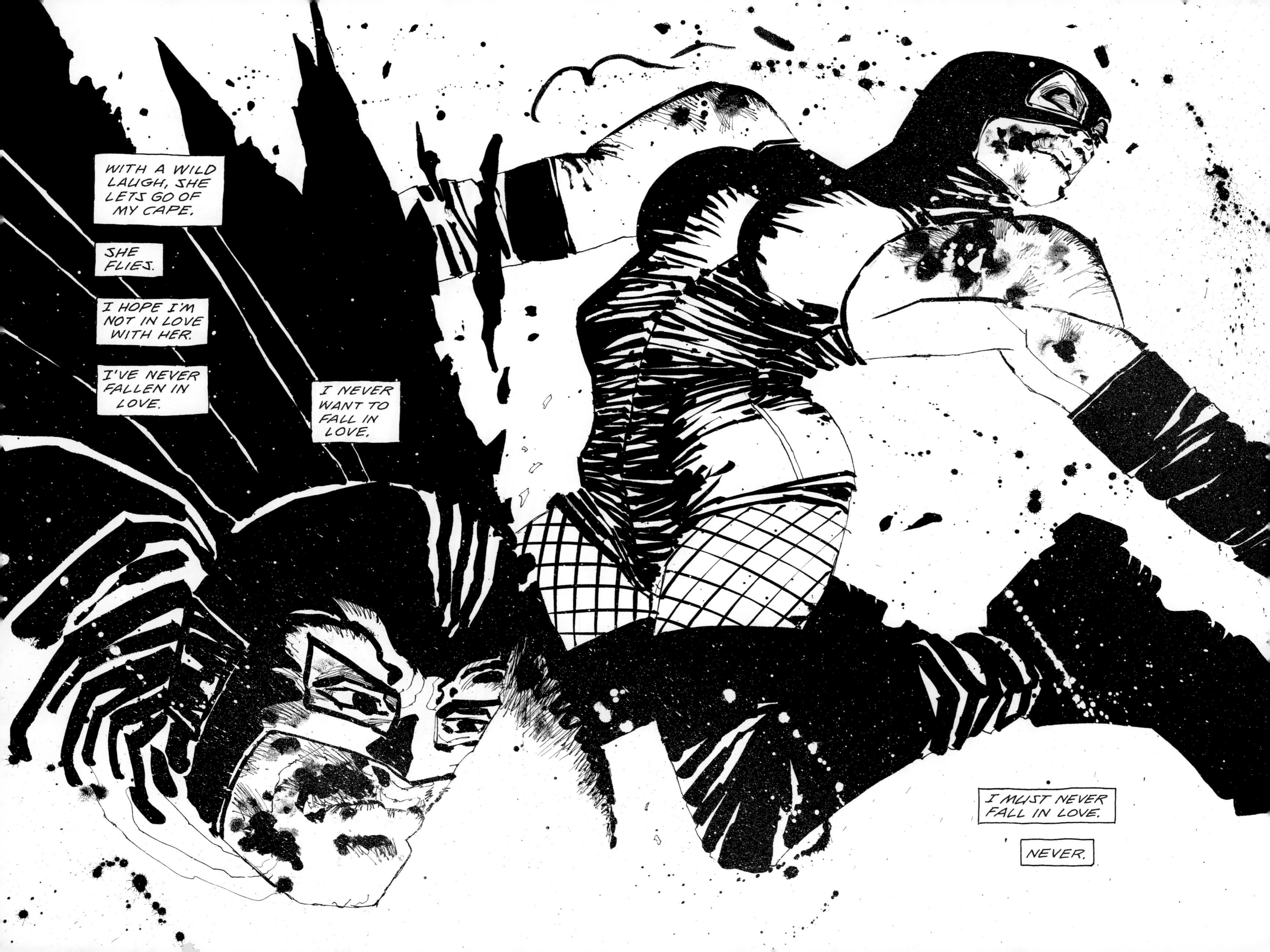
WITH A WILD LAUGH, SHE LETS GO OF MY CAPE.
SHE FLIES.
I HOPE I'M NOT IN LOVE WITH HER.
I'VE NEVER FALLEN IN LOVE.
I NEVER WANT TO FALL IN LOVE.
I MUST NEVER FALL IN LOVE.
NEVER.

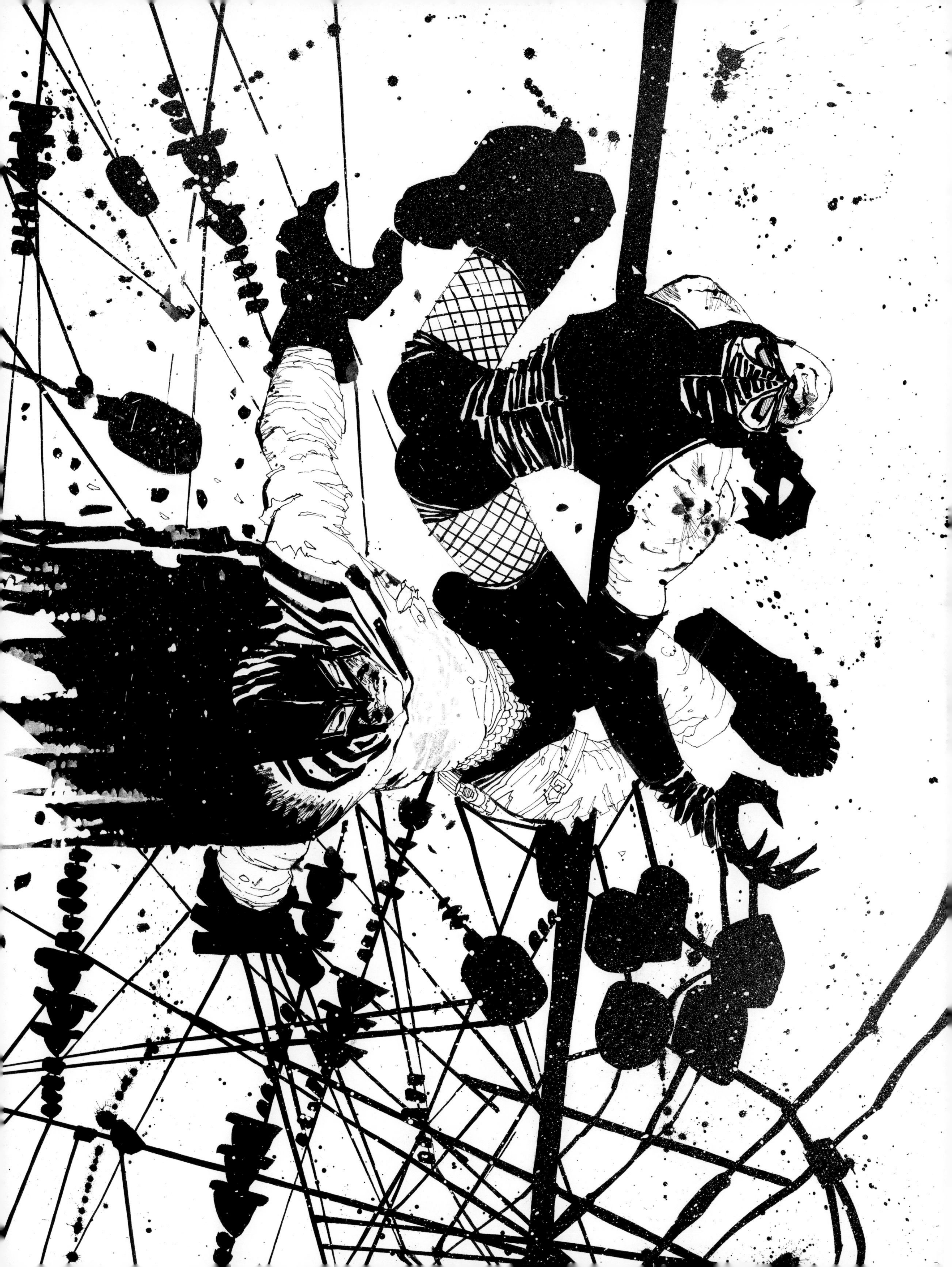

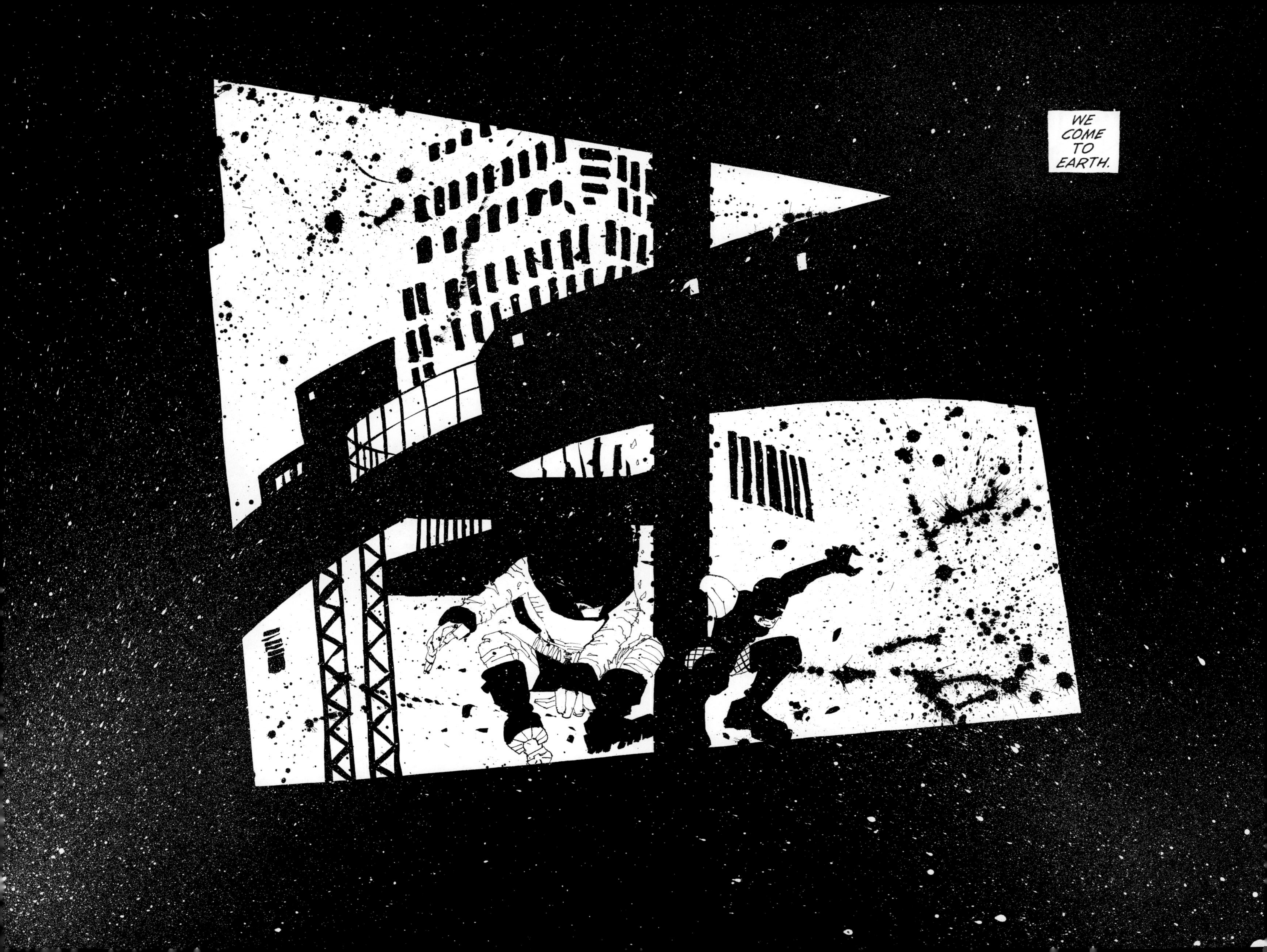
WE COME TO EARTH.

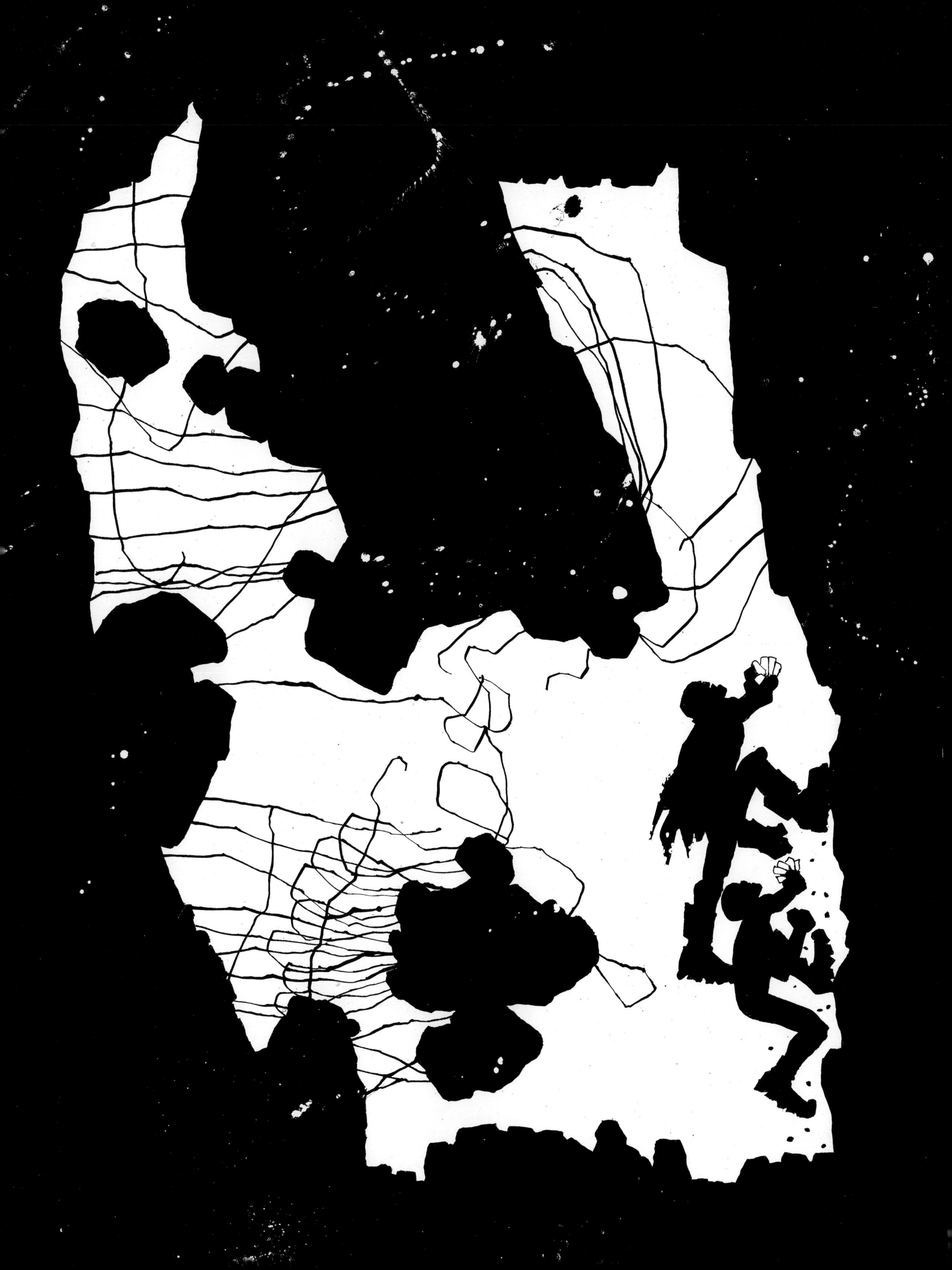

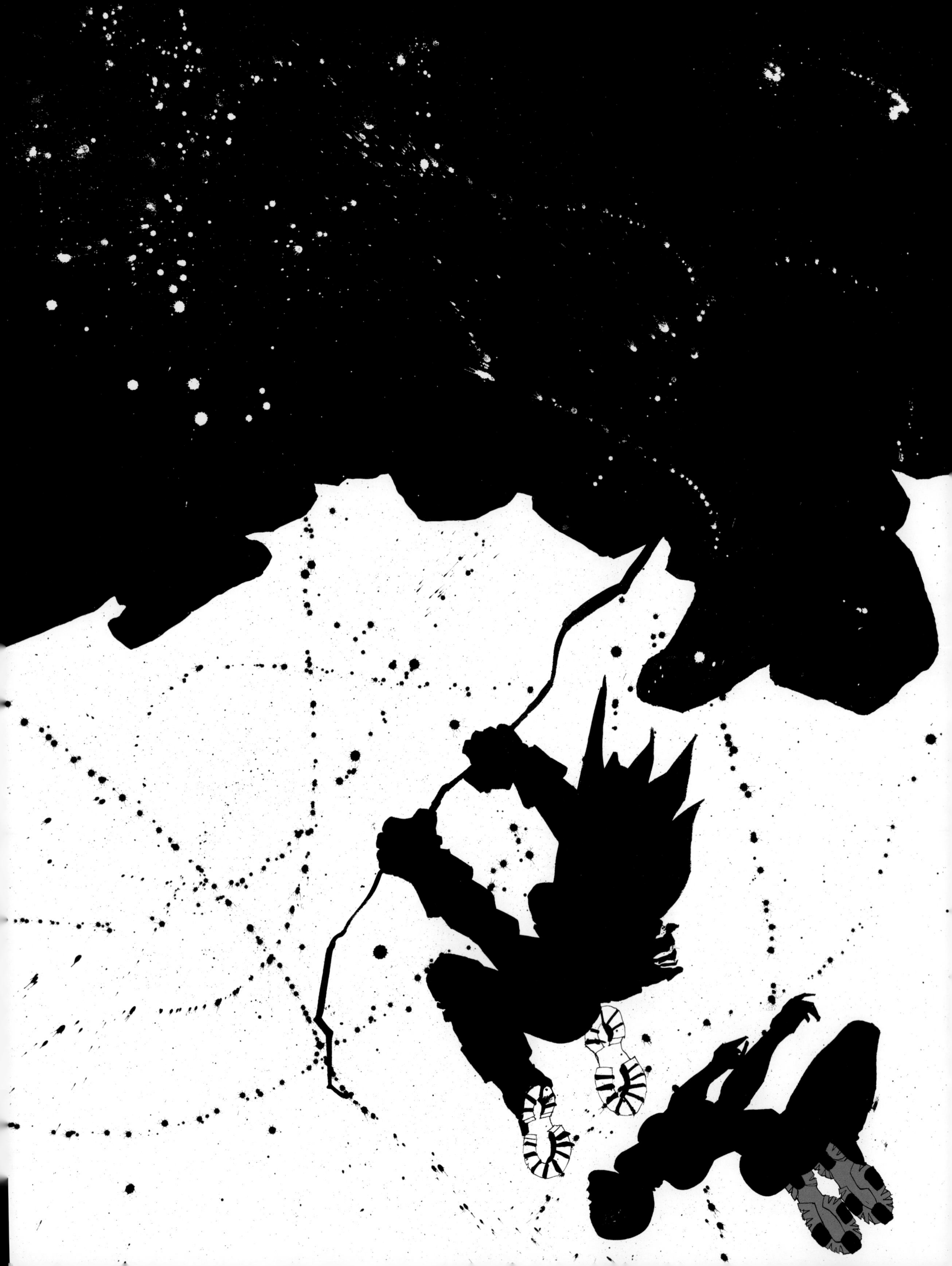

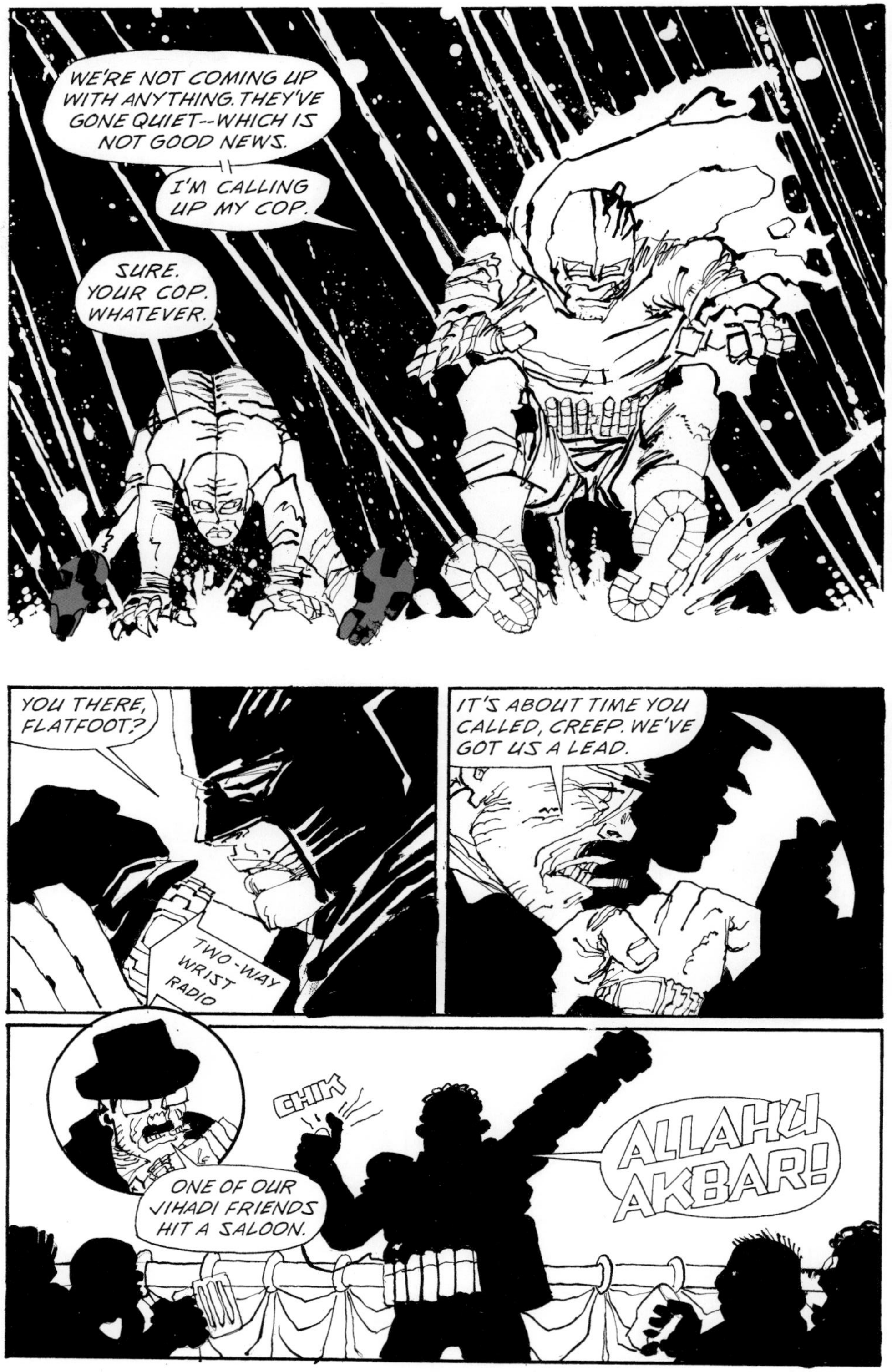
WE'RE NOT COMING UP WITH ANYTHING. THEY'VE GONE QUIET--WHICH IS NOT GOOD NEWS.
I'M CALLING UP MY COP.
SURE. YOUR COP. WHATEVER.
YOU THERE, FLATFOOT?
TWO-WAY WRIST RADIO
IT'S ABOUT TIME YOU CALLED, CREEP. WE'VE GOT US A LEAD.
ONE OF OUR JIHADI FRIENDS HIT A SALOON.
CHIK
ALLAHU AKBAR!

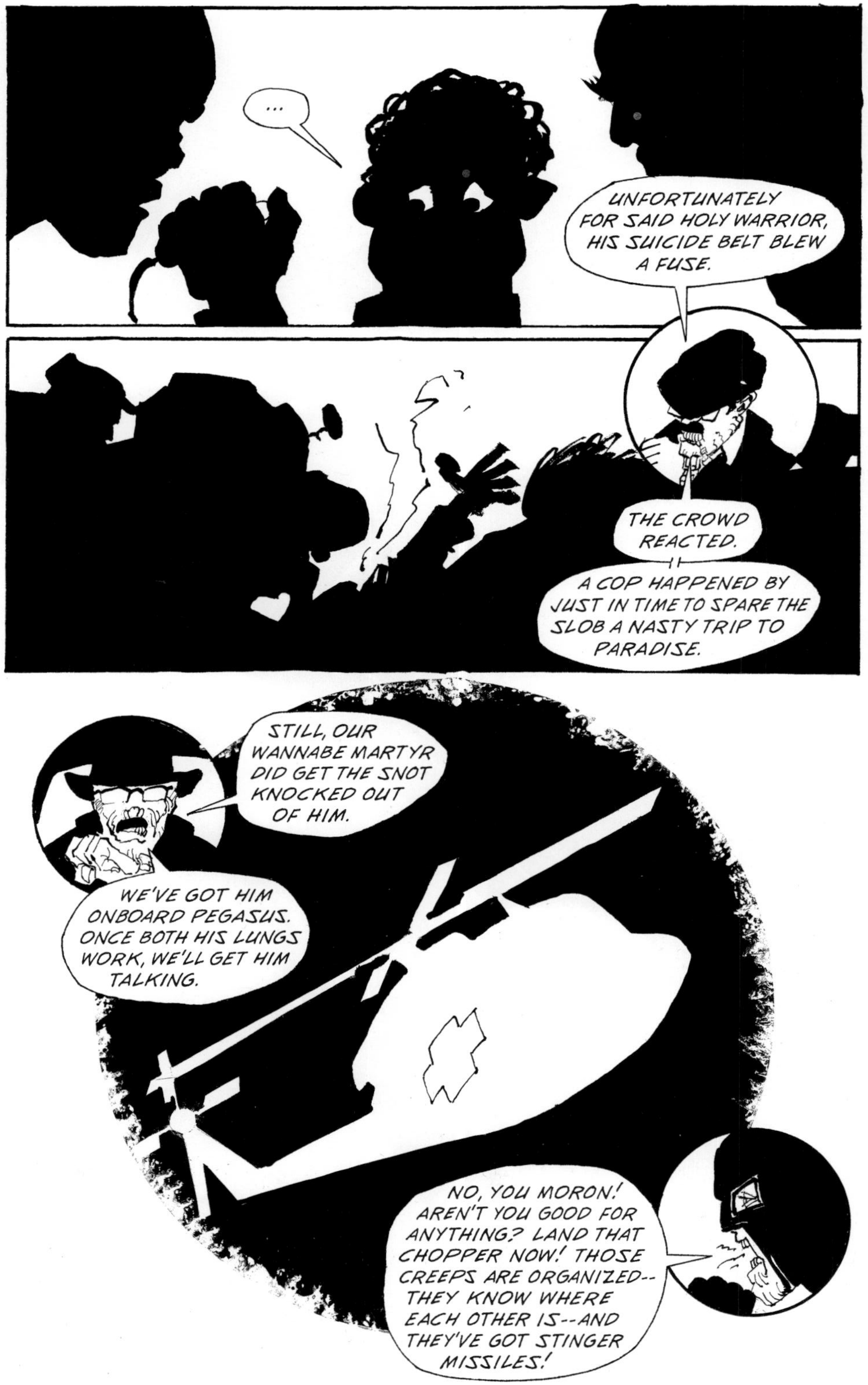
...
UNFORTUNATELY FOR SAID HOLY WARRIOR, HIS SUICIDE BELT BLEW A FUSE.
THE CROWD REACTED.
A COP HAPPENED BY JUST IN TIME TO SPARE THE SLOB A NASTY TRIP TO PARADISE.
STILL, OUR WANNABE MARTYR DID GET THE SNOT KNOCKED OUT OF HIM.
WE'VE GOT HIM ONBOARD PEGASUS. ONCE BOTH HIS LUNGS WORK, WE'LL GET HIM TALKING.
NO, YOU MORON! AREN'T YOU GOOD FOR ANYTHING? LAND THAT CHOPPER NOW! THOSE CREEPS ARE ORGANIZED--THEY KNOW WHERE EACH OTHER IS--AND THEY'VE GOT STINGER MISSILES!

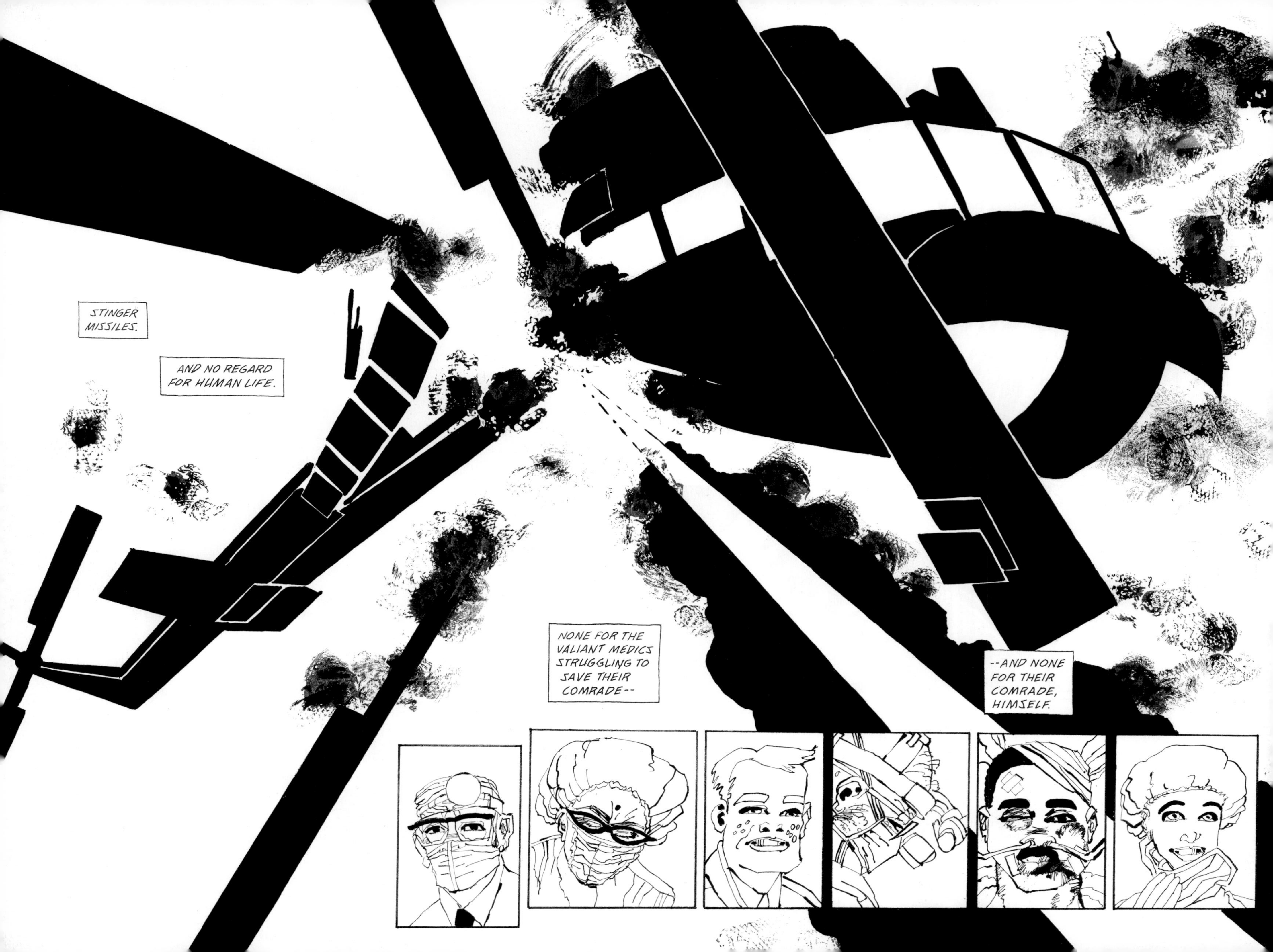
STINGER MISSILES.
AND NO REGARD FOR HUMAN LIFE.
NONE FOR THE VALIANT MEDICS STRUGGLING TO SAVE THEIR COMRADE--
--AND NONE FOR THEIR COMRADE, HIMSELF.

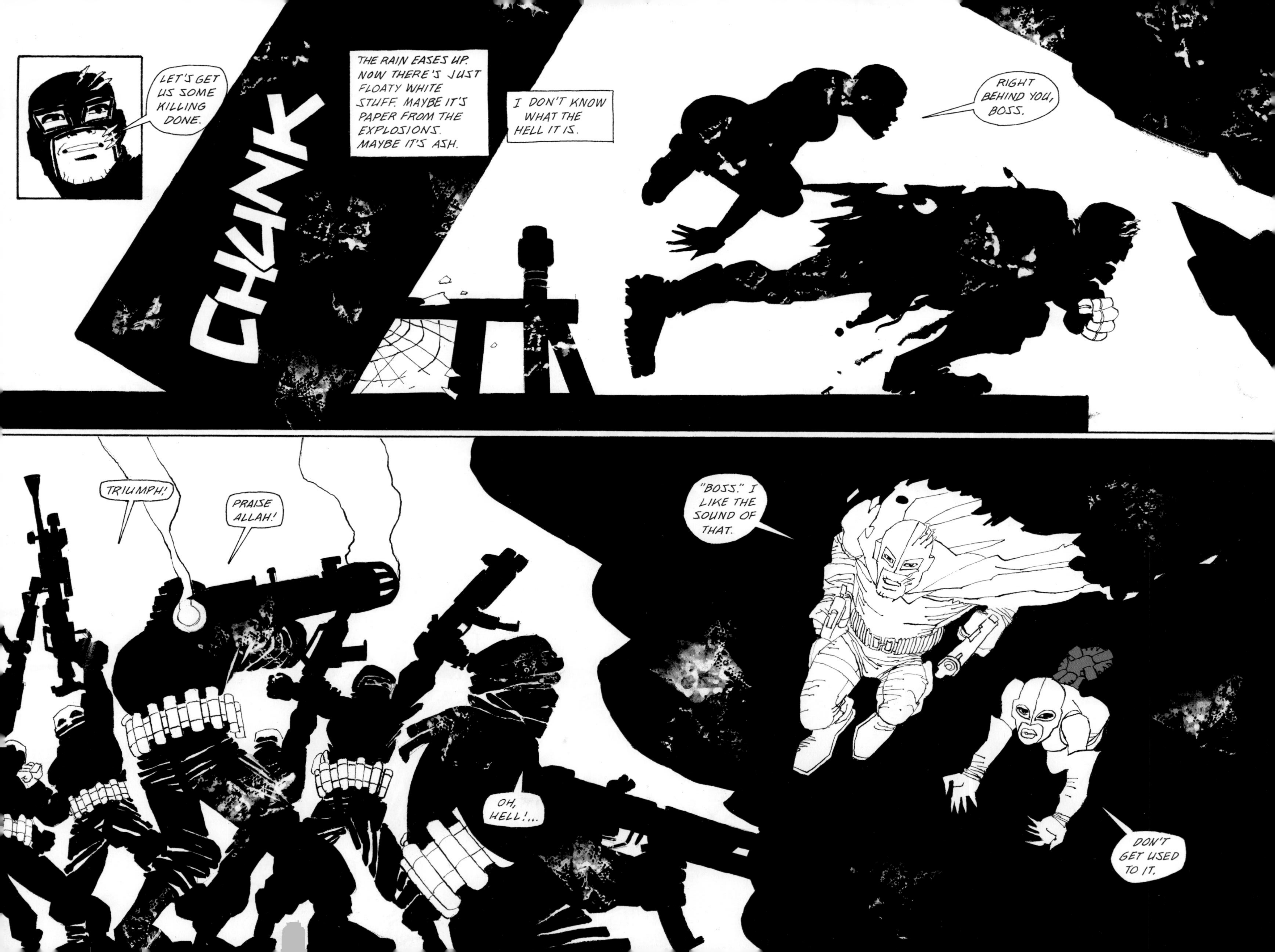
LET'S GET US SOME KILLING DONE.
CHUNK
THE RAIN EASES UP. NOW THERE'S JUST FLOATY WHITE STUFF. MAYBE IT'S PAPER FROM THE EXPLOSIONS. MAYBE IT'S ASH.
I DON'T KNOW WHAT THE HELL IT IS.
RIGHT BEHIND YOU, BOSS.
TRIUMPH!
PRAISE ALLAH!
OH, HELL!...
"BOSS." I LIKE THE SOUND OF THAT.
DON'T GET USED TO IT.

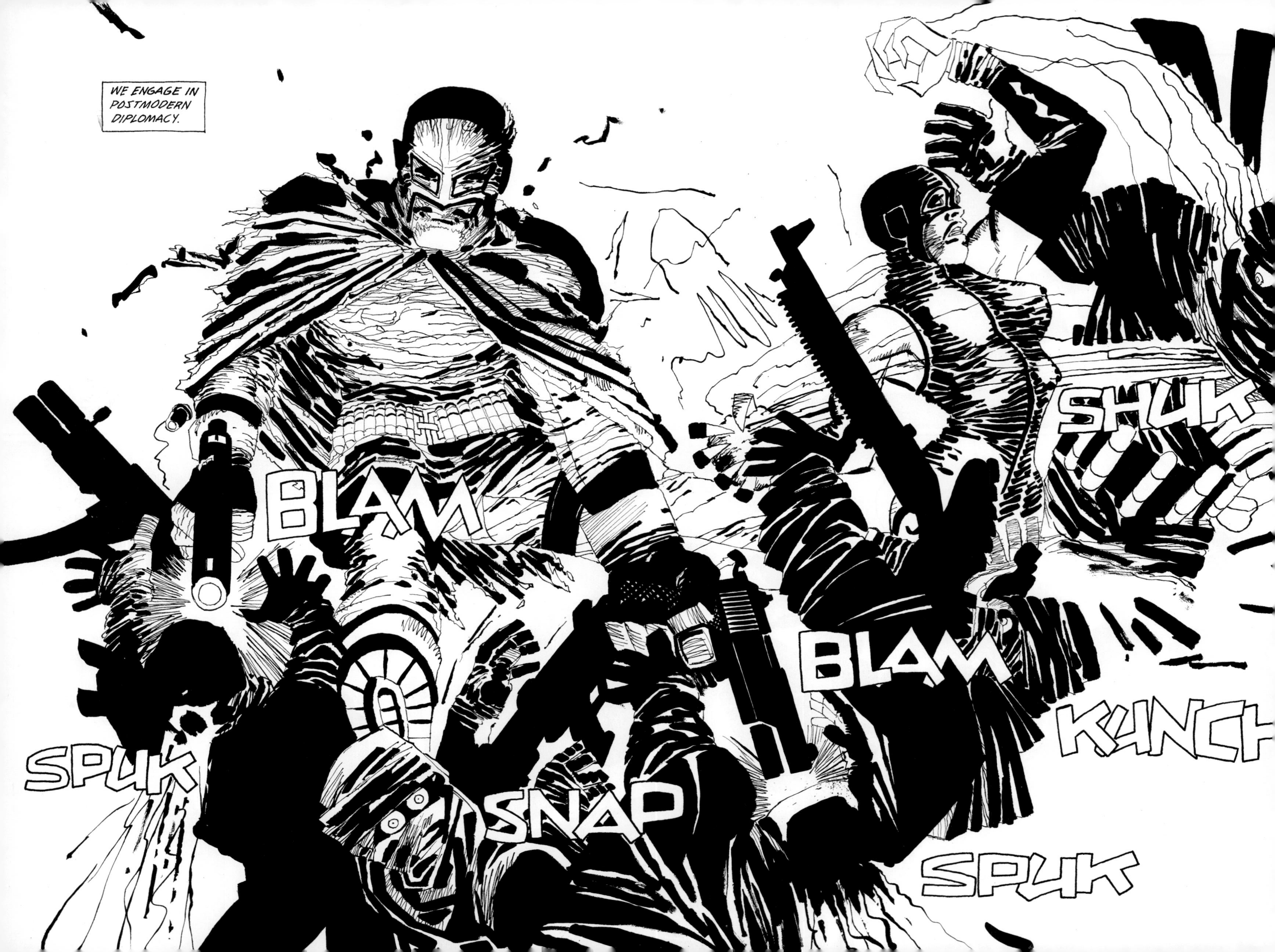
WE ENGAGE IN POSTMODERN DIPLOMACY.
BLAM
SPUK
SNAP
BLAM
SHUK
KUNCH
SPUK

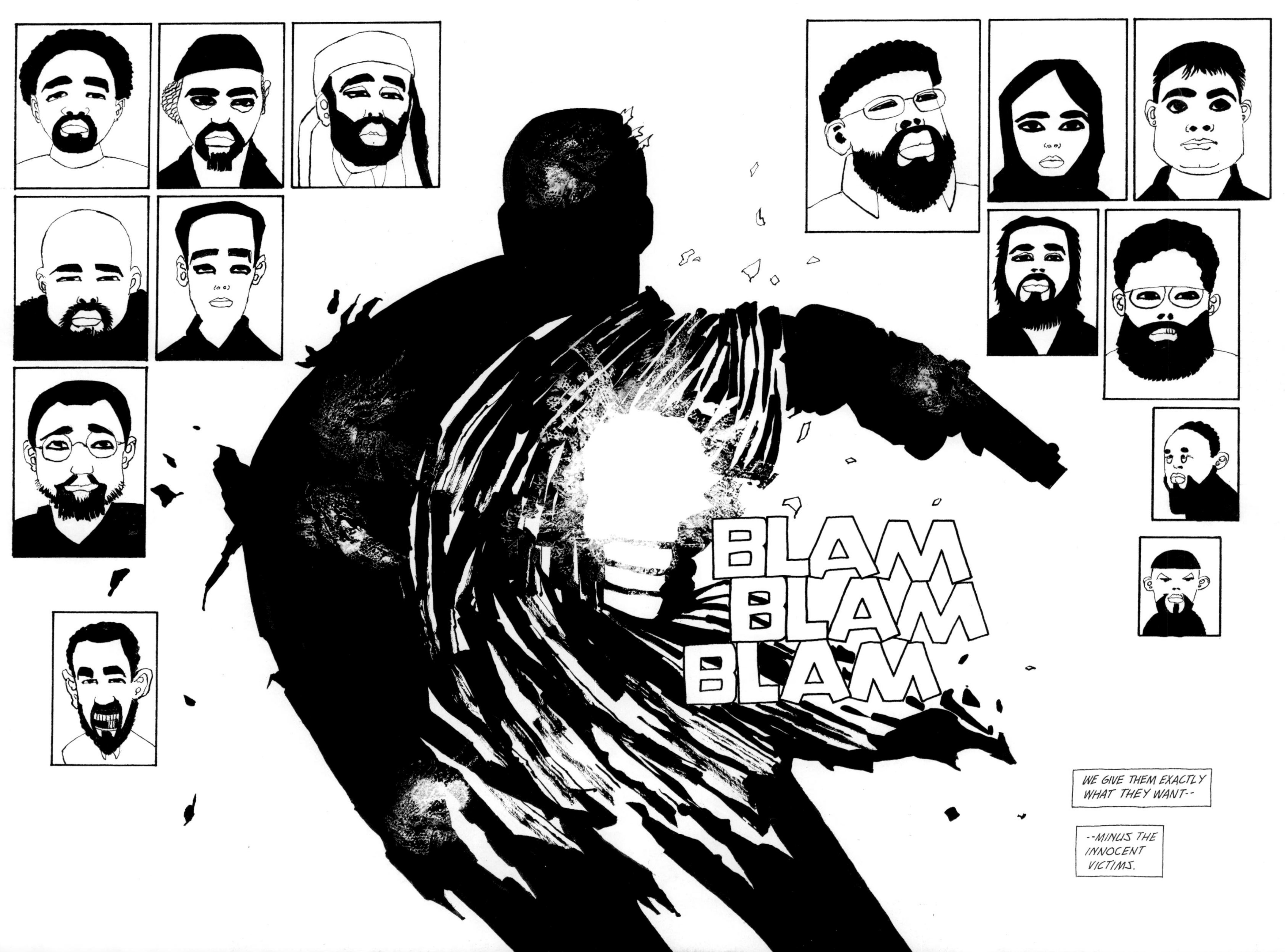
BLAM
BLAM
BLAM
WE GIVE THEM EXACTLY WHAT THEY WANT--
--MINUS THE INNOCENT VICTIMS.

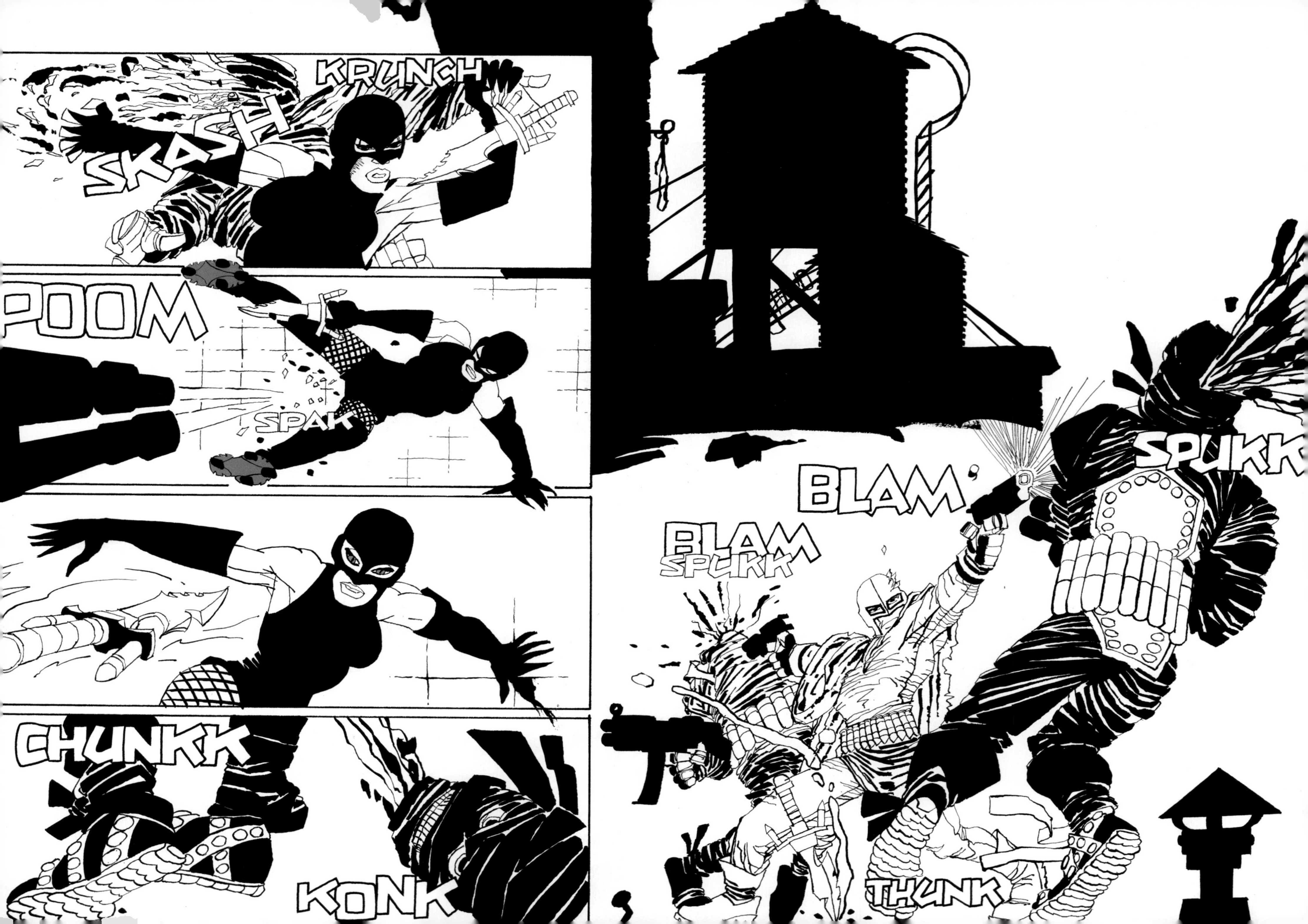
KRUNCH
SKASH
POOM
SPAK
CHUNKK
KONK
BLAM
BLAM
SPUKK
SPUKK
THUNK

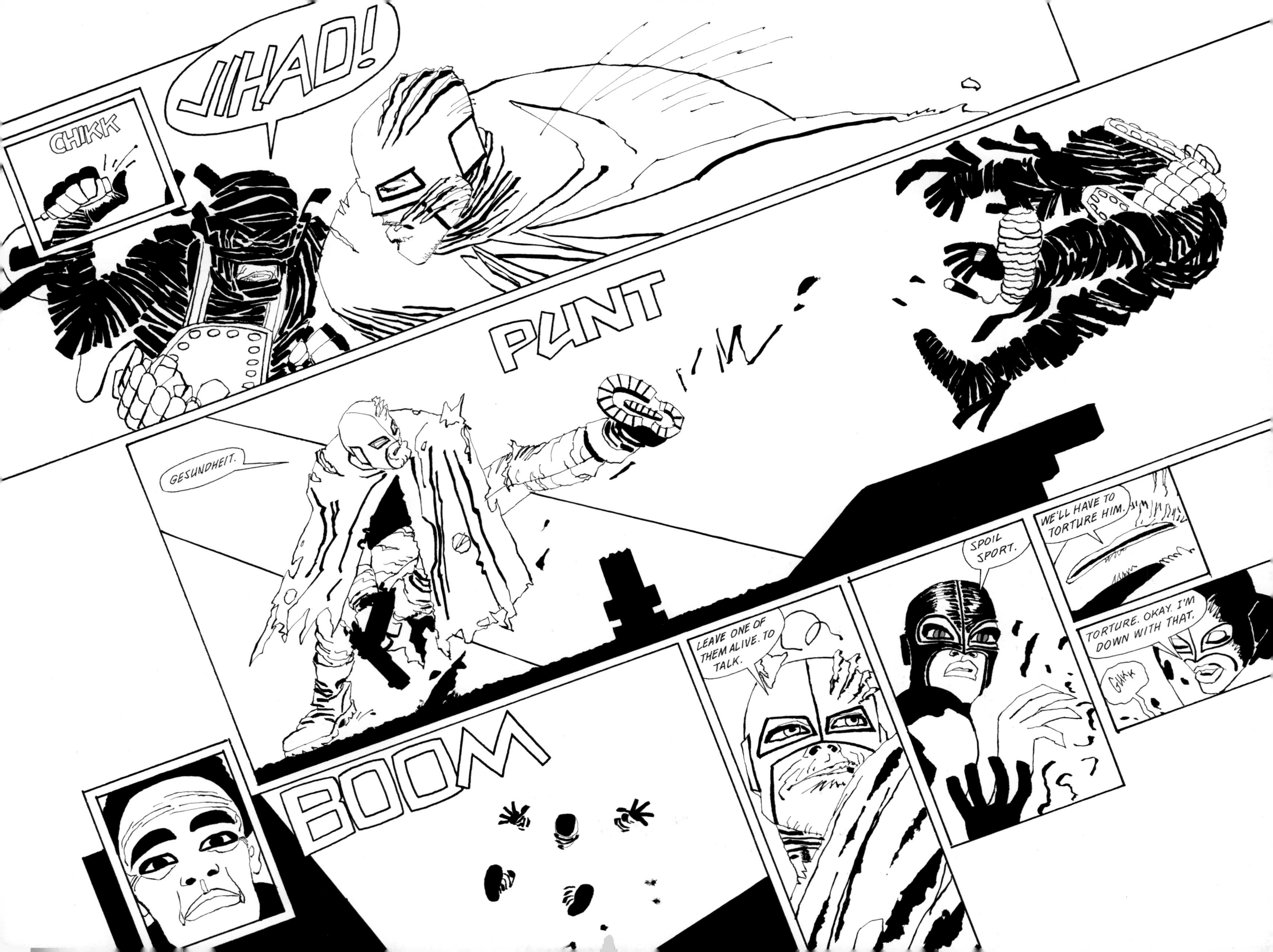
CHIKK
JIHAD!
PUNT
GESUNDHEIT.
BOOM
LEAVE ONE OF THEM ALIVE. TO TALK.
SPOIL SPORT.
WE'LL HAVE TO TORTURE HIM.
TORTURE. OKAY. I'M DOWN WITH THAT.
GAKK

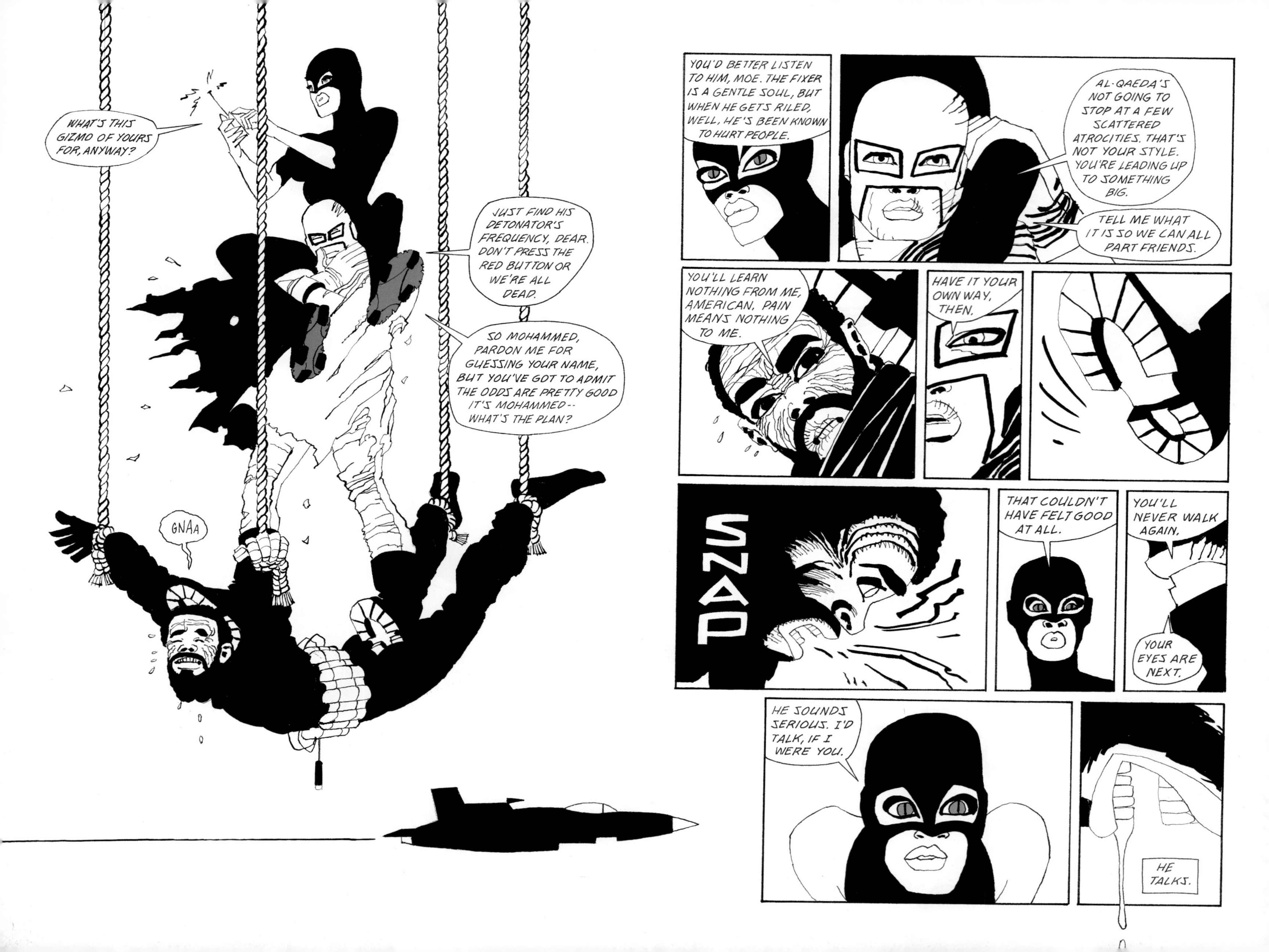
WHAT'S THIS GIZMO OF YOURS FOR, ANYWAY?
JUST FIND HIS DETONATOR'S FREQUENCY, DEAR. DON'T PRESS THE RED BUTTON OR WE'RE ALL DEAD.
SO MOHAMMED, PARDON ME FOR GUESSING YOUR NAME, BUT YOU'VE GOT TO ADMIT THE ODDS ARE PRETTY GOOD IT'S MOHAMMED-- WHAT'S THE PLAN?
GNAA
YOU'D BETTER LISTEN TO HIM, MOE. THE FIXER IS A GENTLE SOUL, BUT WHEN HE GETS RILED, WELL, HE'S BEEN KNOWN TO HURT PEOPLE.
AL-QAEDA'S NOT GOING TO STOP AT A FEW SCATTERED ATROCITIES. THAT'S NOT YOUR STYLE. YOU'RE LEADING UP TO SOMETHING BIG.
TELL ME WHAT IT IS SO WE CAN ALL PART FRIENDS.
YOU'LL LEARN NOTHING FROM ME, AMERICAN. PAIN MEANS NOTHING TO ME.
HAVE IT YOUR OWN WAY, THEN.
SNAP
THAT COULDN'T HAVE FELT GOOD AT ALL.
YOU'LL NEVER WALK AGAIN.
YOUR EYES ARE NEXT.
HE SOUNDS SERIOUS. I'D TALK, IF I WERE YOU.
HE TALKS.

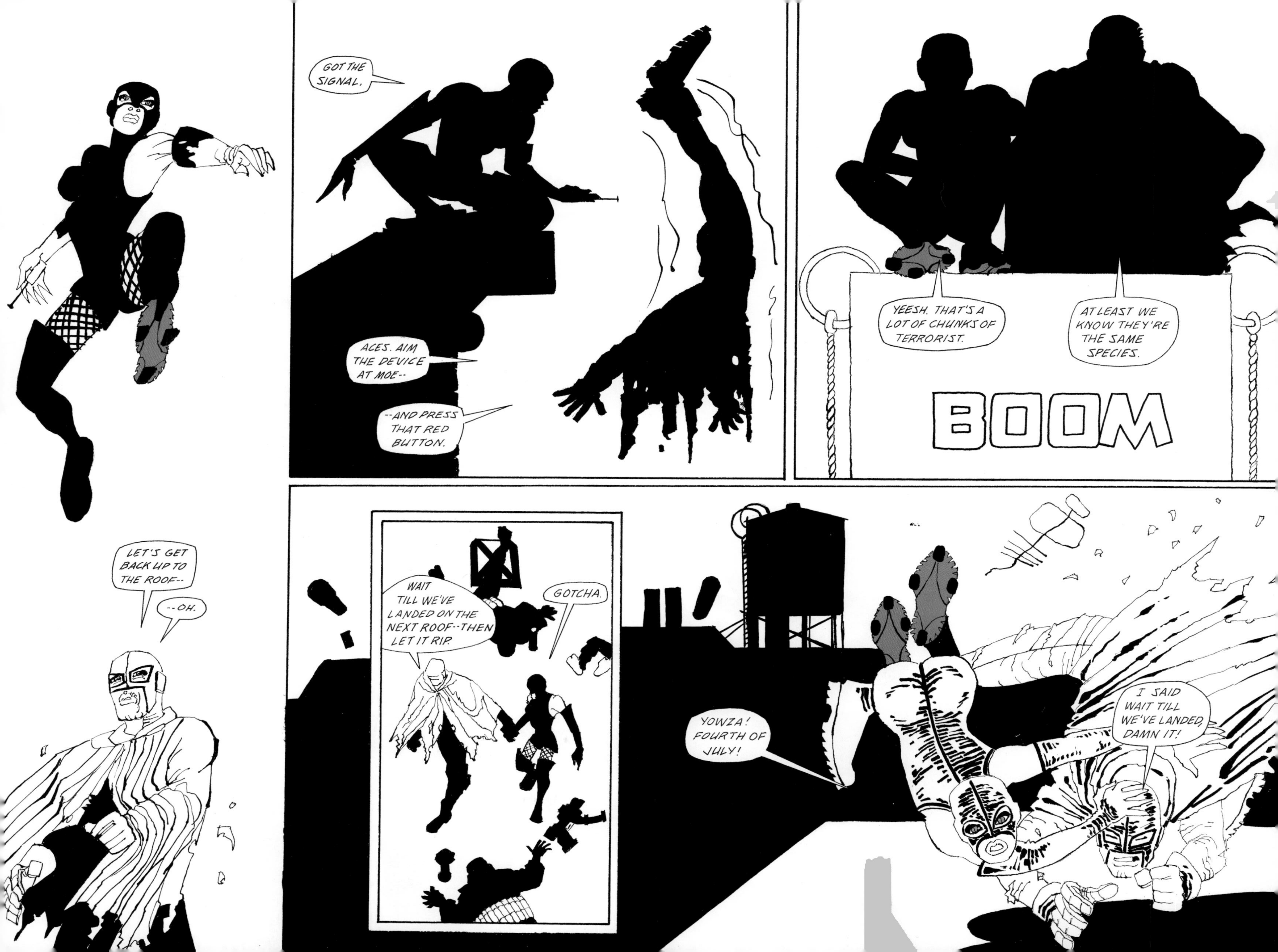
GOT THE SIGNAL.
ACES. AIM THE DEVICE AT MOE--
--AND PRESS THAT RED BUTTON.
YEESH. THAT'S A LOT OF CHUNKS OF TERRORIST.
AT LEAST WE KNOW THEY'RE THE SAME SPECIES.
BOOM
LET'S GET BACK UP TO THE ROOF--
--OH.
WAIT TILL WE'VE LANDED ON THE NEXT ROOF--THEN LET IT RIP.
GOTCHA.
YOWZA! FOURTH OF JULY!
I SAID WAIT TILL WE'VE LANDED, DAMN IT!

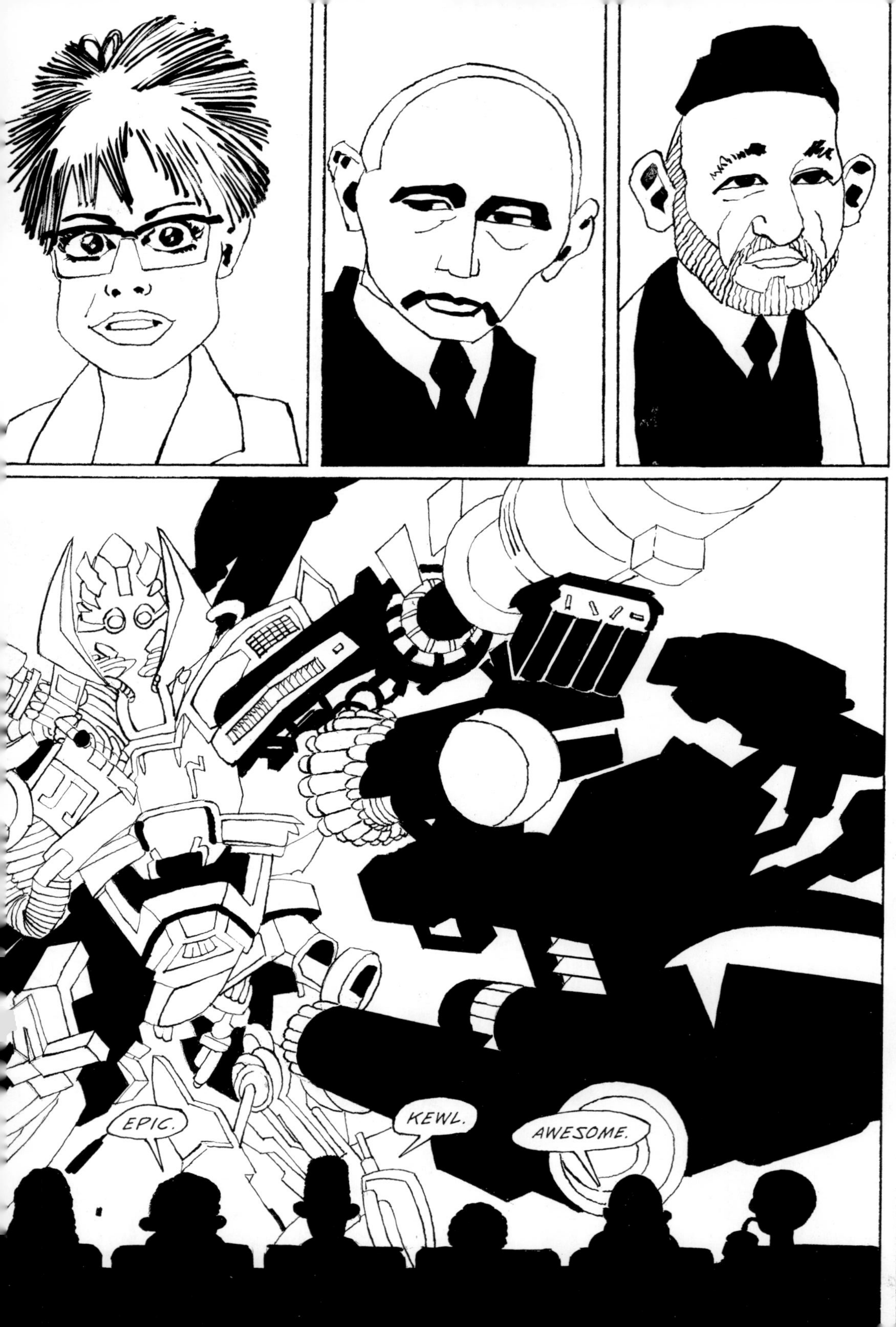
EPIC.
KEWL.
AWESOME.

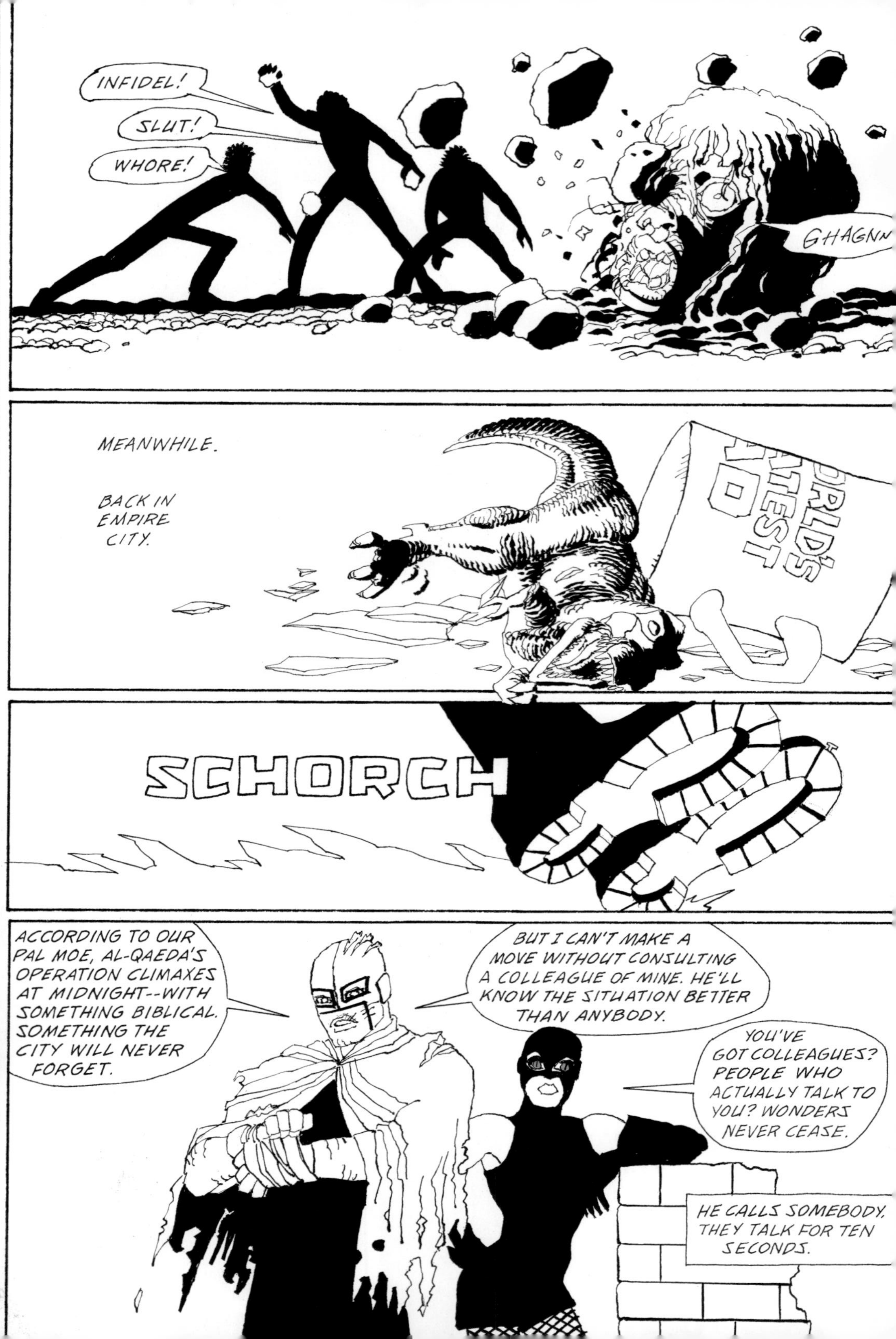
INFIDEL!
SLUT!
WHORE!
GHAGNN
MEANWHILE.
BACK IN EMPIRE CITY.
SCHORCH
ACCORDING TO OUR PAL MOE, AL-QAEDA'S OPERATION CLIMAXES AT MIDNIGHT--WITH SOMETHING BIBLICAL. SOMETHING THE CITY WILL NEVER FORGET.
BUT I CAN'T MAKE A MOVE WITHOUT CONSULTING A COLLEAGUE OF MINE. HE'LL KNOW THE SITUATION BETTER THAN ANYBODY.
YOU'VE GOT COLLEAGUES? PEOPLE WHO ACTUALLY TALK TO YOU? WONDERS NEVER CEASE.
HE CALLS SOMEBODY. THEY TALK FOR TEN SECONDS.

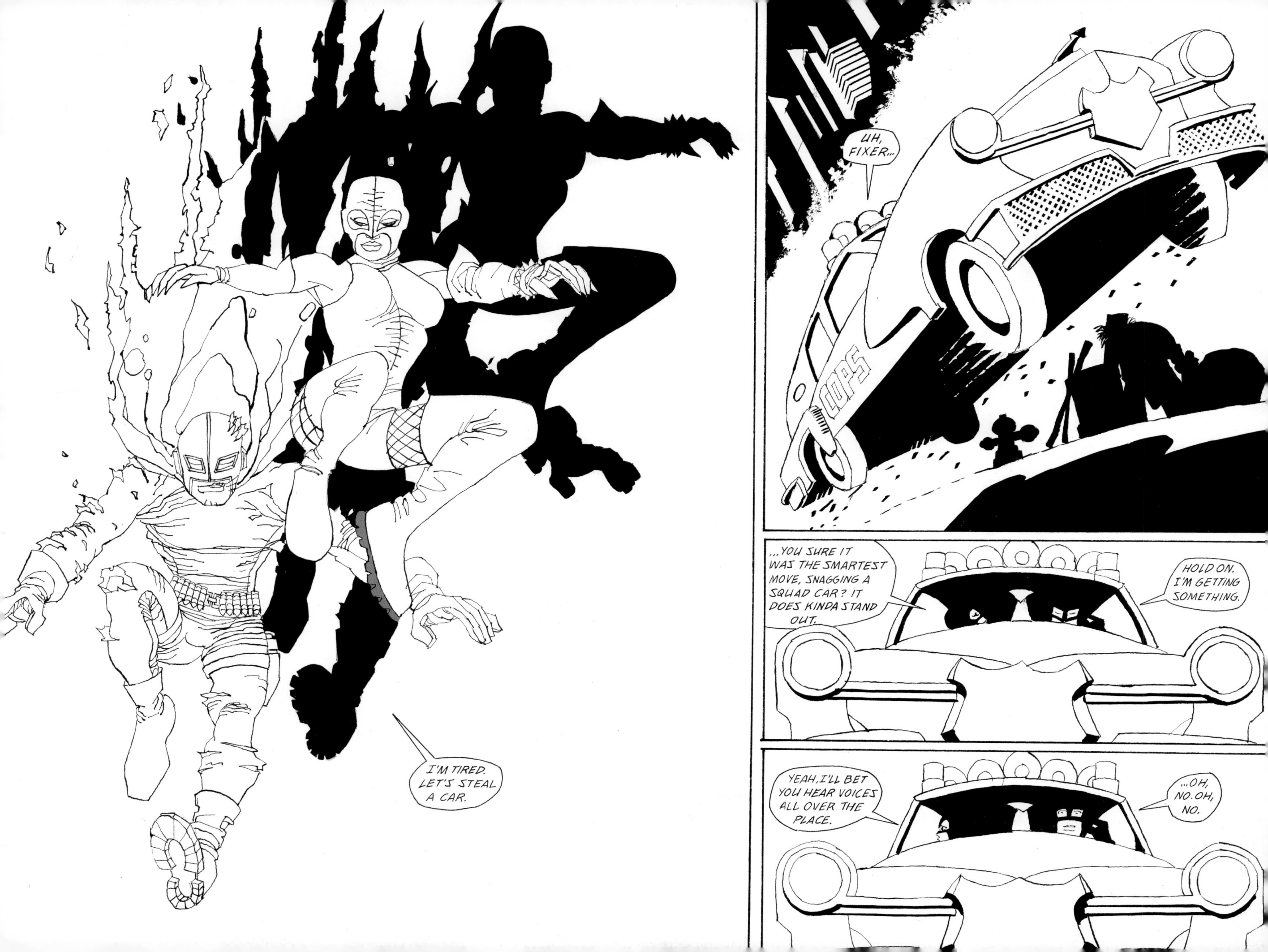

I'M TIRED. LET'S STEAL A CAR.
UH, FIXER...
...YOU SURE IT WAS THE SMARTEST MOVE, SNAGGING A SQUAD CAR? IT DOES KINDA STAND OUT.
HOLD ON. I'M GETTING SOMETHING.
YEAH, I'LL BET YOU HEAR VOICES ALL OVER THE PLACE.
...OH, NO. OH, NO.

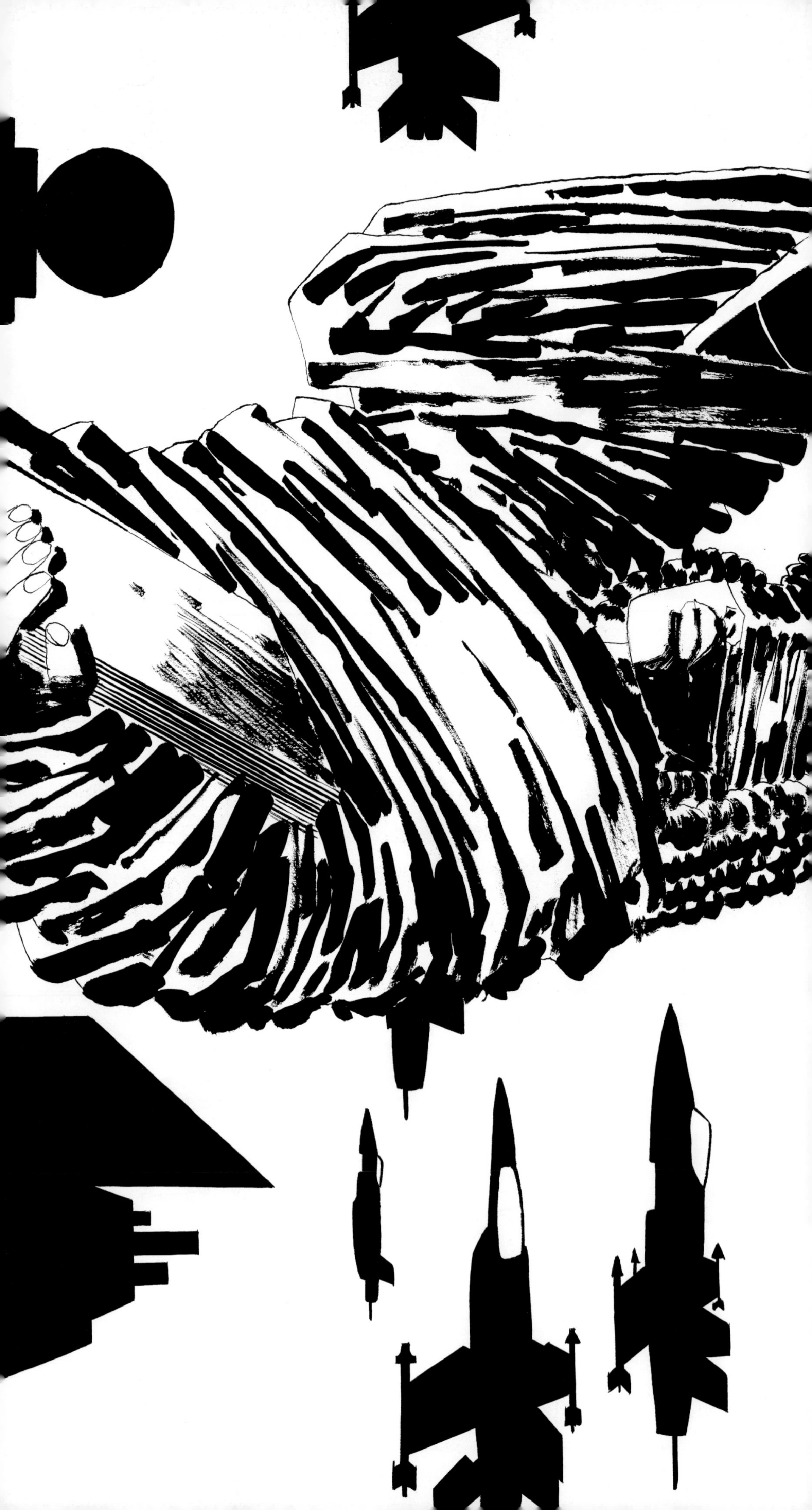

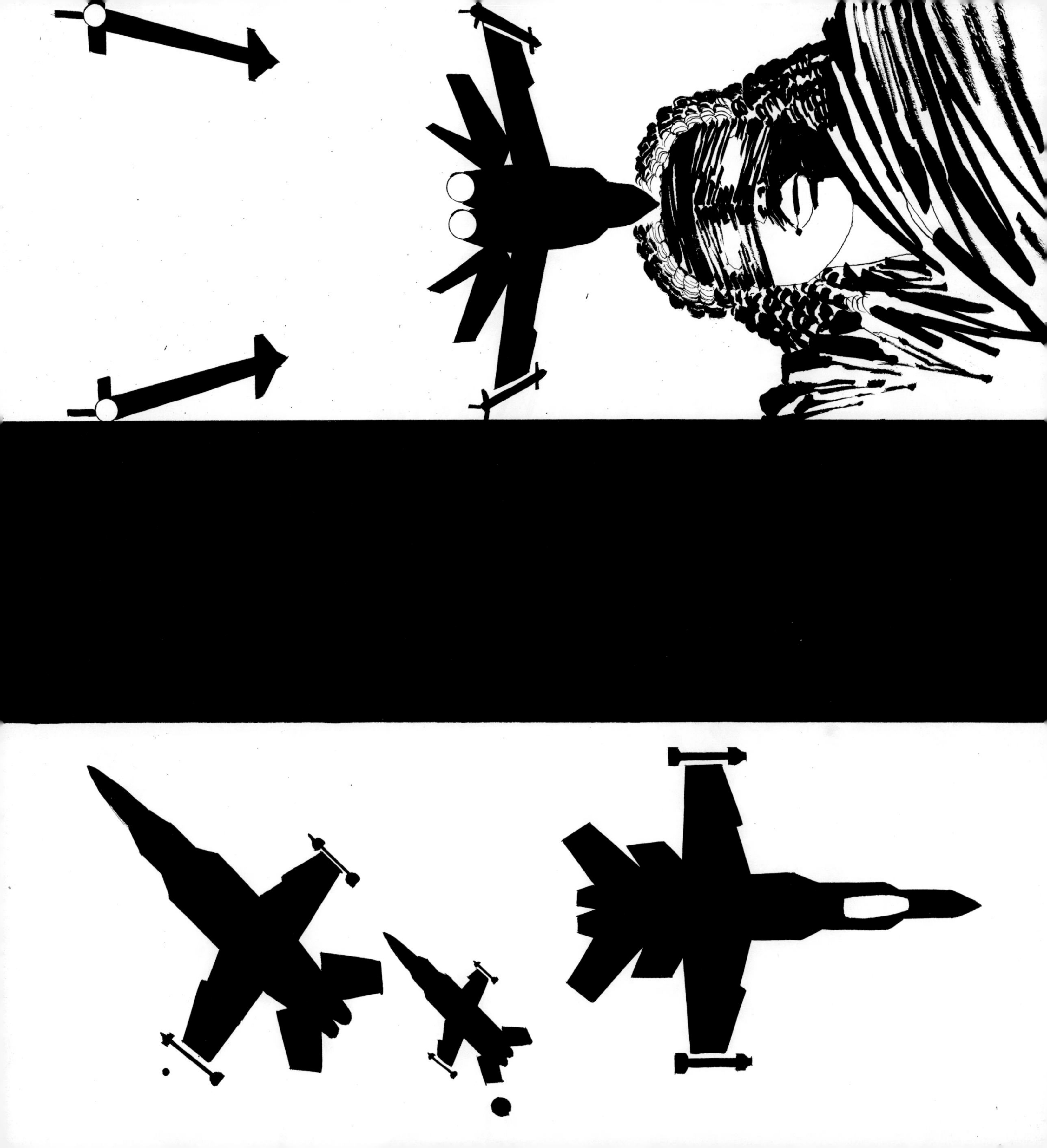

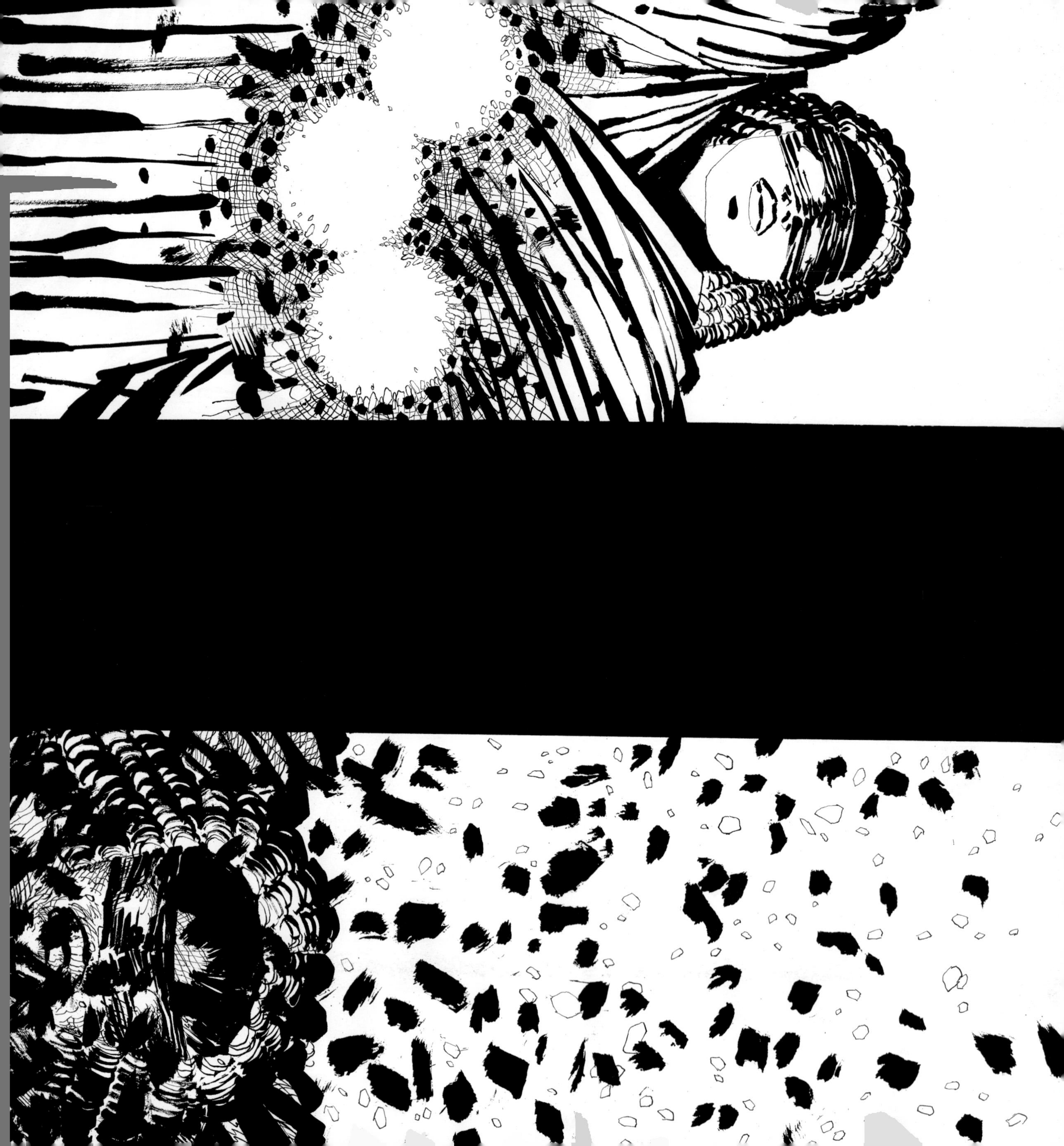

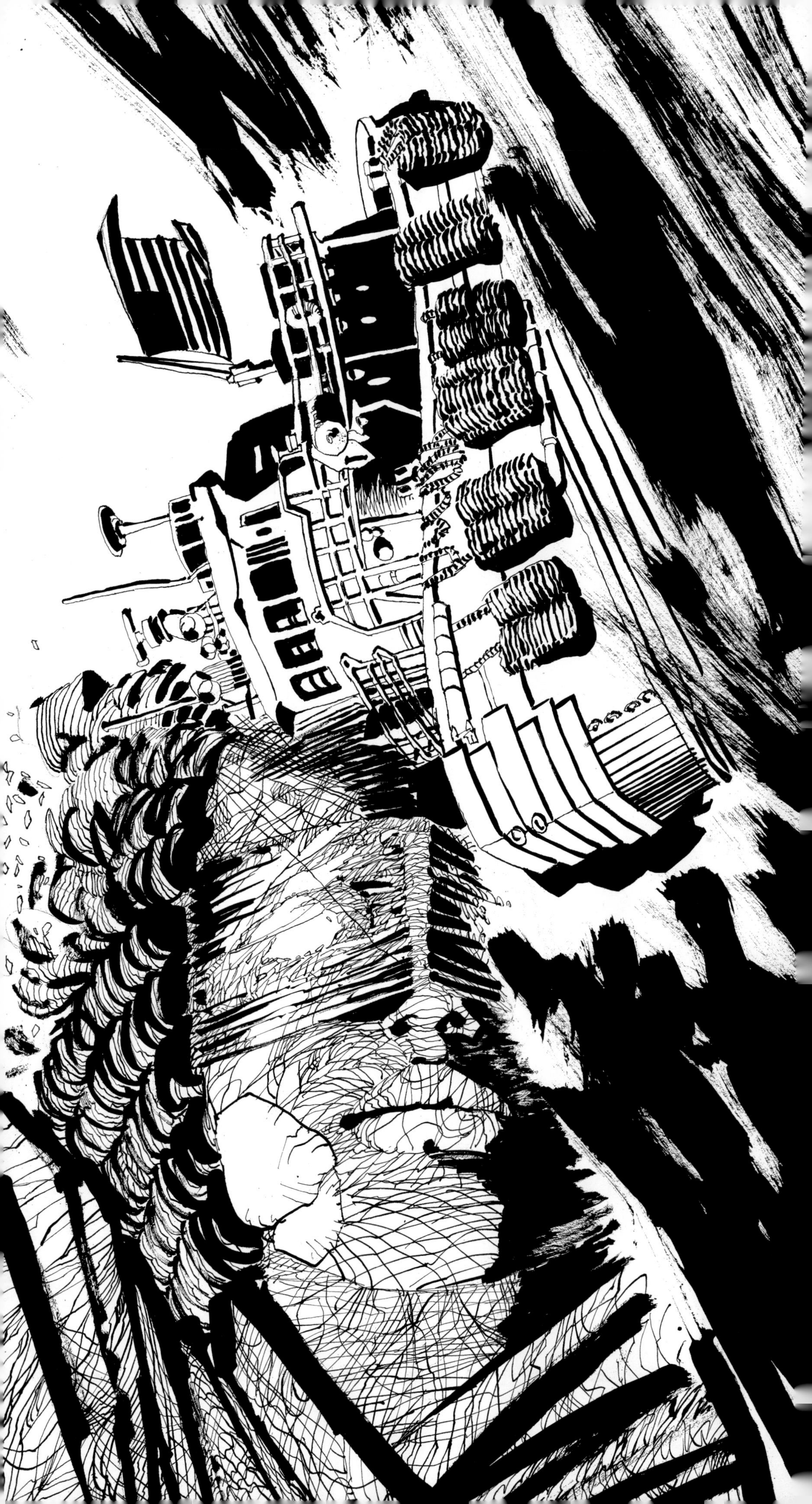

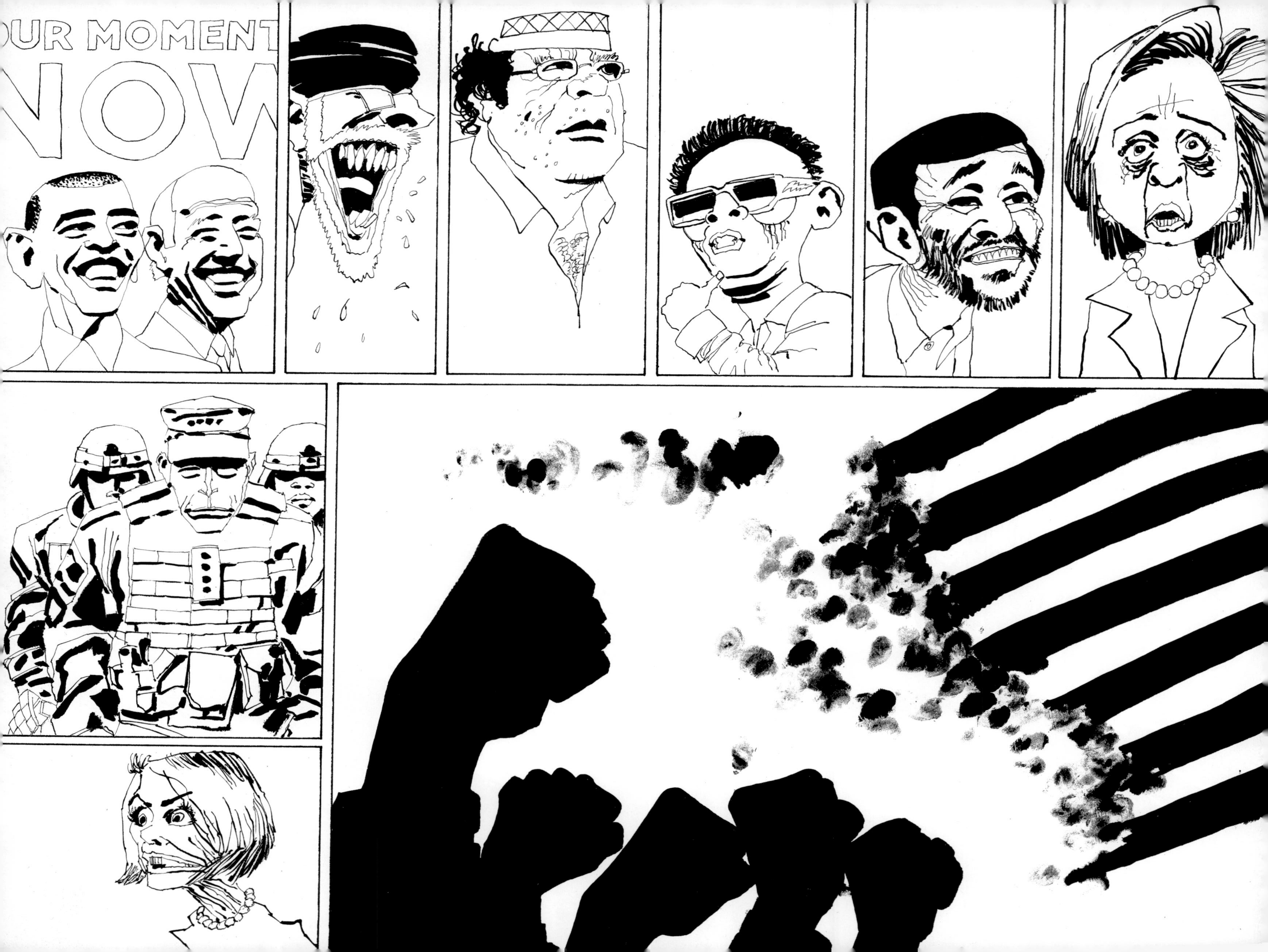
OUR MOMENT
NOW

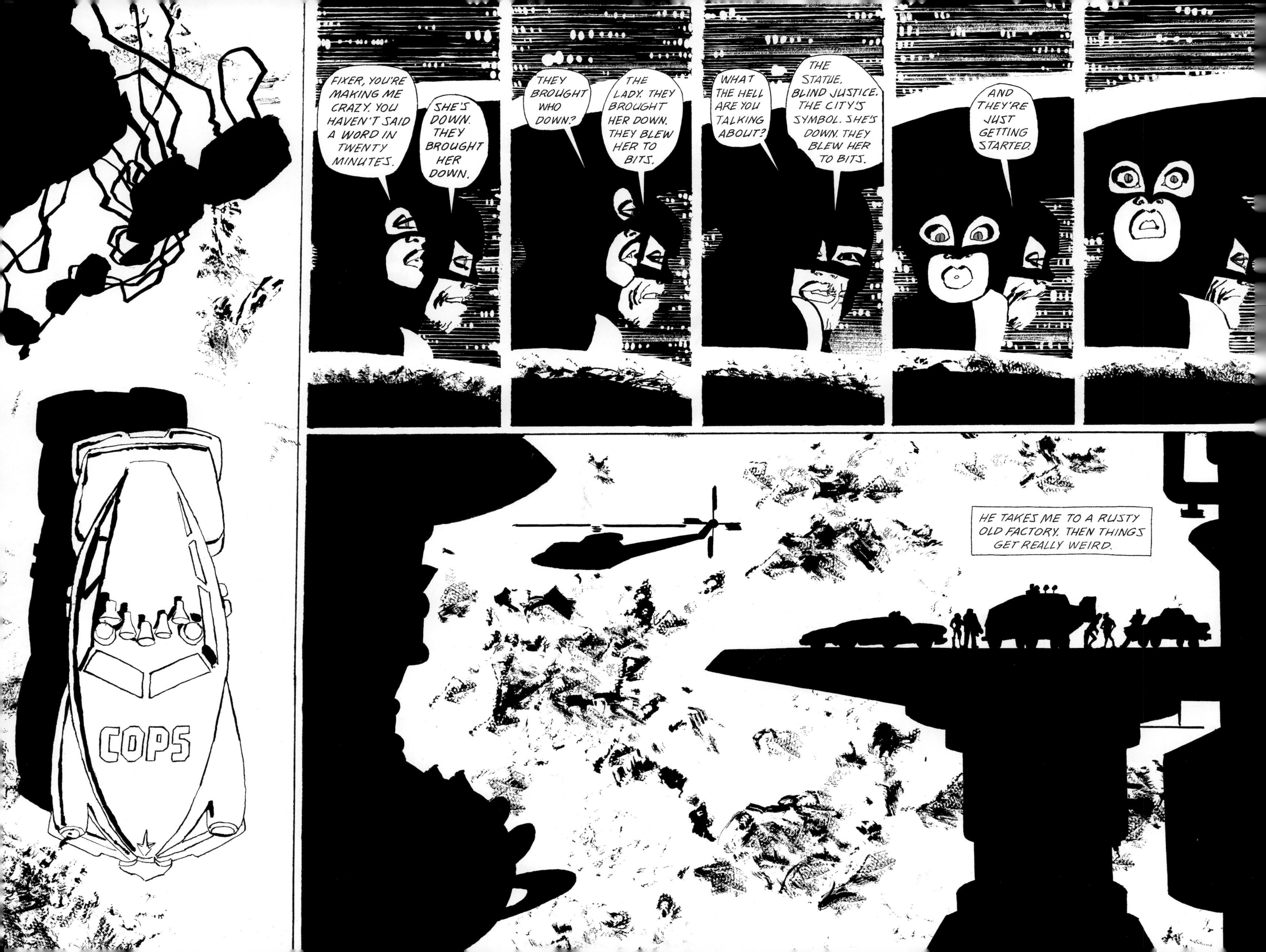

COPS
FIXER, YOU'RE MAKING ME CRAZY. YOU HAVEN'T SAID A WORD IN TWENTY MINUTES.
SHE'S DOWN. THEY BROUGHT HER DOWN.
THEY BROUGHT WHO DOWN?
THE LADY. THEY BROUGHT HER DOWN. THEY BLEW HER TO BITS.
WHAT THE HELL ARE YOU TALKING ABOUT?
THE STATUE. BLIND JUSTICE. THE CITY'S SYMBOL. SHE'S DOWN. THEY BLEW HER TO BITS.
AND THEY'RE JUST GETTING STARTED.
HE TAKES ME TO A RUSTY OLD FACTORY. THEN THINGS GET REALLY WEIRD.

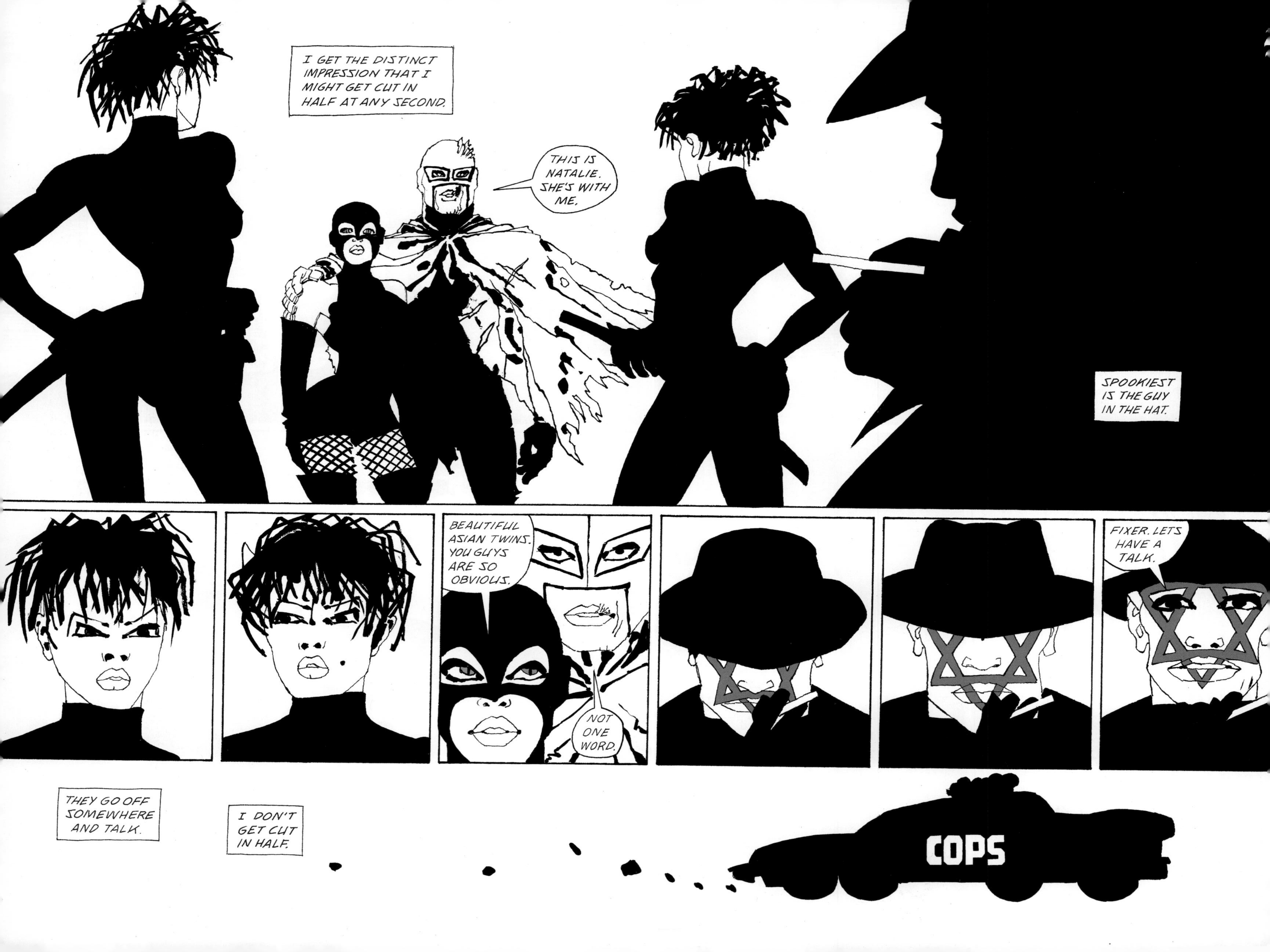
I GET THE DISTINCT IMPRESSION THAT I MIGHT GET CUT IN HALF AT ANY SECOND.
THIS IS NATALIE. SHE'S WITH ME.
SPOOKIEST IS THE GUY IN THE HAT.
BEAUTIFUL ASIAN TWINS. YOU GUYS ARE SO OBVIOUS.
NOT ONE WORD.
FIXER. LETS HAVE A TALK.
THEY GO OFF SOMEWHERE AND TALK.
I DON'T GET CUT IN HALF.
COPS

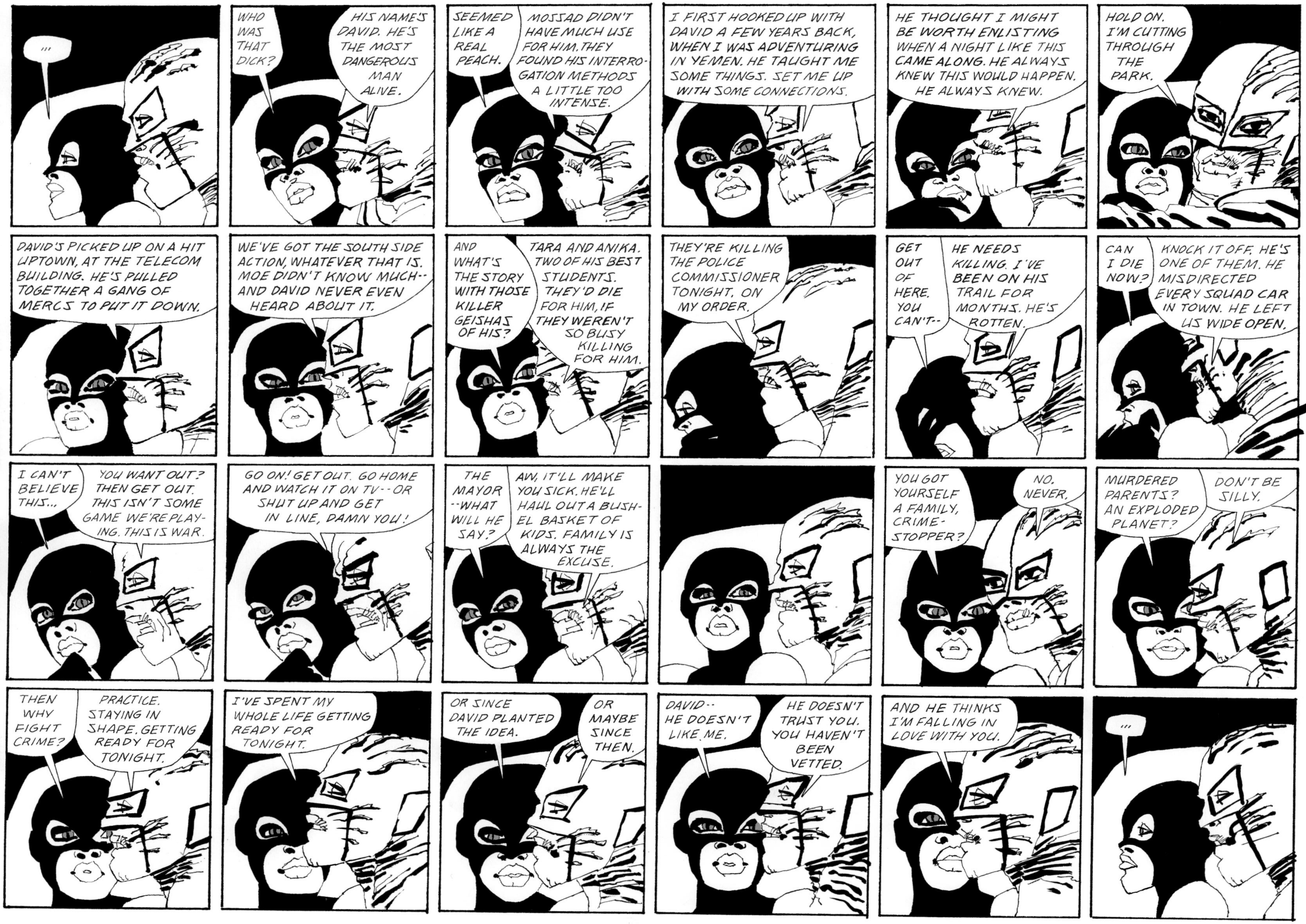
...
WHO WAS THAT DICK?
HIS NAME'S DAVID. HE'S THE MOST DANGEROUS MAN ALIVE.
SEEMED LIKE A REAL PEACH.
MOSSAD DIDN'T HAVE MUCH USE FOR HIM. THEY FOUND HIS INTERROGATION METHODS A LITTLE TOO INTENSE.
I FIRST HOOKED UP WITH DAVID A FEW YEARS BACK, WHEN I WAS ADVENTURING IN YEMEN. HE TAUGHT ME SOME THINGS. SET ME UP WITH SOME CONNECTIONS.
HE THOUGHT I MIGHT BE WORTH ENLISTING WHEN A NIGHT LIKE THIS CAME ALONG. HE ALWAYS KNEW THIS WOULD HAPPEN. HE ALWAYS KNEW.
HOLD ON. I'M CUTTING THROUGH THE PARK.
DAVID'S PICKED UP ON A HIT UPTOWN, AT THE TELECOM BUILDING. HE'S PULLED TOGETHER A GANG OF MERCS TO PUT IT DOWN.
WE'VE GOT THE SOUTH SIDE ACTION, WHATEVER THAT IS. MOE DIDN'T KNOW MUCH-- AND DAVID NEVER EVEN HEARD ABOUT IT.
AND WHAT'S THE STORY WITH THOSE KILLER GEISHAS OF HIS?
TARA AND ANIKA. TWO OF HIS BEST STUDENTS. THEY'D DIE FOR HIM, IF THEY WEREN'T SO BUSY KILLING FOR HIM.
THEY'RE KILLING THE POLICE COMMISSIONER TONIGHT. ON MY ORDER.
GET OUT OF HERE. YOU CAN'T--
HE NEEDS KILLING. I'VE BEEN ON HIS TRAIL FOR MONTHS. HE'S ROTTEN.
CAN I DIE NOW?
KNOCK IT OFF. HE'S ONE OF THEM. HE MISDIRECTED EVERY SQUAD CAR IN TOWN. HE LEFT US WIDE OPEN.
I CAN'T BELIEVE THIS...
YOU WANT OUT? THEN GET OUT. THIS ISN'T SOME GAME WE'RE PLAYING. THIS IS WAR.
GO ON! GET OUT. GO HOME AND WATCH IT ON TV--OR SHUT UP AND GET IN LINE, DAMN YOU!
THE MAYOR --WHAT WILL HE SAY?
AW, IT'LL MAKE YOU SICK. HE'LL HAUL OUT A BUSHEL BASKET OF KIDS. FAMILY IS ALWAYS THE EXCUSE.
YOU GOT YOURSELF A FAMILY, CRIME-STOPPER?
NO. NEVER.
MURDERED PARENTS? AN EXPLODED PLANET?
DON'T BE SILLY.
THEN WHY FIGHT CRIME?
PRACTICE. STAYING IN SHAPE. GETTING READY FOR TONIGHT.
I'VE SPENT MY WHOLE LIFE GETTING READY FOR TONIGHT.
OR SINCE DAVID PLANTED THE IDEA.
OR MAYBE SINCE THEN.
DAVID-- HE DOESN'T LIKE ME.
HE DOESN'T TRUST YOU. YOU HAVEN'T BEEN VETTED.
AND HE THINKS I'M FALLING IN LOVE WITH YOU.
...

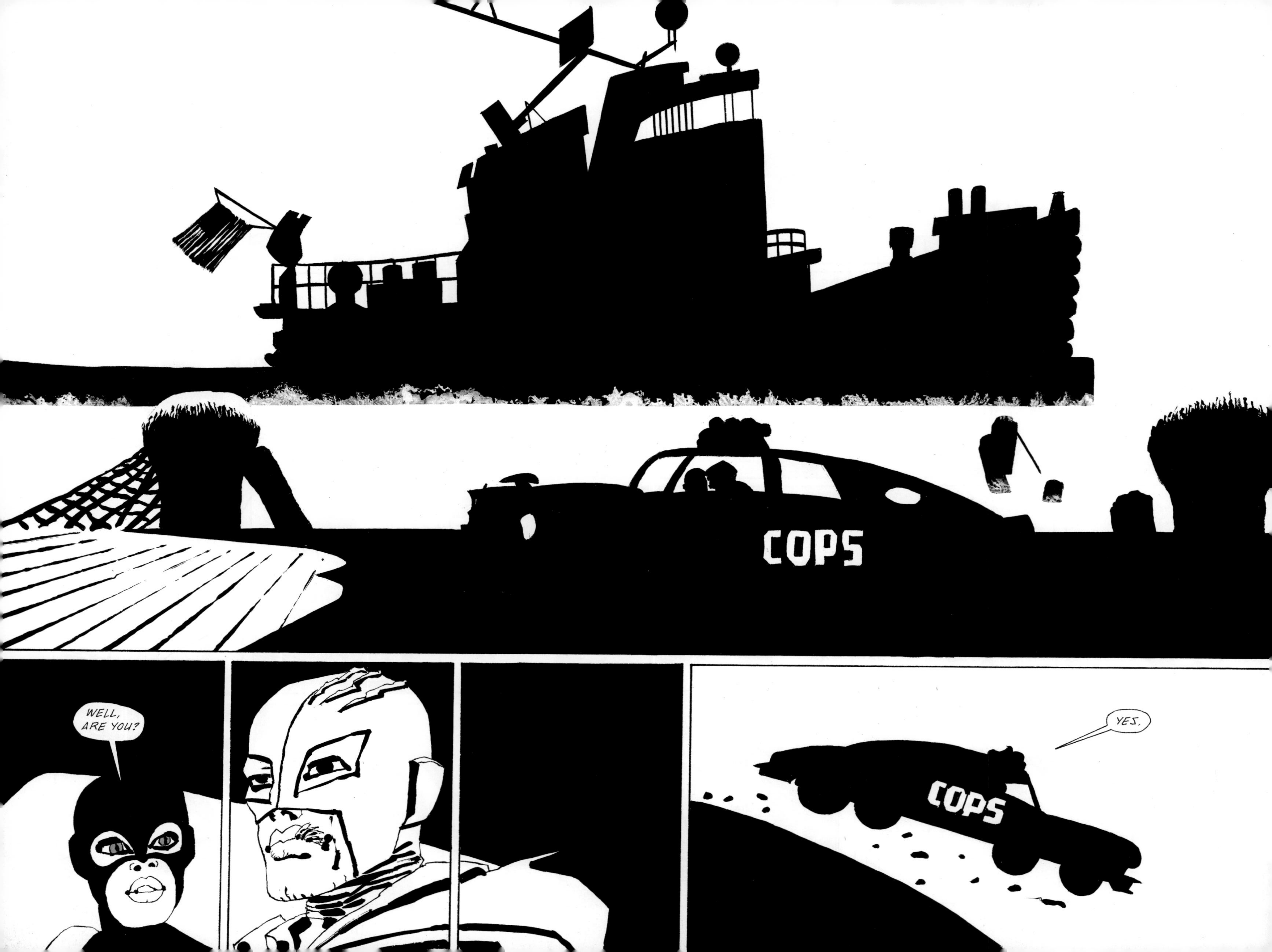
COPS
WELL, ARE YOU?
YES.
COPS

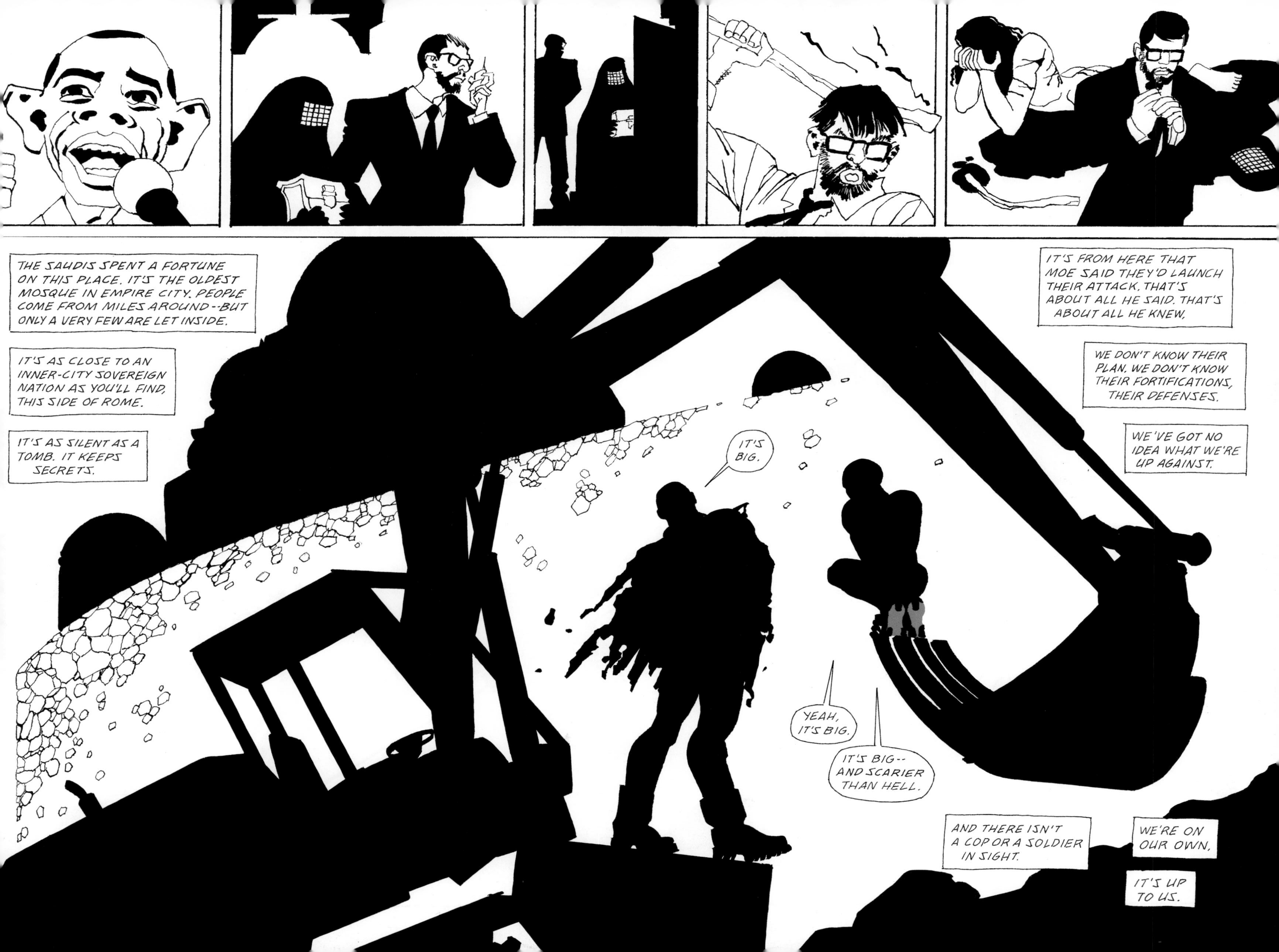
THE SAUDIS SPENT A FORTUNE ON THIS PLACE. IT'S THE OLDEST MOSQUE IN EMPIRE CITY. PEOPLE COME FROM MILES AROUND--BUT ONLY A VERY FEW ARE LET INSIDE.
IT'S AS CLOSE TO AN INNER-CITY SOVEREIGN NATION AS YOU'LL FIND, THIS SIDE OF ROME.
IT'S AS SILENT AS A TOMB. IT KEEPS SECRETS.
IT'S FROM HERE THAT MOE SAID THEY'D LAUNCH THEIR ATTACK. THAT'S ABOUT ALL HE SAID. THAT'S ABOUT ALL HE KNEW.
WE DON'T KNOW THEIR PLAN. WE DON'T KNOW THEIR FORTIFICATIONS, THEIR DEFENSES.
WE'VE GOT NO IDEA WHAT WE'RE UP AGAINST.
IT'S BIG.
YEAH, IT'S BIG.
IT'S BIG--AND SCARIER THAN HELL.
AND THERE ISN'T A COP OR A SOLDIER IN SIGHT.
WE'RE ON OUR OWN.
IT'S UP TO US.

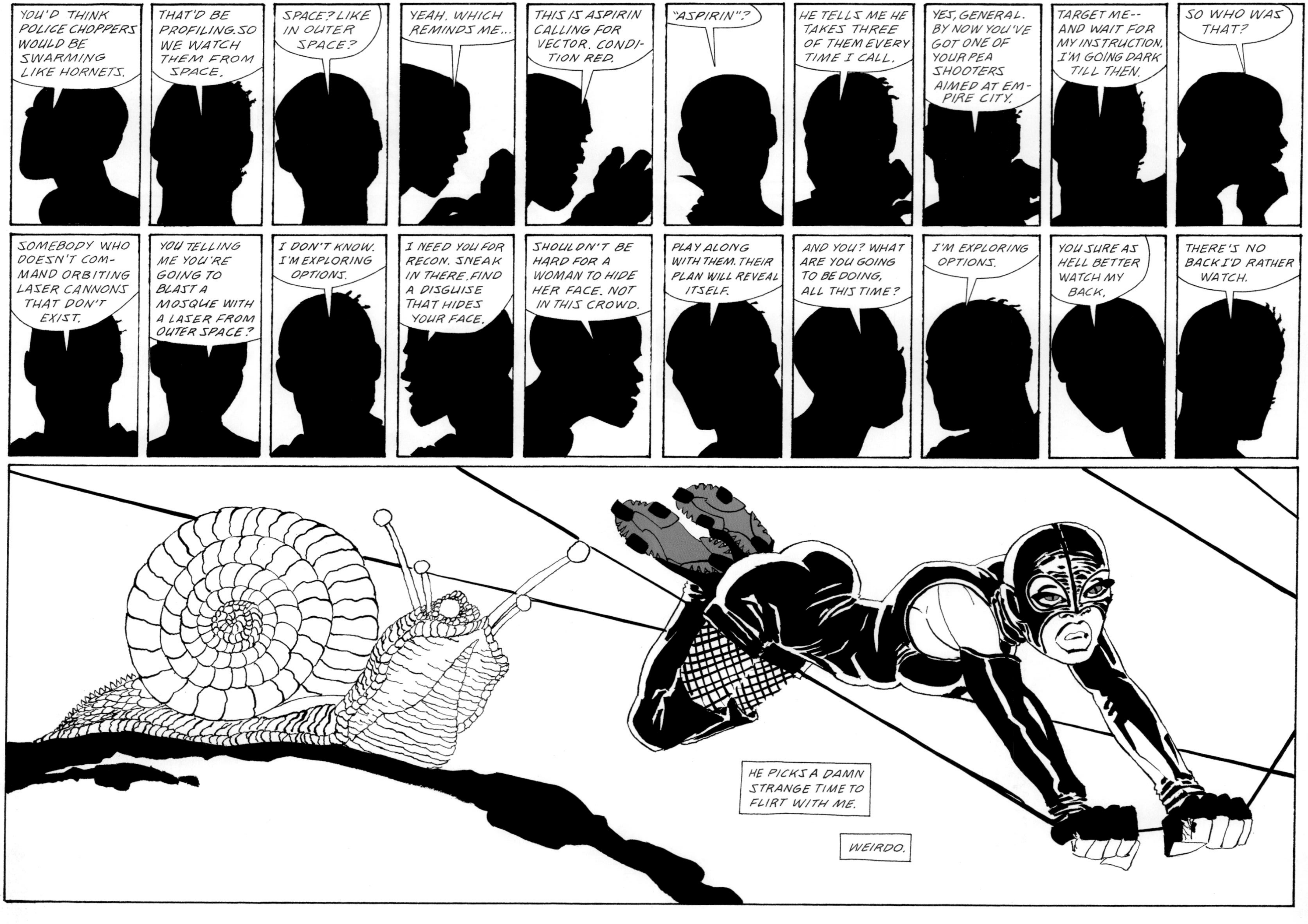
YOU'D THINK POLICE CHOPPERS WOULD BE SWARMING LIKE HORNETS.
THAT'D BE PROFILING. SO WE WATCH THEM FROM SPACE.
SPACE? LIKE IN OUTER SPACE?
YEAH. WHICH REMINDS ME...
THIS IS ASPIRIN CALLING FOR VECTOR. CONDITION RED.
"ASPIRIN"?
HE TELLS ME HE TAKES THREE OF THEM EVERY TIME I CALL.
YES, GENERAL. BY NOW YOU'VE GOT ONE OF YOUR PEA SHOOTERS AIMED AT EMPIRE CITY.
TARGET ME-- AND WAIT FOR MY INSTRUCTION. I'M GOING DARK TILL THEN.
SO WHO WAS THAT?
SOMEBODY WHO DOESN'T COMMAND ORBITING LASER CANNONS THAT DON'T EXIST.
YOU TELLING ME YOU'RE GOING TO BLAST A MOSQUE WITH A LASER FROM OUTER SPACE?
I DON'T KNOW. I'M EXPLORING OPTIONS.
I NEED YOU FOR RECON. SNEAK IN THERE. FIND A DISGUISE THAT HIDES YOUR FACE.
SHOULDN'T BE HARD FOR A WOMAN TO HIDE HER FACE. NOT IN THIS CROWD.
PLAY ALONG WITH THEM. THEIR PLAN WILL REVEAL ITSELF.
AND YOU? WHAT ARE YOU GOING TO BE DOING, ALL THIS TIME?
I'M EXPLORING OPTIONS.
YOU SURE AS HELL BETTER WATCH MY BACK.
THERE'S NO BACK I'D RATHER WATCH.
HE PICKS A DAMN STRANGE TIME TO FLIRT WITH ME.
WEIRDO.

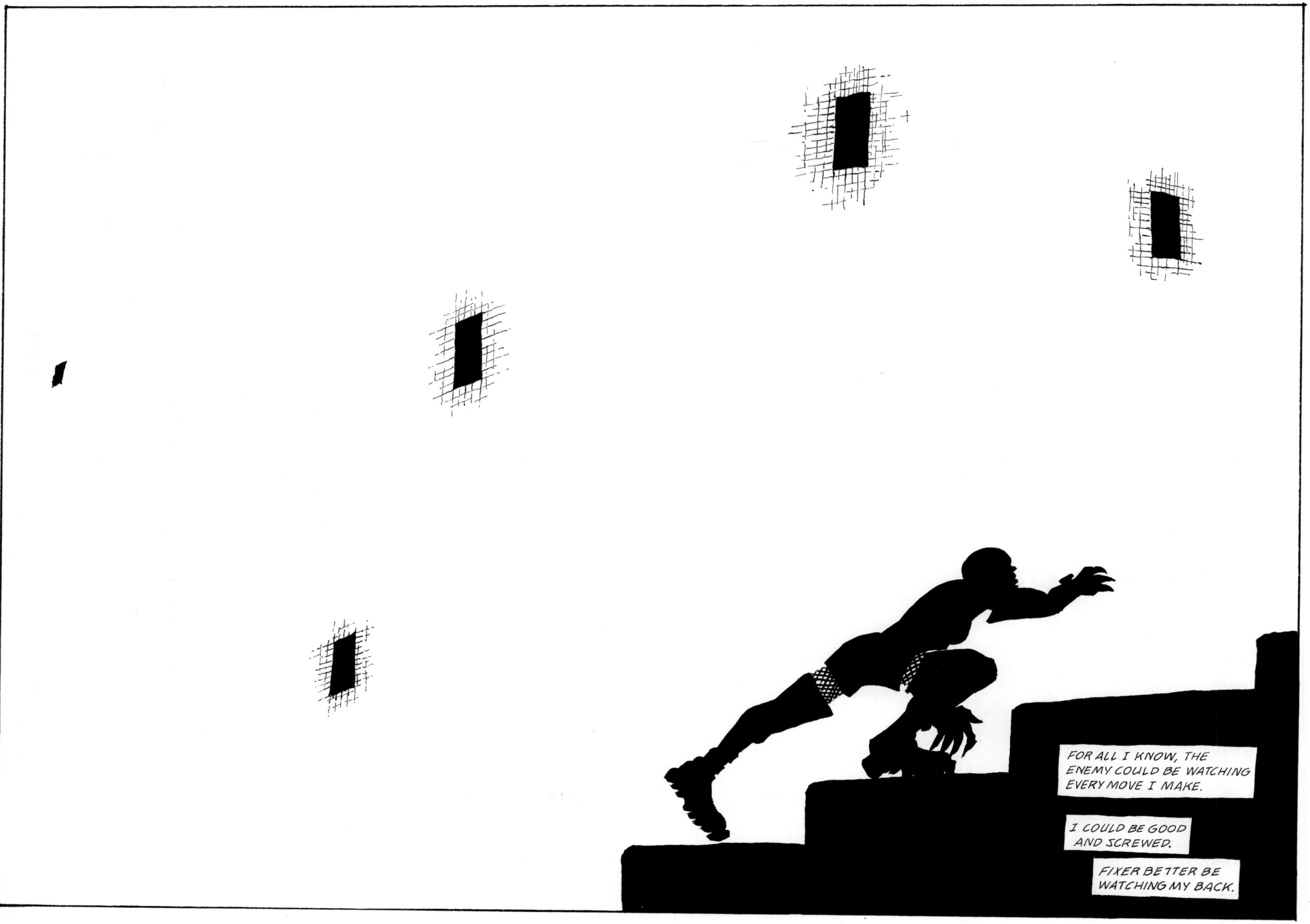
FOR ALL I KNOW, THE ENEMY COULD BE WATCHING EVERY MOVE I MAKE.
I COULD BE GOOD AND SCREWED.
FIXER BETTER BE WATCHING MY BACK.

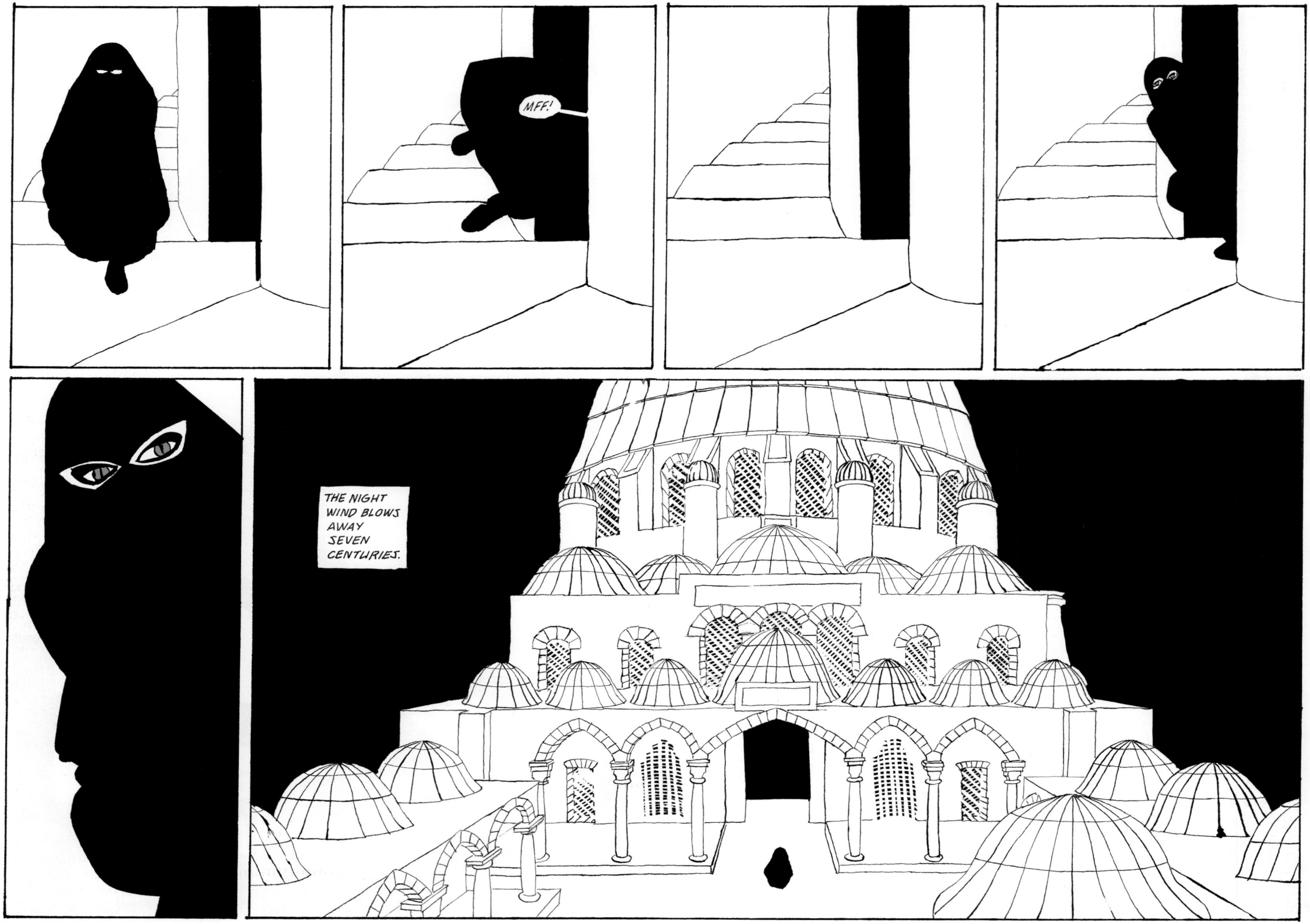
MFF!
THE NIGHT WIND BLOWS AWAY SEVEN CENTURIES.

I TRY TO WALK HUMBLE.
WHATEVER THAT MEANS.

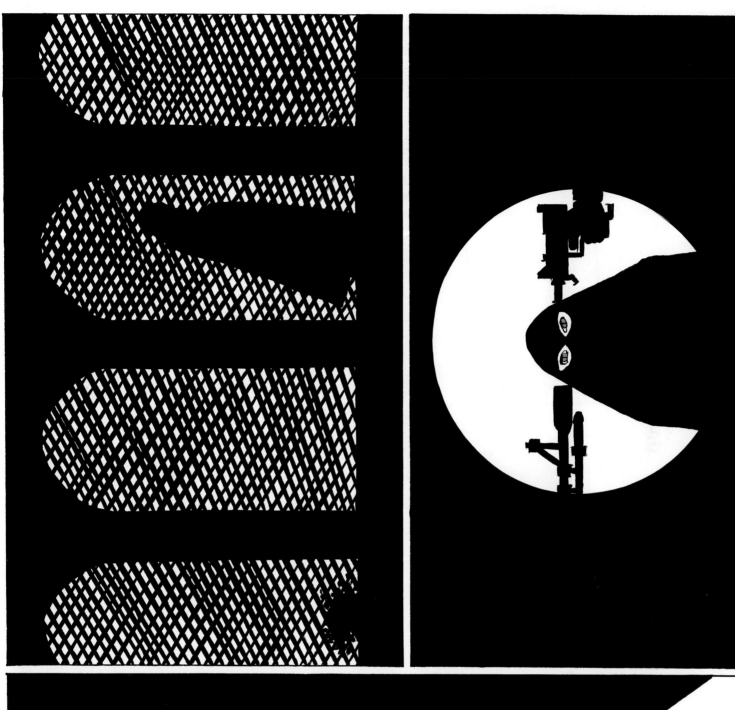

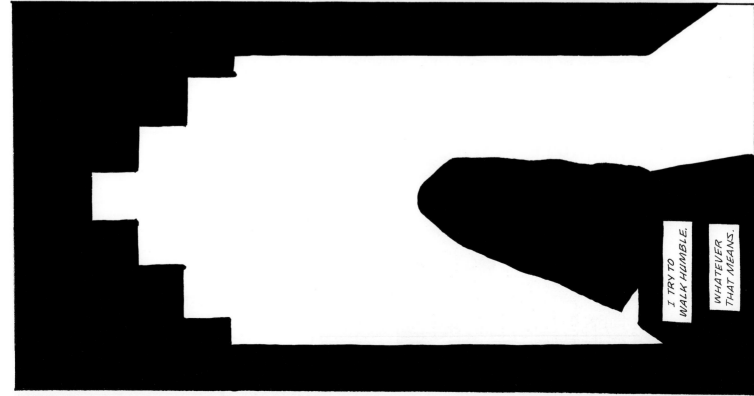

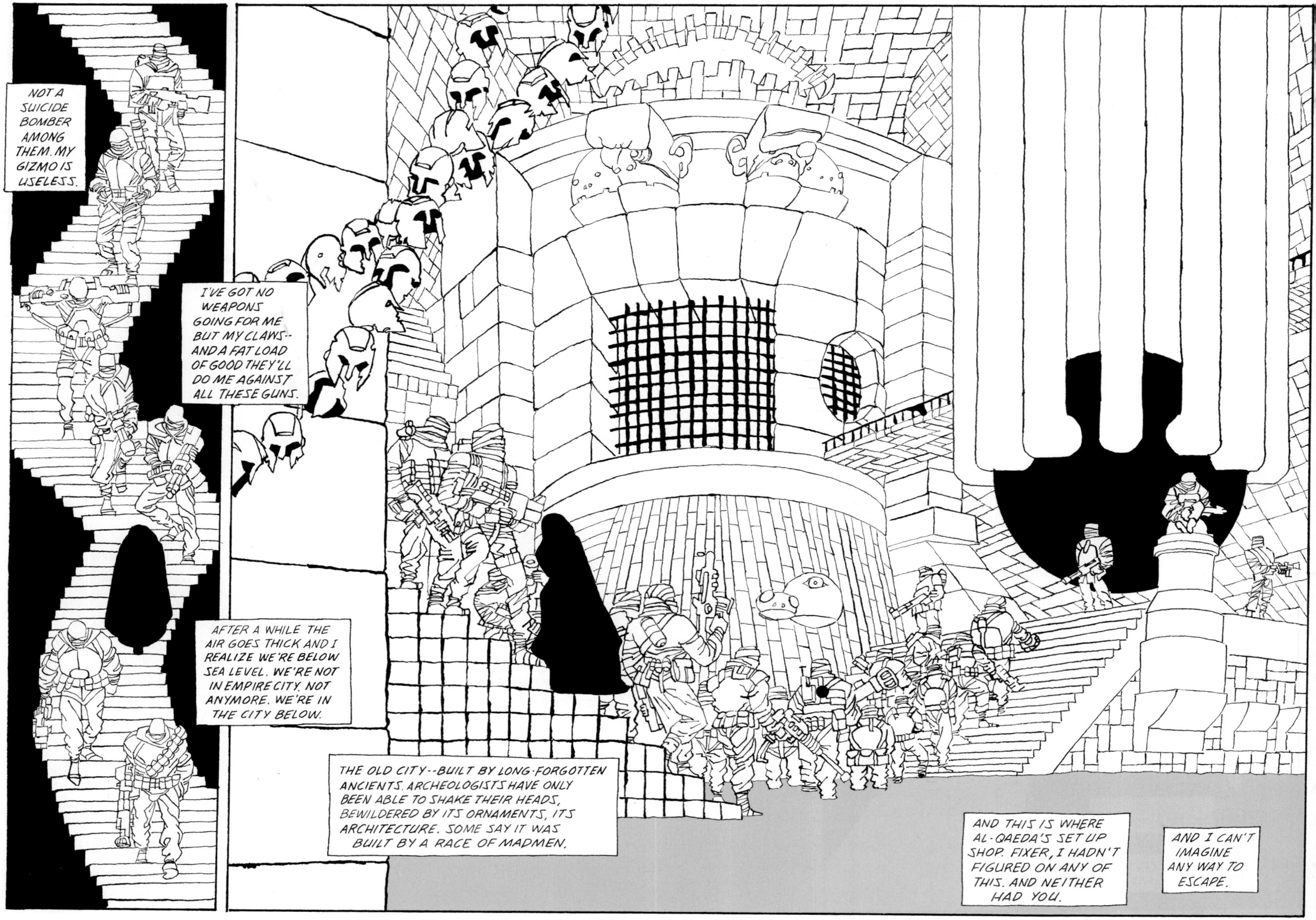
NOT A SUICIDE BOMBER AMONG THEM. MY GIZMO IS USELESS.
I'VE GOT NO WEAPONS GOING FOR ME BUT MY CLAWS-- AND A FAT LOAD OF GOOD THEY'LL DO ME AGAINST ALL THESE GUNS.
AFTER A WHILE THE AIR GOES THICK AND I REALIZE WE'RE BELOW SEA LEVEL. WE'RE NOT IN EMPIRE CITY. NOT ANYMORE. WE'RE IN THE CITY BELOW.
THE OLD CITY--BUILT BY LONG-FORGOTTEN ANCIENTS. ARCHEOLOGISTS HAVE ONLY BEEN ABLE TO SHAKE THEIR HEADS, BEWILDERED BY ITS ORNAMENTS, ITS ARCHITECTURE. SOME SAY IT WAS BUILT BY A RACE OF MADMEN.
AND THIS IS WHERE AL-QAEDA'S SET UP SHOP. FIXER, I HADN'T FIGURED ON ANY OF THIS. AND NEITHER HAD YOU.
AND I CAN'T IMAGINE ANY WAY TO ESCAPE.

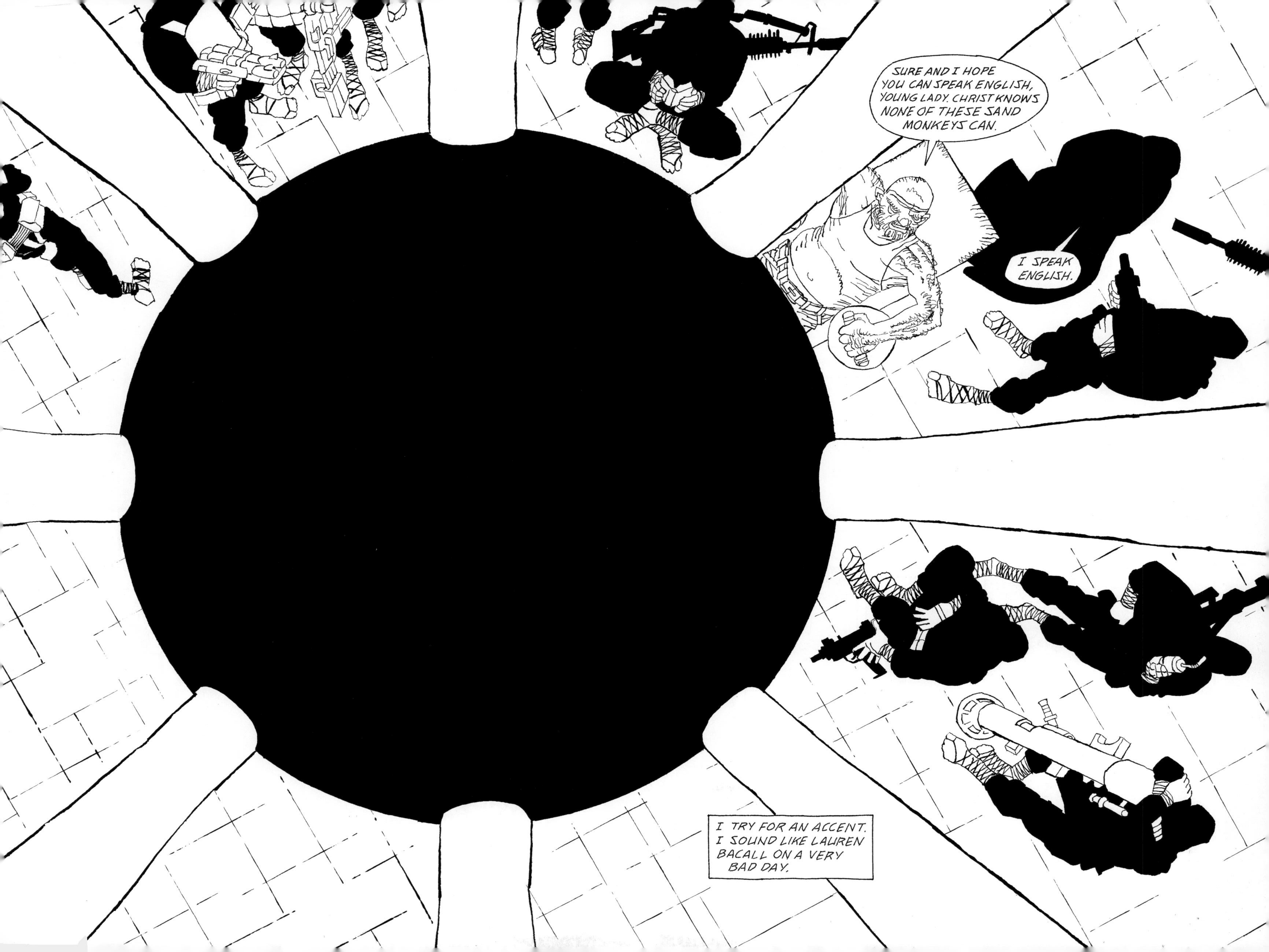
SURE AND I HOPE YOU CAN SPEAK ENGLISH, YOUNG LADY. CHRIST KNOWS NONE OF THESE SAND MONKEYS CAN.
I SPEAK ENGLISH.
I TRY FOR AN ACCENT. I SOUND LIKE LAUREN BACALL ON A VERY BAD DAY.

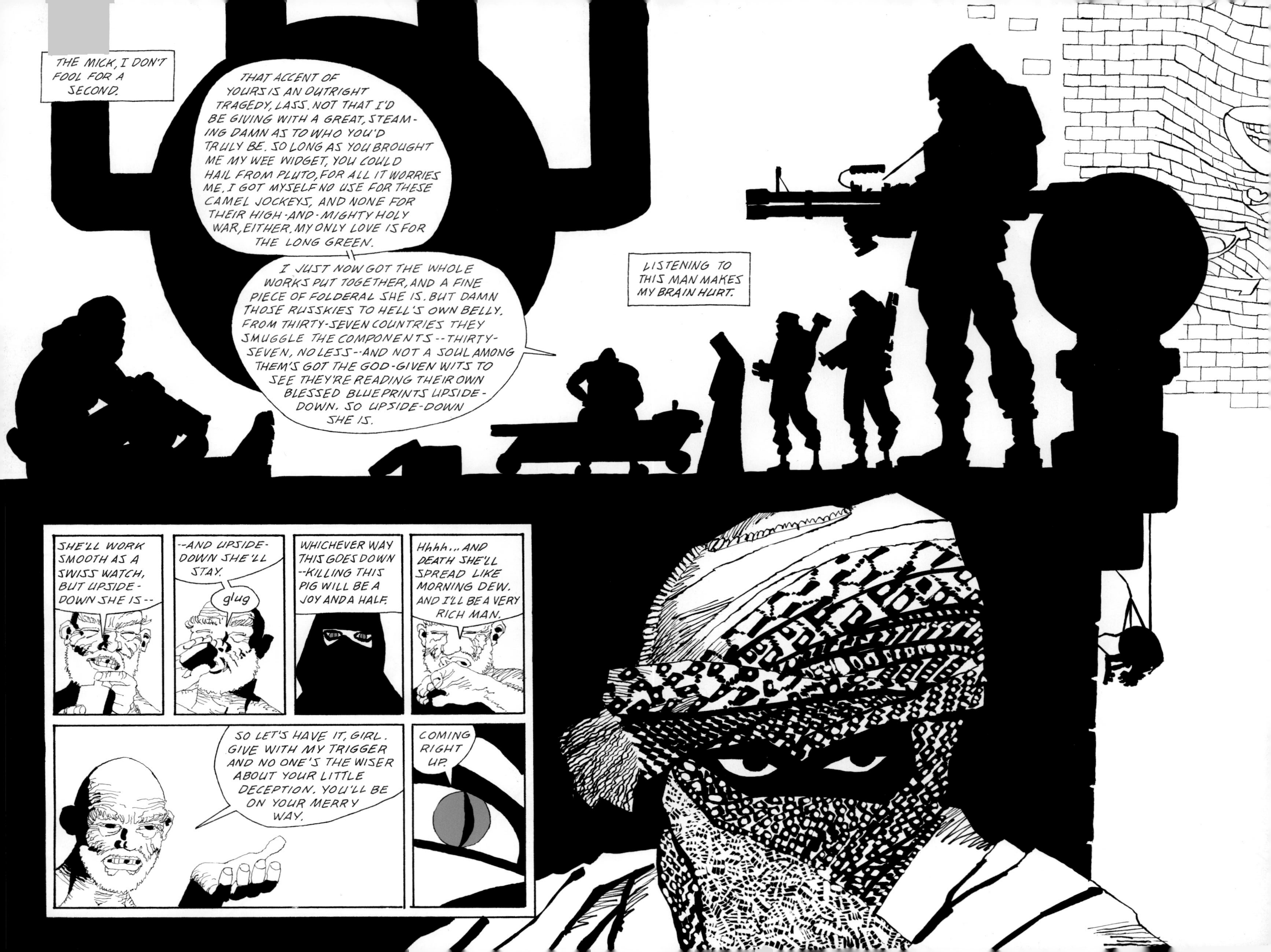
THE MICK, I DON'T FOOL FOR A SECOND.
THAT ACCENT OF YOURS IS AN OUTRIGHT TRAGEDY, LASS. NOT THAT I'D BE GIVING WITH A GREAT, STEAMING DAMN AS TO WHO YOU'D TRULY BE. SO LONG AS YOU BROUGHT ME MY WEE WIDGET, YOU COULD HAIL FROM PLUTO, FOR ALL IT WORRIES ME. I GOT MYSELF NO USE FOR THESE CAMEL JOCKEYS, AND NONE FOR THEIR HIGH-AND-MIGHTY HOLY WAR, EITHER. MY ONLY LOVE IS FOR THE LONG GREEN.
I JUST NOW GOT THE WHOLE WORKS PUT TOGETHER, AND A FINE PIECE OF FOLDERAL SHE IS. BUT DAMN THOSE RUSSKIES TO HELL'S OWN BELLY. FROM THIRTY-SEVEN COUNTRIES THEY SMUGGLE THE COMPONENTS--THIRTY-SEVEN, NO LESS--AND NOT A SOUL AMONG THEM'S GOT THE GOD-GIVEN WITS TO SEE THEY'RE READING THEIR OWN BLESSED BLUEPRINTS UPSIDE-DOWN. SO UPSIDE-DOWN SHE IS.
LISTENING TO THIS MAN MAKES MY BRAIN HURT.
SHE'LL WORK SMOOTH AS A SWISS WATCH, BUT UPSIDE-DOWN SHE IS--
--AND UPSIDE-DOWN SHE'LL STAY.
glug
WHICHEVER WAY THIS GOES DOWN --KILLING THIS PIG WILL BE A JOY AND A HALF.
Hhhh... AND DEATH SHE'LL SPREAD LIKE MORNING DEW. AND I'LL BE A VERY RICH MAN.
SO LET'S HAVE IT, GIRL. GIVE WITH MY TRIGGER AND NO ONE'S THE WISER ABOUT YOUR LITTLE DECEPTION. YOU'LL BE ON YOUR MERRY WAY.
COMING RIGHT UP.

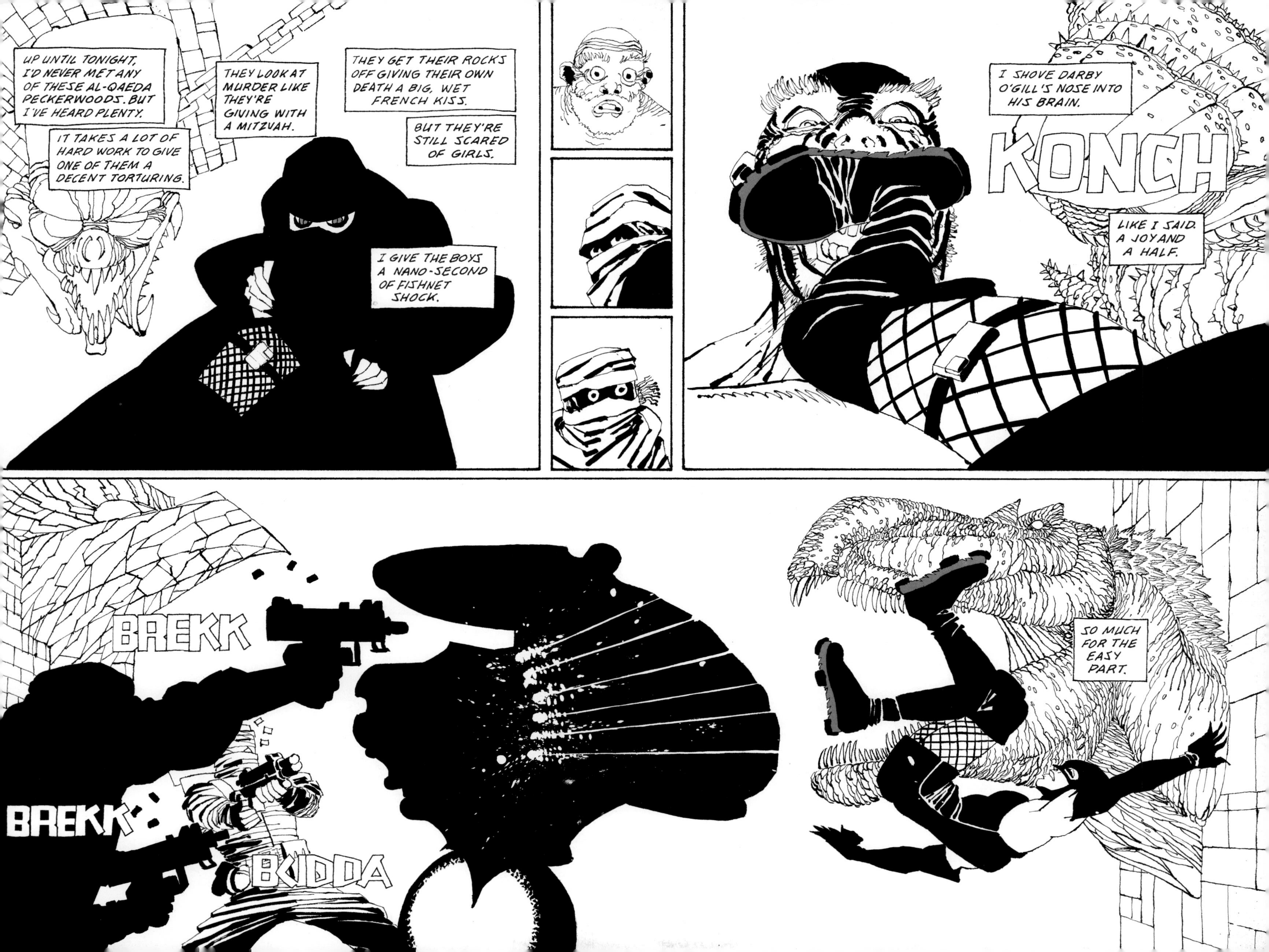
UP UNTIL TONIGHT, I'D NEVER MET ANY OF THESE AL-QAEDA PECKERWOODS. BUT I'VE HEARD PLENTY.
IT TAKES A LOT OF HARD WORK TO GIVE ONE OF THEM A DECENT TORTURING.
THEY LOOK AT MURDER LIKE THEY'RE GIVING WITH A MITZVAH.
THEY GET THEIR ROCKS OFF GIVING THEIR OWN DEATH A BIG, WET FRENCH KISS.
BUT THEY'RE STILL SCARED OF GIRLS.
I GIVE THE BOYS A NANO-SECOND OF FISHNET SHOCK.
I SHOVE DARBY O'GILL'S NOSE INTO HIS BRAIN.
KONCH
LIKE I SAID. A JOY AND A HALF.
BREKK
BREKK
BUDDA
SO MUCH FOR THE EASY PART.

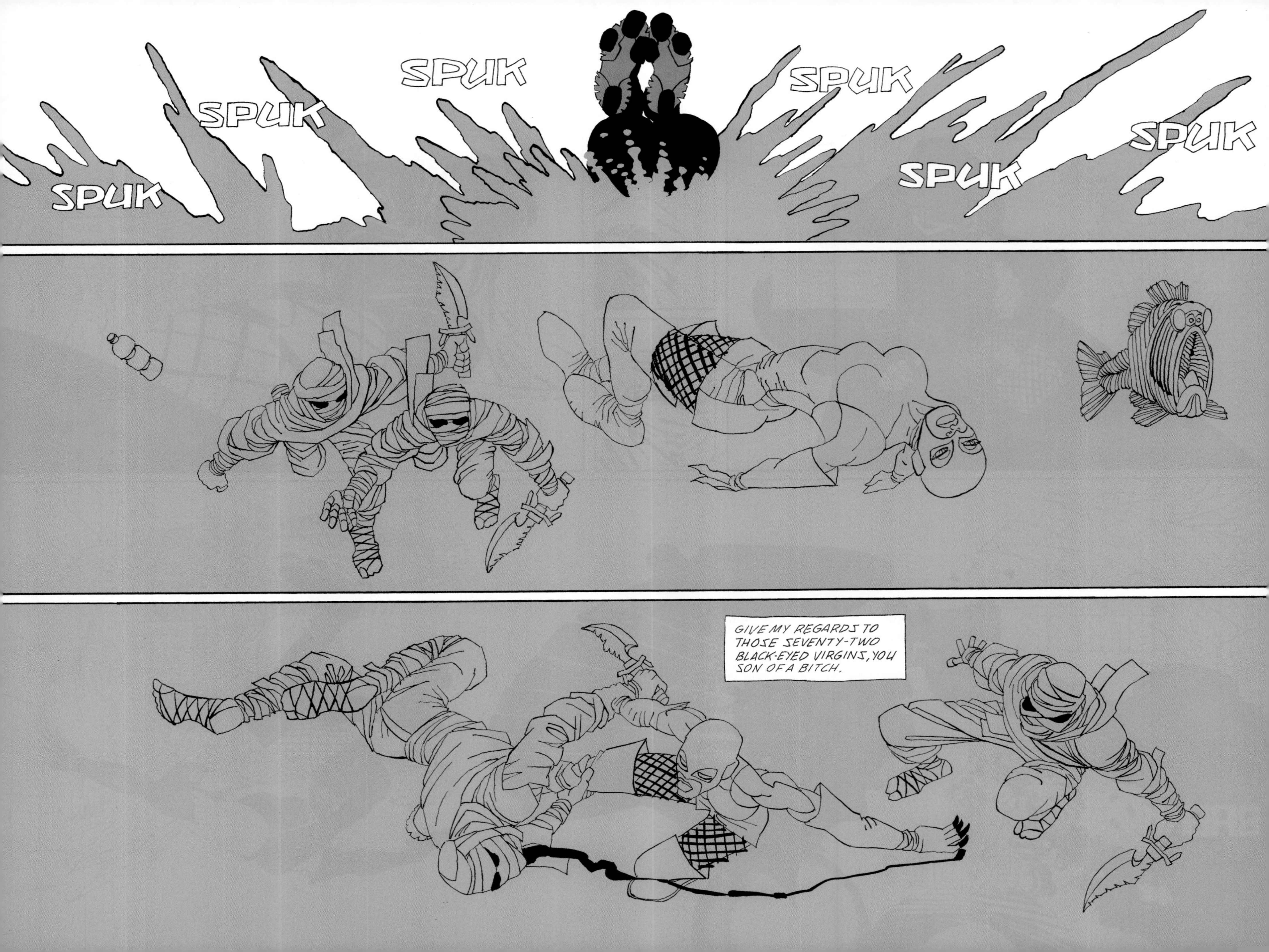
SPUK
SPUK
SPUK
SPUK
SPUK
SPUK
GIVE MY REGARDS TO THOSE SEVENTY-TWO BLACK-EYED VIRGINS, YOU SON OF A BITCH.

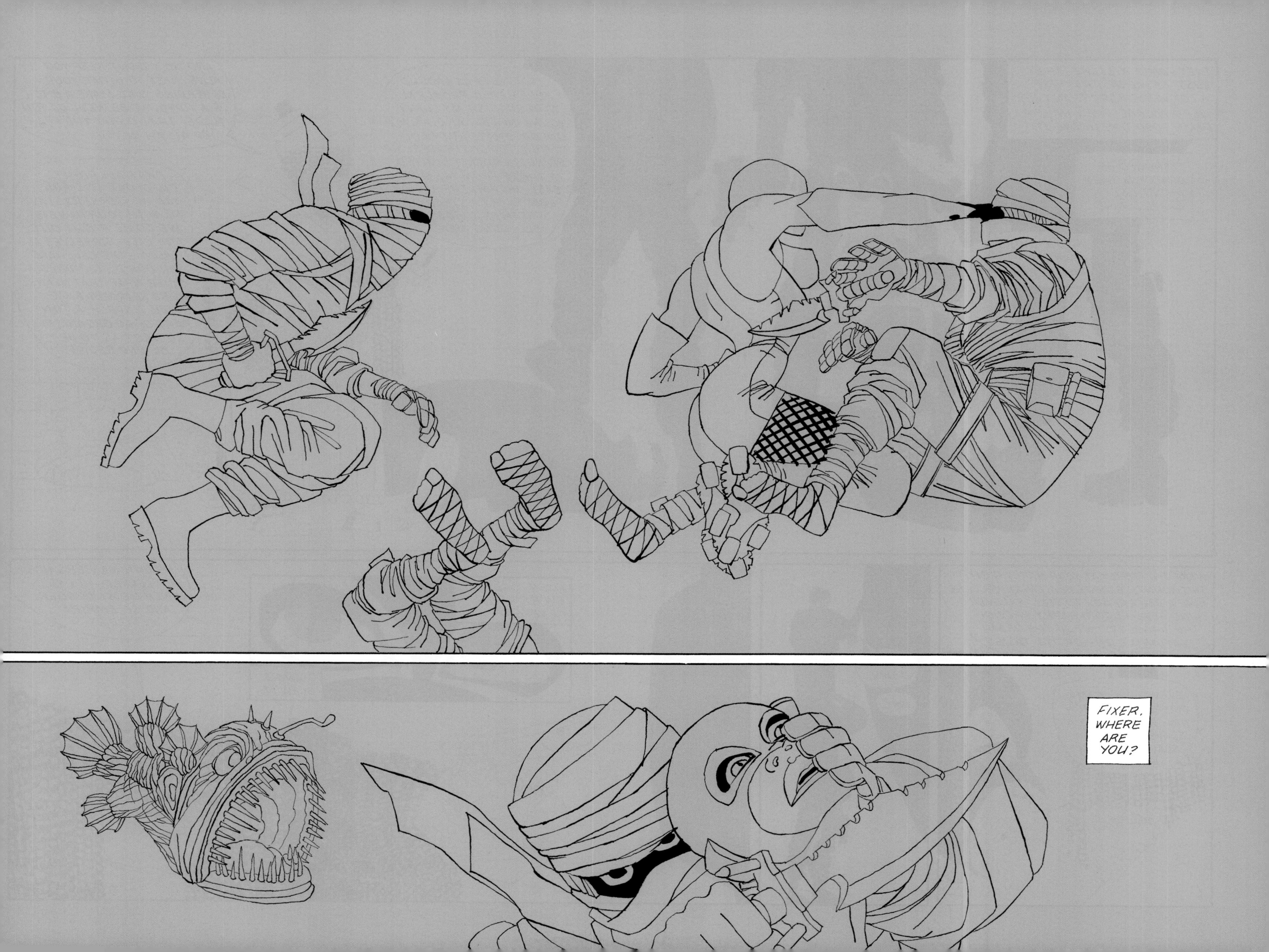
FIXER. WHERE ARE YOU?

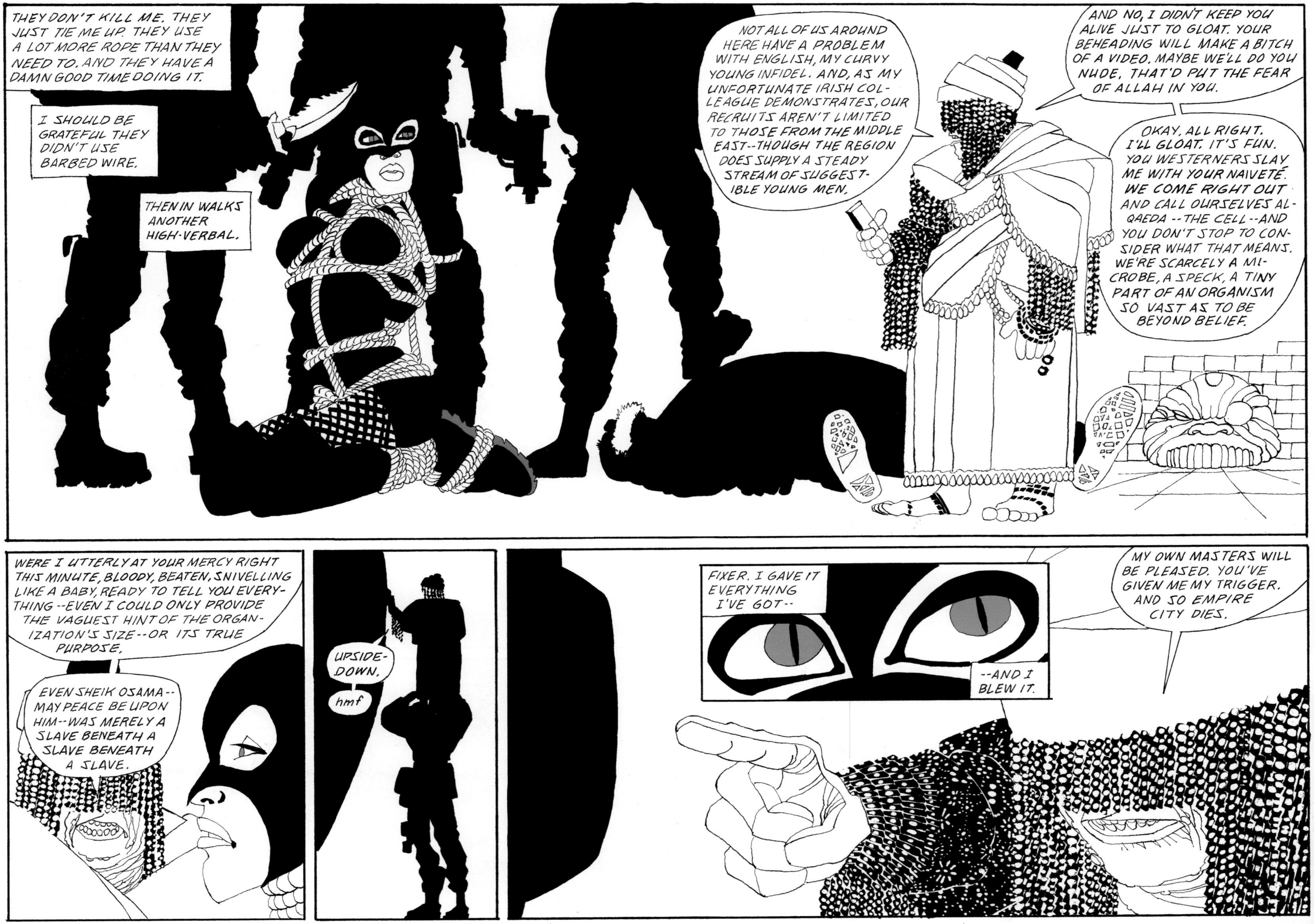
THEY DON'T KILL ME. THEY JUST TIE ME UP. THEY USE A LOT MORE ROPE THAN THEY NEED TO. AND THEY HAVE A DAMN GOOD TIME DOING IT.
I SHOULD BE GRATEFUL THEY DIDN'T USE BARBED WIRE.
THEN IN WALKS ANOTHER HIGH-VERBAL.
NOT ALL OF US AROUND HERE HAVE A PROBLEM WITH ENGLISH, MY CURVY YOUNG INFIDEL. AND, AS MY UNFORTUNATE IRISH COL-LEAGUE DEMONSTRATES, OUR RECRUITS AREN'T LIMITED TO THOSE FROM THE MIDDLE EAST--THOUGH THE REGION DOES SUPPLY A STEADY STREAM OF SUGGEST-IBLE YOUNG MEN.
AND NO, I DIDN'T KEEP YOU ALIVE JUST TO GLOAT. YOUR BEHEADING WILL MAKE A BITCH OF A VIDEO. MAYBE WE'LL DO YOU NUDE. THAT'D PUT THE FEAR OF ALLAH IN YOU.
OKAY, ALL RIGHT. I'LL GLOAT. IT'S FUN. YOU WESTERNERS SLAY ME WITH YOUR NAIVETÉ. WE COME RIGHT OUT AND CALL OURSELVES AL-QAEDA --THE CELL--AND YOU DON'T STOP TO CON-SIDER WHAT THAT MEANS. WE'RE SCARCELY A MI-CROBE, A SPECK, A TINY PART OF AN ORGANISM SO VAST AS TO BE BEYOND BELIEF.
WERE I UTTERLY AT YOUR MERCY RIGHT THIS MINUTE, BLOODY, BEATEN, SNIVELLING LIKE A BABY, READY TO TELL YOU EVERY-THING --EVEN I COULD ONLY PROVIDE THE VAGUEST HINT OF THE ORGAN-IZATION'S SIZE--OR ITS TRUE PURPOSE.
EVEN SHEIK OSAMA--MAY PEACE BE UPON HIM--WAS MERELY A SLAVE BENEATH A SLAVE BENEATH A SLAVE.
UPSIDE-DOWN.
hmf
FIXER. I GAVE IT EVERYTHING I'VE GOT--
--AND I BLEW IT.
MY OWN MASTERS WILL BE PLEASED. YOU'VE GIVEN ME MY TRIGGER. AND SO EMPIRE CITY DIES.

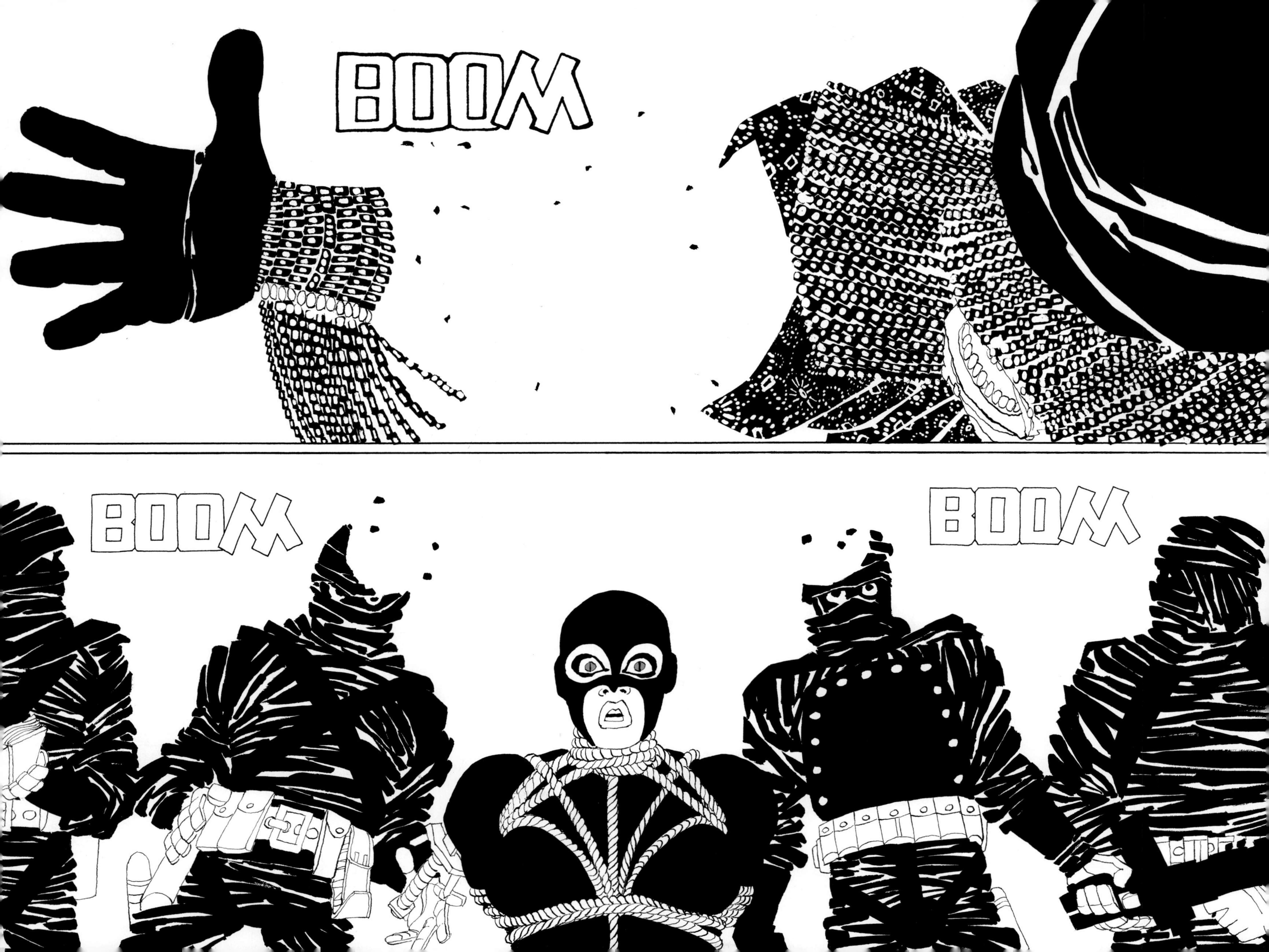
BOOM
BOOM
BOOM

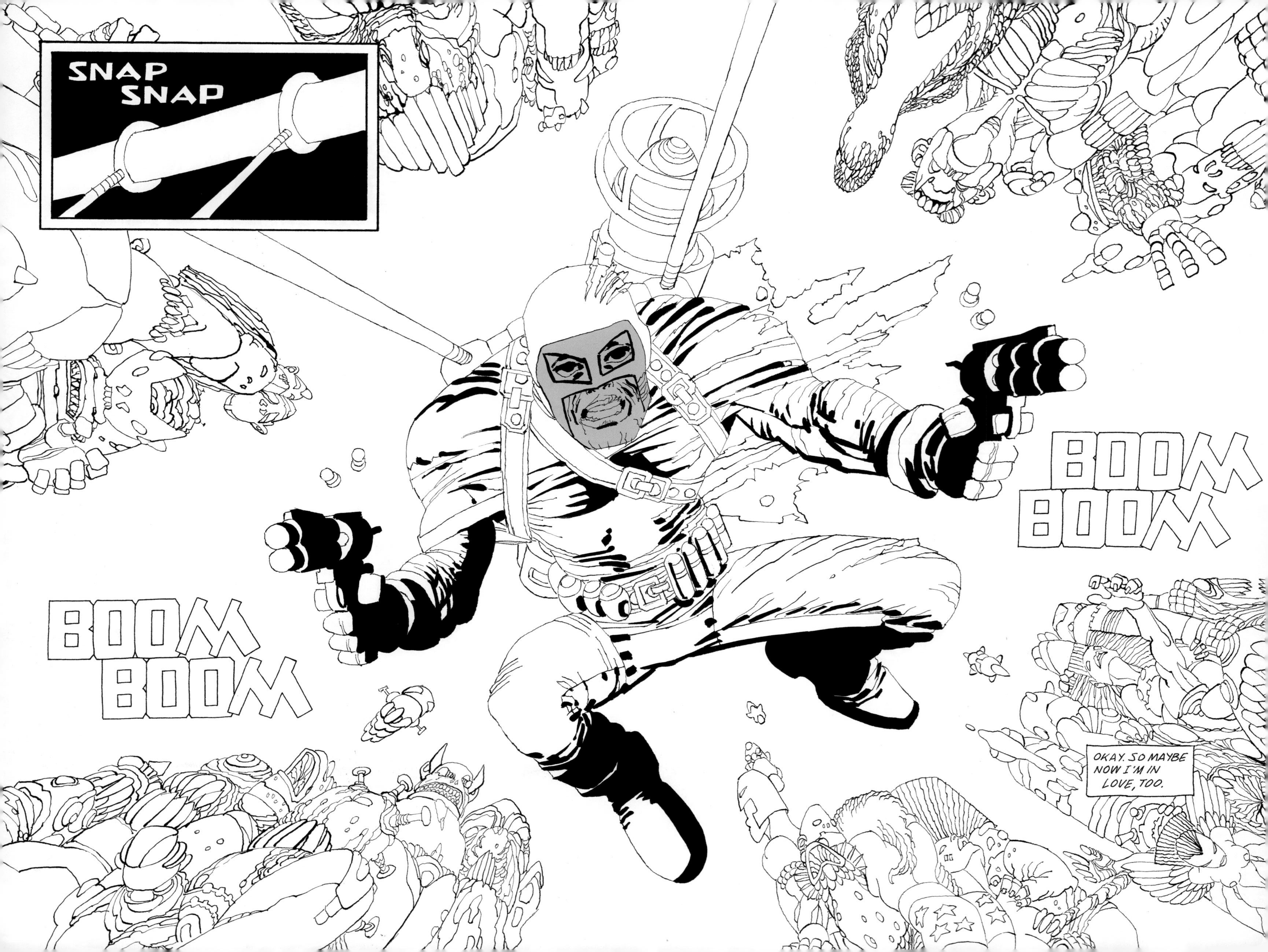
SNAP
SNAP
BOOM
BOOM
BOOM
BOOM
OKAY. SO MAYBE NOW I'M IN LOVE, TOO.

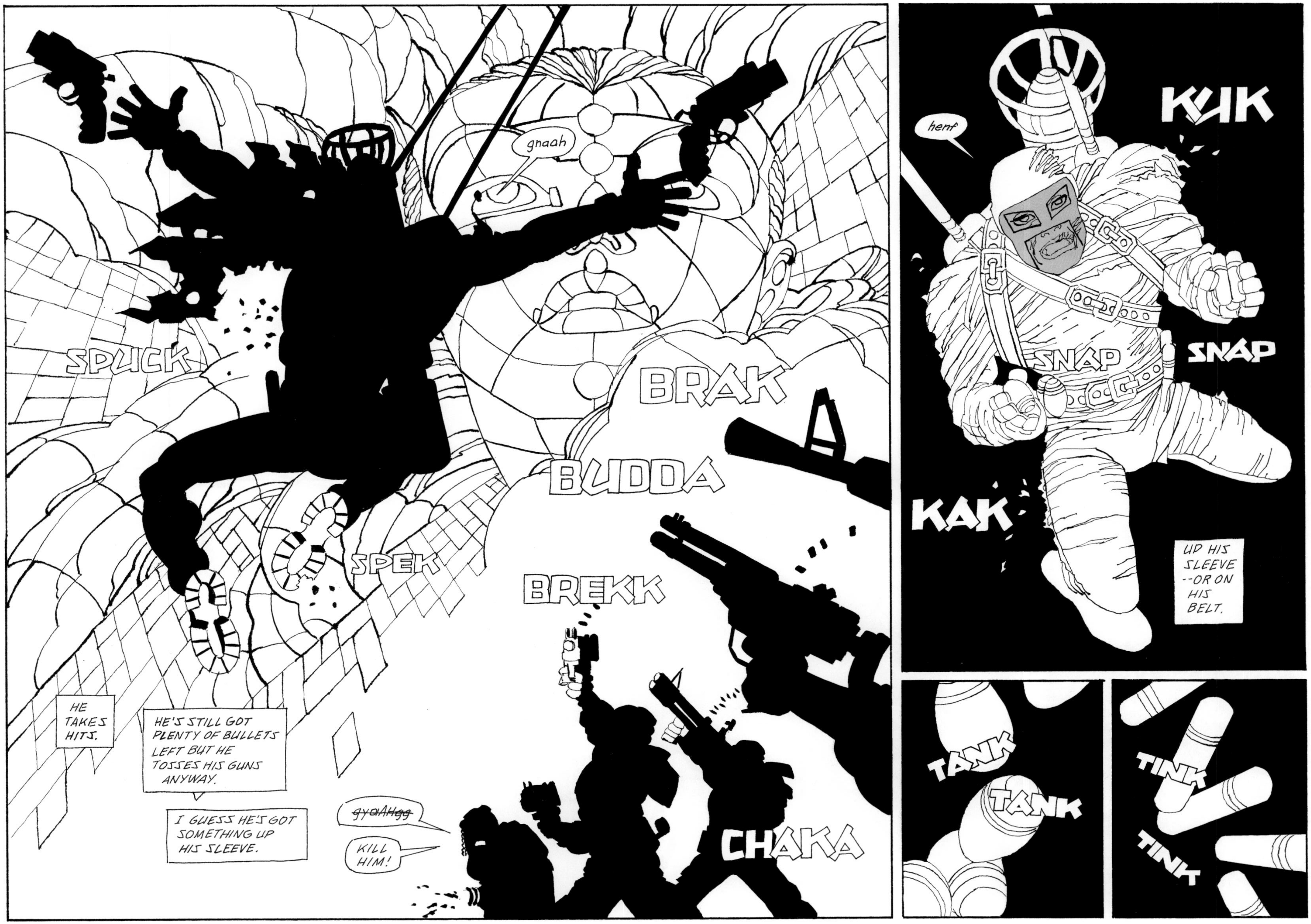
gnaah
SPUCK
BRAK
BUDDA
SPEK
BREKK
HE TAKES HITS.
HE'S STILL GOT PLENTY OF BULLETS LEFT BUT HE TOSSES HIS GUNS ANYWAY.
I GUESS HE'S GOT SOMETHING UP HIS SLEEVE.
gyaAHgg
KILL HIM!
CHAKA
henf
KUK
SNAP
SNAP
KAK
UP HIS SLEEVE --OR ON HIS BELT.
TANK
TANK
TINK
TINK

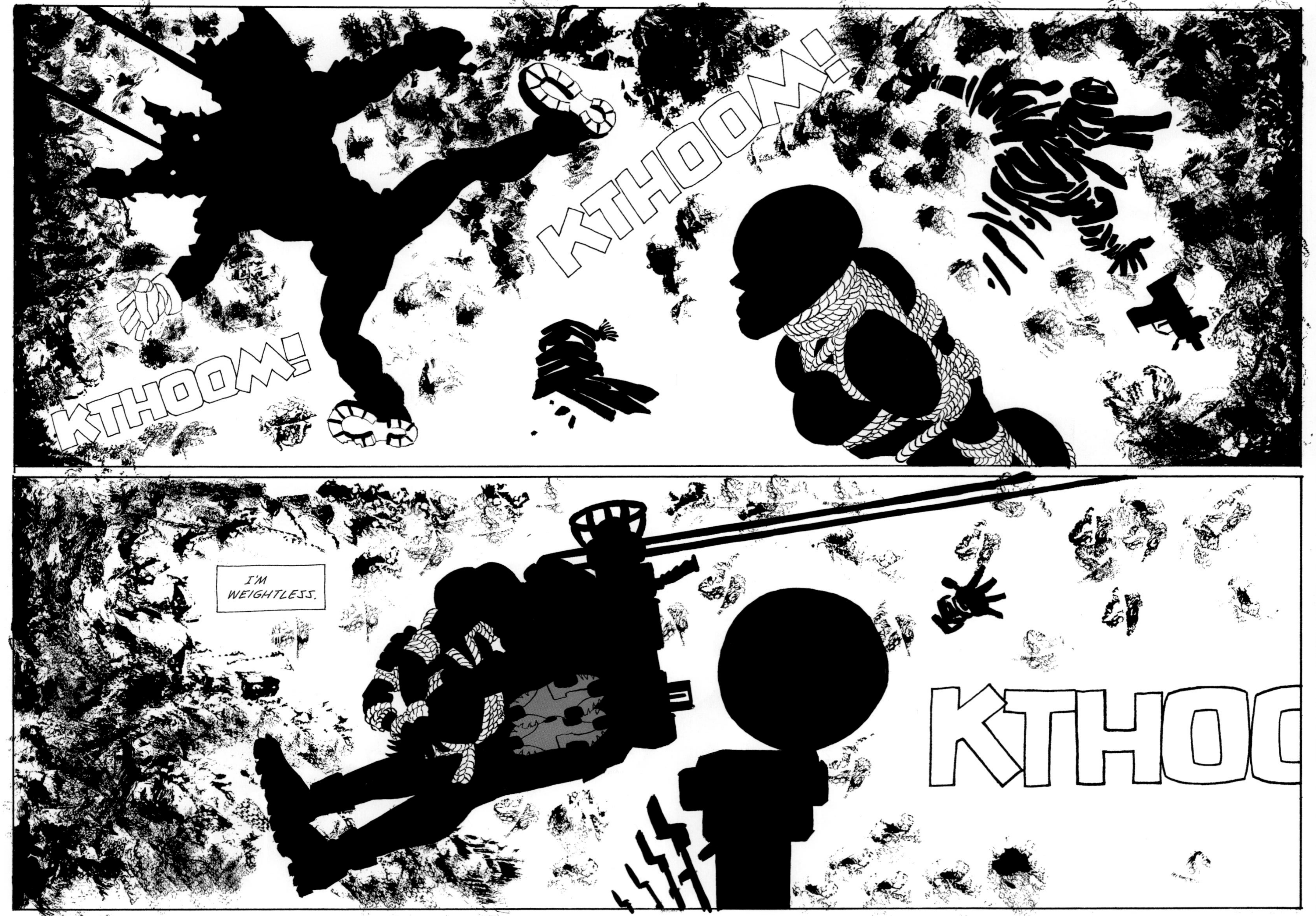
KTHOOM!
KTHOOM!
I'M WEIGHTLESS.
KTHOO

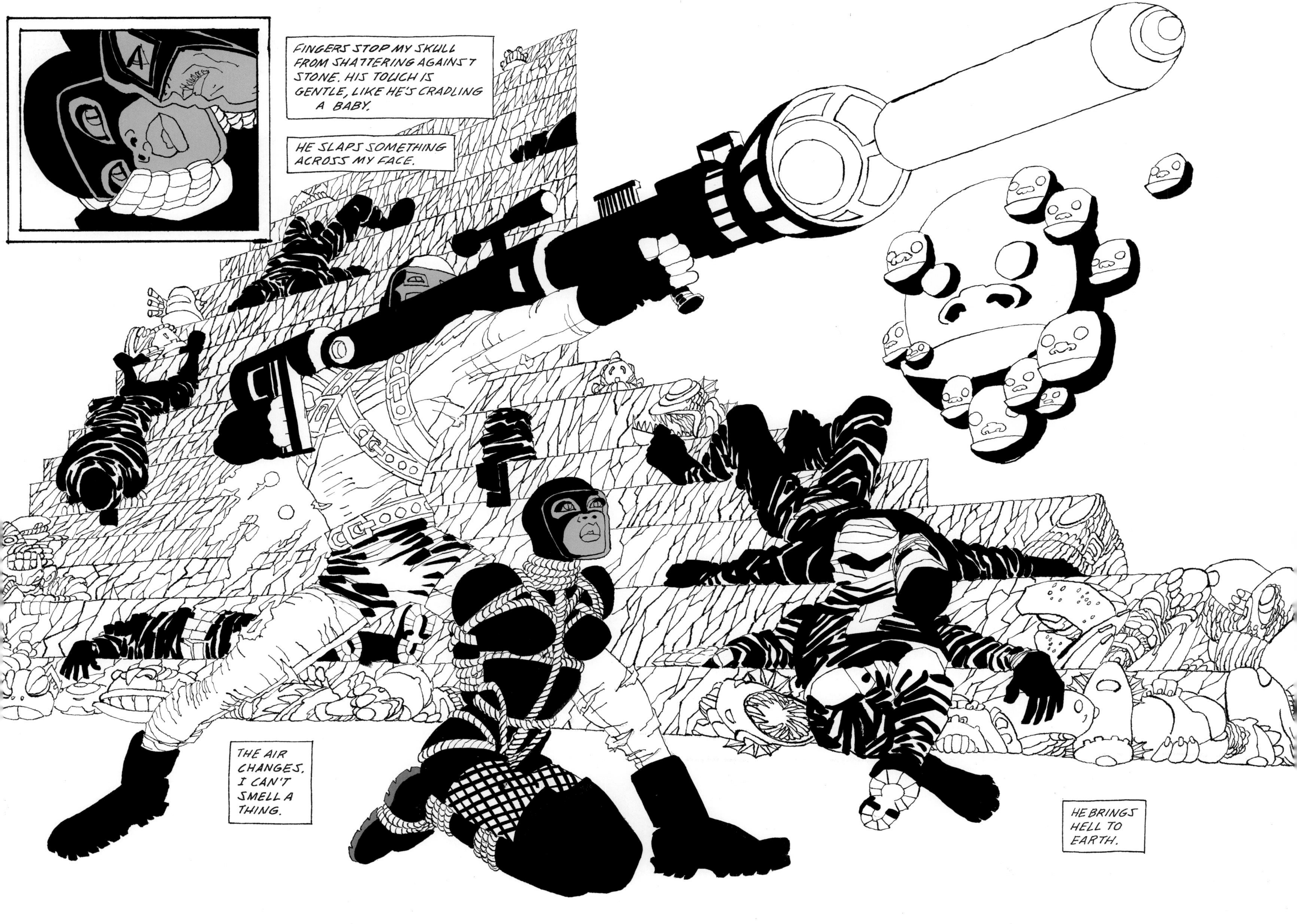
FINGERS STOP MY SKULL FROM SHATTERING AGAINST STONE. HIS TOUCH IS GENTLE, LIKE HE'S CRADLING A BABY.
HE SLAPS SOMETHING ACROSS MY FACE.
THE AIR CHANGES. I CAN'T SMELL A THING.
HE BRINGS HELL TO EARTH.

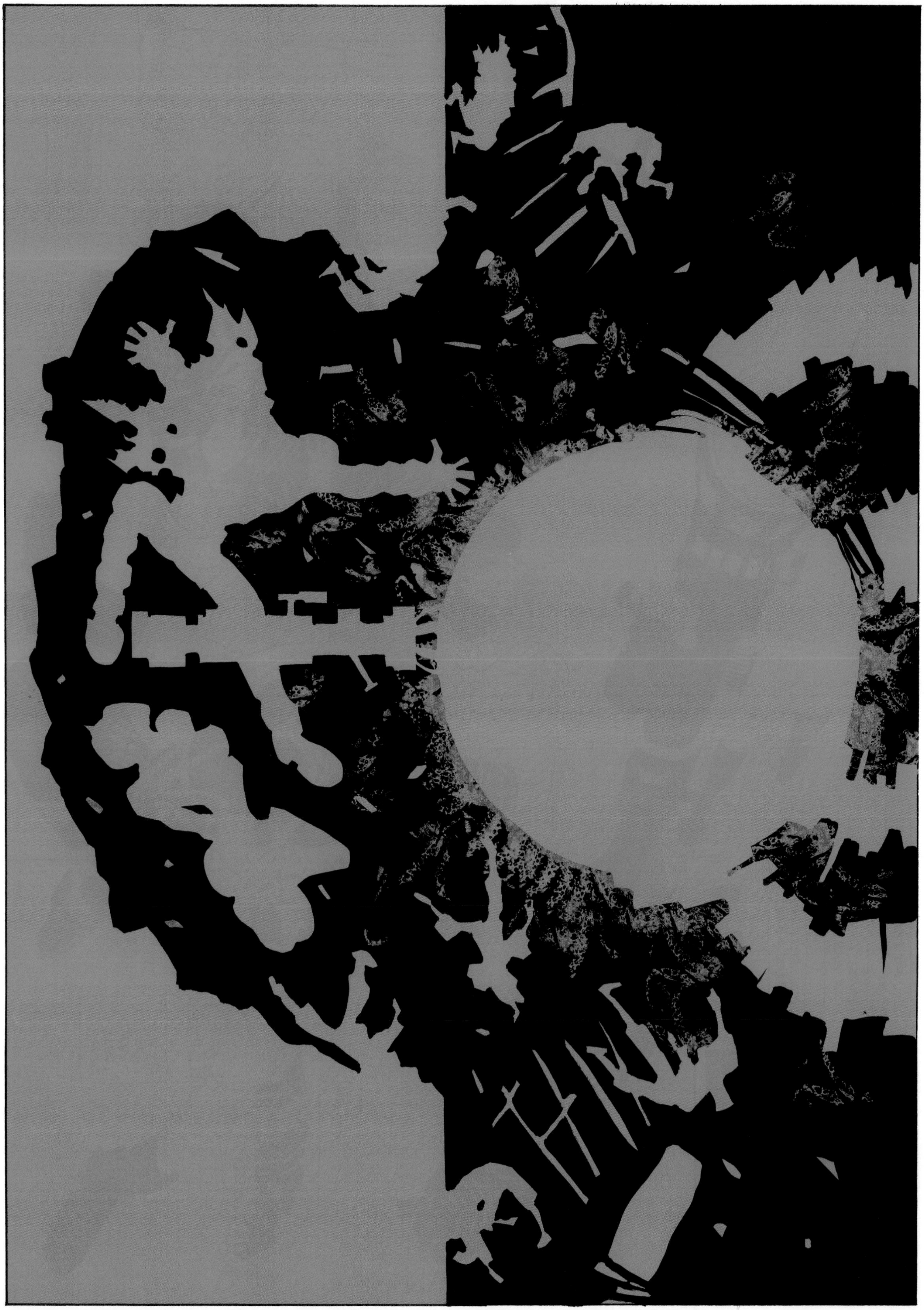

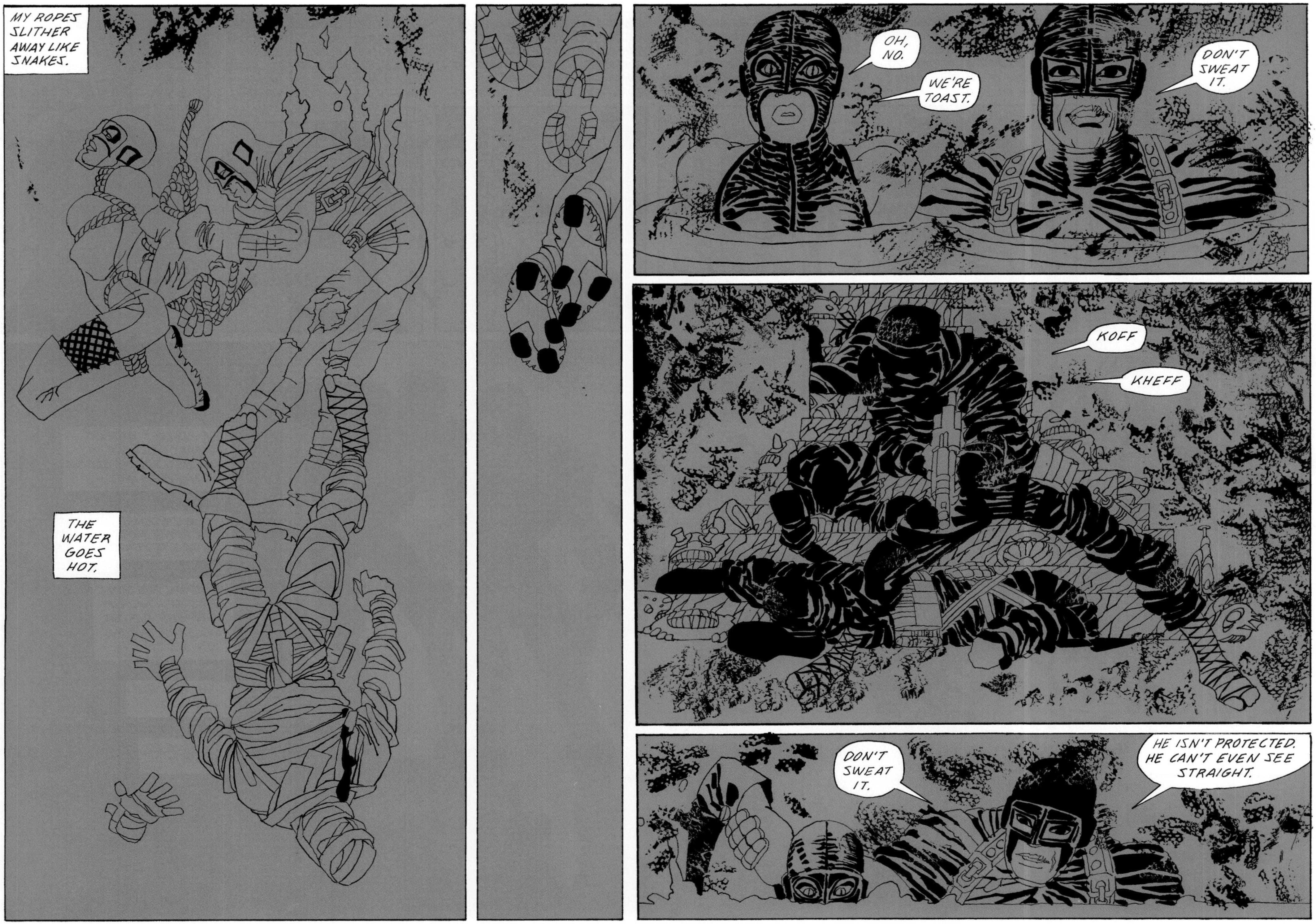
MY ROPES SLITHER AWAY LIKE SNAKES.
THE WATER GOES HOT.
OH, NO.
WE'RE TOAST.
DON'T SWEAT IT.
KOFF
KHEFF
HE ISN'T PROTECTED. HE CAN'T EVEN SEE STRAIGHT.
DON'T SWEAT IT.

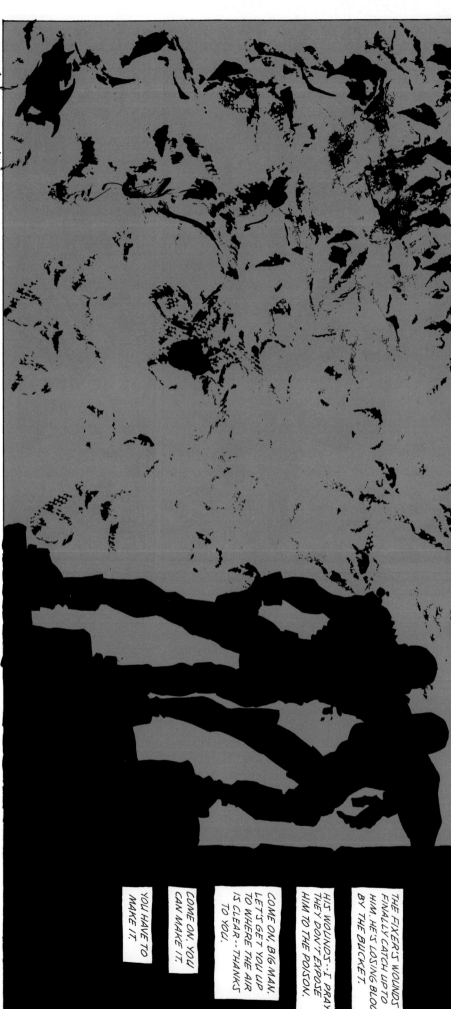

HE DROPS HIS GUN, JUST LIKE THAT.

HIS KNEES HIT THE FLOOR. THEY DRAG THE REST OF HIM DOWN WITH THEM. THE SOUND IS SOGGY, ALL WRONG. HE VOMITS BLOOD A WHOLE LOT OF BLOOD. IT TAKES AWHILE FOR HIM TO STOP.

HE GURGLES OUT WHAT SHOULD BE A SCREAM. HE STARTS SCRATCHING HIMSELF ALL OVER, LIKE HE'S COVERED WITH BEETLES. HE DOESN'T STOP GURGLING. HE RIPS AT HIS CLOTHES.

HIS NOSE AND EARS AND EYES START BLEEDING. HE KEEPS SCRATCHING, HE PULLS HIS HAIR OUT IN CLUMPS. HE CLAWS AT HIS FACE. HE WRENCHES HIS RIGHT EYE FROM ITS SOCKET.

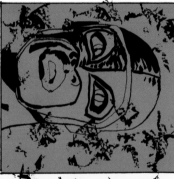

HE DIGS INTO HIS DOUGHY FLESH, HIS SKIN COMES OFF IN SHEETS, HIS STOMACH SPLITS OPEN, HIS GUTS SPILL OUT. HIS LEFT EYE GOES DEAD. HIS RIGHT EYE DANGLES ON HIS CHEEK, STARING AT NOTHING. HE GOES LIMP.

THIS IS WHAT THEY PLANNED FOR US.

LET'S GET THE HELL OUT OF HERE.

THE FIXER'S WOUNDS FINALLY CATCH UP TO HIM. HE'S LOSING BLOOD BY THE BUCKET.

HIS WOUNDS--I PRAY THEY DON'T EXPOSE HIM TO THE POISON.

COME ON, BIG MAN. LET'S GET YOU UP TO WHERE THE AIR IS CLEAR--THANKS TO YOU.

COME ON, YOU CAN MAKE IT.

YOU HAVE TO MAKE IT.

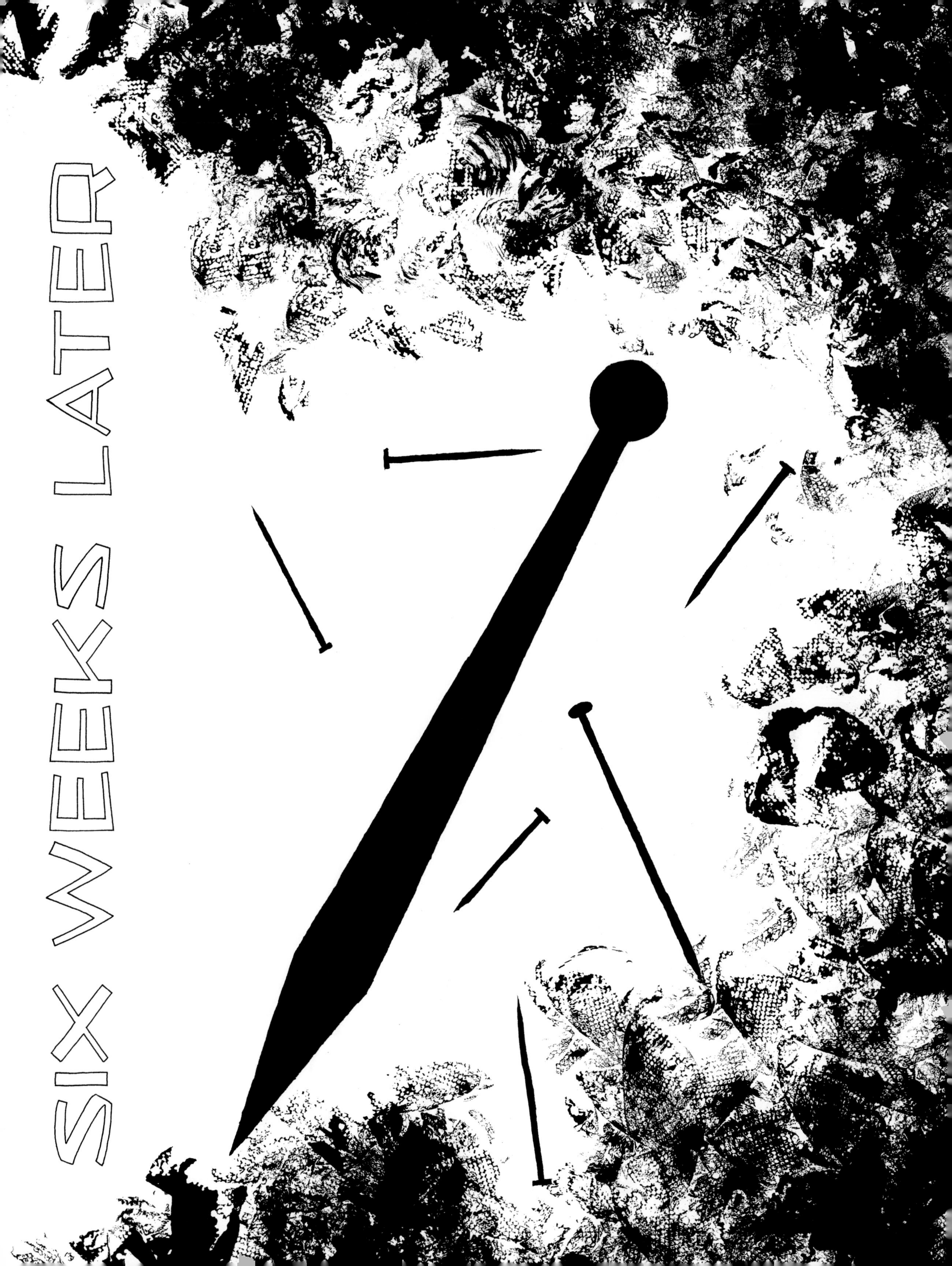
SIX WEEKS LATER

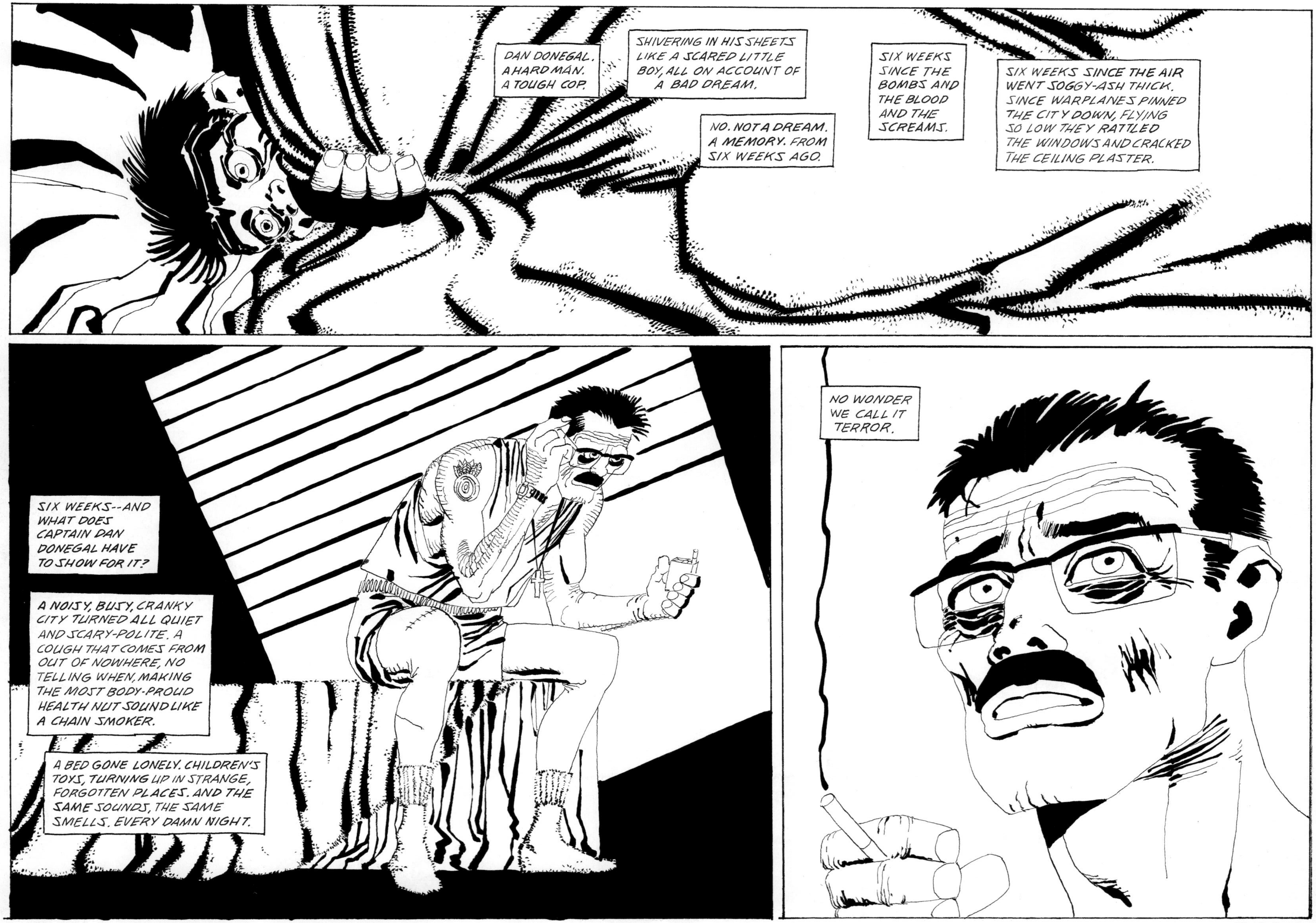
DAN DONEGAL. A HARD MAN. A TOUGH COP.
SHIVERING IN HIS SHEETS LIKE A SCARED LITTLE BOY, ALL ON ACCOUNT OF A BAD DREAM.
NO. NOT A DREAM. A MEMORY. FROM SIX WEEKS AGO.
SIX WEEKS SINCE THE BOMBS AND THE BLOOD AND THE SCREAMS.
SIX WEEKS SINCE THE AIR WENT SOGGY-ASH THICK. SINCE WARPLANES PINNED THE CITY DOWN, FLYING SO LOW THEY RATTLED THE WINDOWS AND CRACKED THE CEILING PLASTER.
SIX WEEKS--AND WHAT DOES CAPTAIN DAN DONEGAL HAVE TO SHOW FOR IT?
A NOISY, BUSY, CRANKY CITY TURNED ALL QUIET AND SCARY-POLITE. A COUGH THAT COMES FROM OUT OF NOWHERE, NO TELLING WHEN, MAKING THE MOST BODY-PROUD HEALTH NUT SOUND LIKE A CHAIN SMOKER.
A BED GONE LONELY. CHILDREN'S TOYS, TURNING UP IN STRANGE, FORGOTTEN PLACES. AND THE SAME SOUNDS, THE SAME SMELLS. EVERY DAMN NIGHT.
NO WONDER WE CALL IT TERROR.

THE END

Respectfully dedicated to THEO VAN GOGH
(1957-2004)

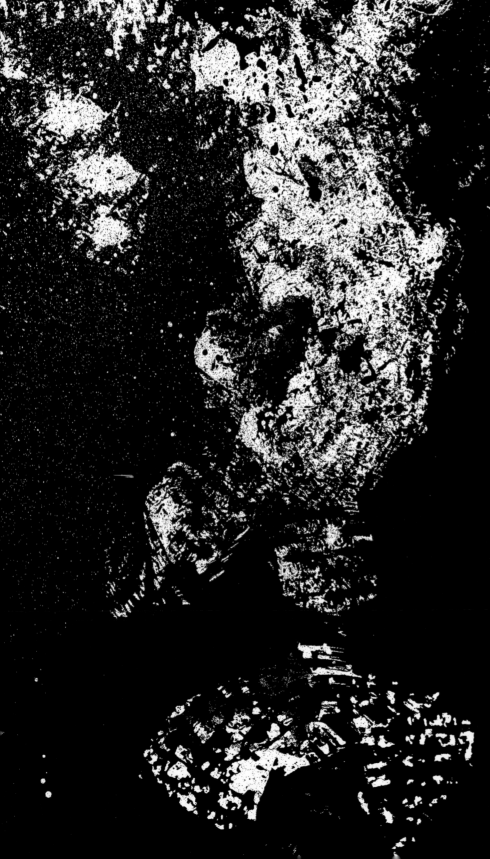

FRANK MILLER

Frank Miller is one of the seminal creative talents who sparked today's onslaught of motion pictures featuring comic book characters & concepts. He single-handedly re-defined the presentation of comic book characters and heroic fiction with his grand-daddy of graphic novels, **THE DARK KNIGHT RETURNS** and his other graphic novels, turned box-office hits, include **300** and **SIN CITY** (the film version of which Miller co-directed with Robert Rodriguez), proving that success does not always come wrapped in spandex. Miller also created **RONIN**, and wrote **BATMAN: YEAR ONE**, **BATMAN: THE DARK KNIGHT STRIKES AGAIN**, and **ALL-STAR BATMAN AND ROBIN THE BOY WONDER** all for DC Comics, and **THE BIG GUY AND RUSTY THE BOY ROBOT, HARD BOILED, and MARTHA WASHINGTON** at Dark Horse Comics. The motion picture, **THE SPIRIT**, marked Miller's solo feature film directorial debut.

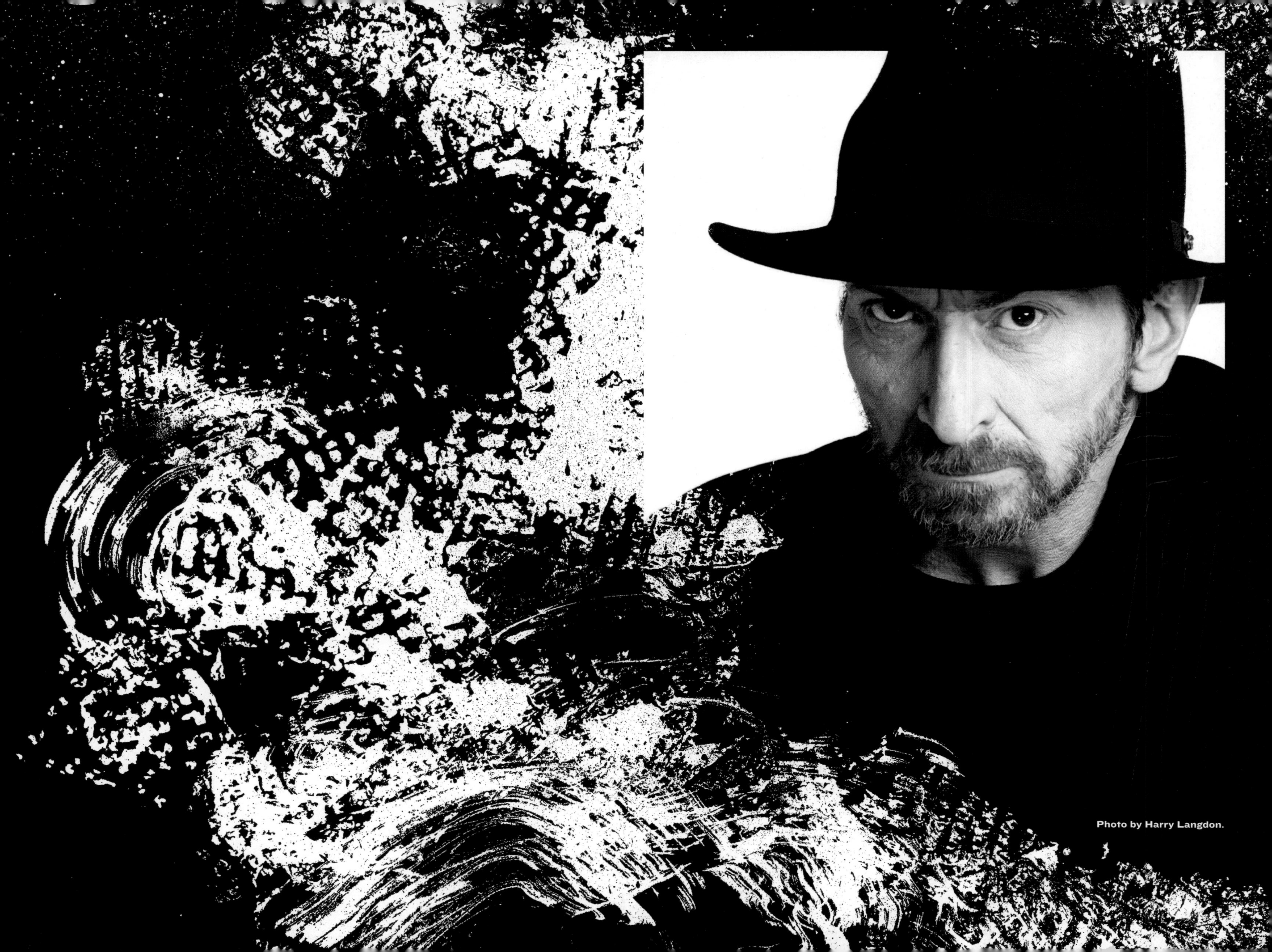

Photo by Harry Langdon.

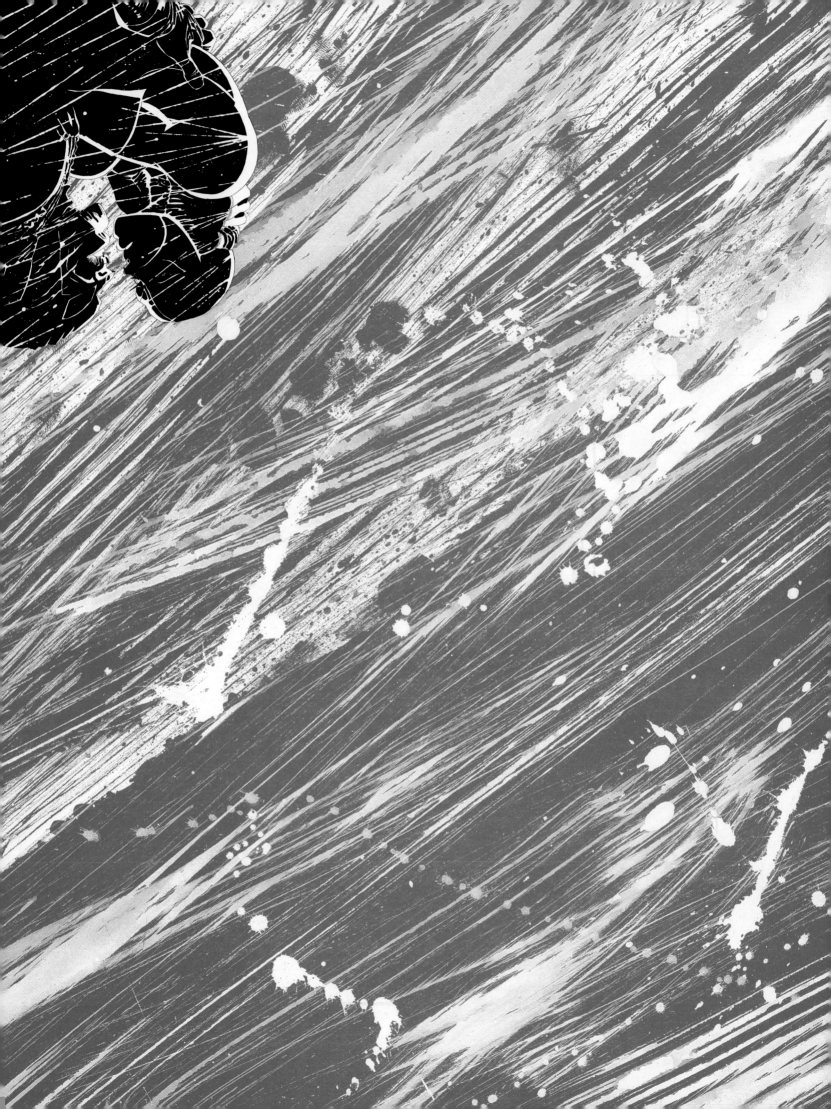

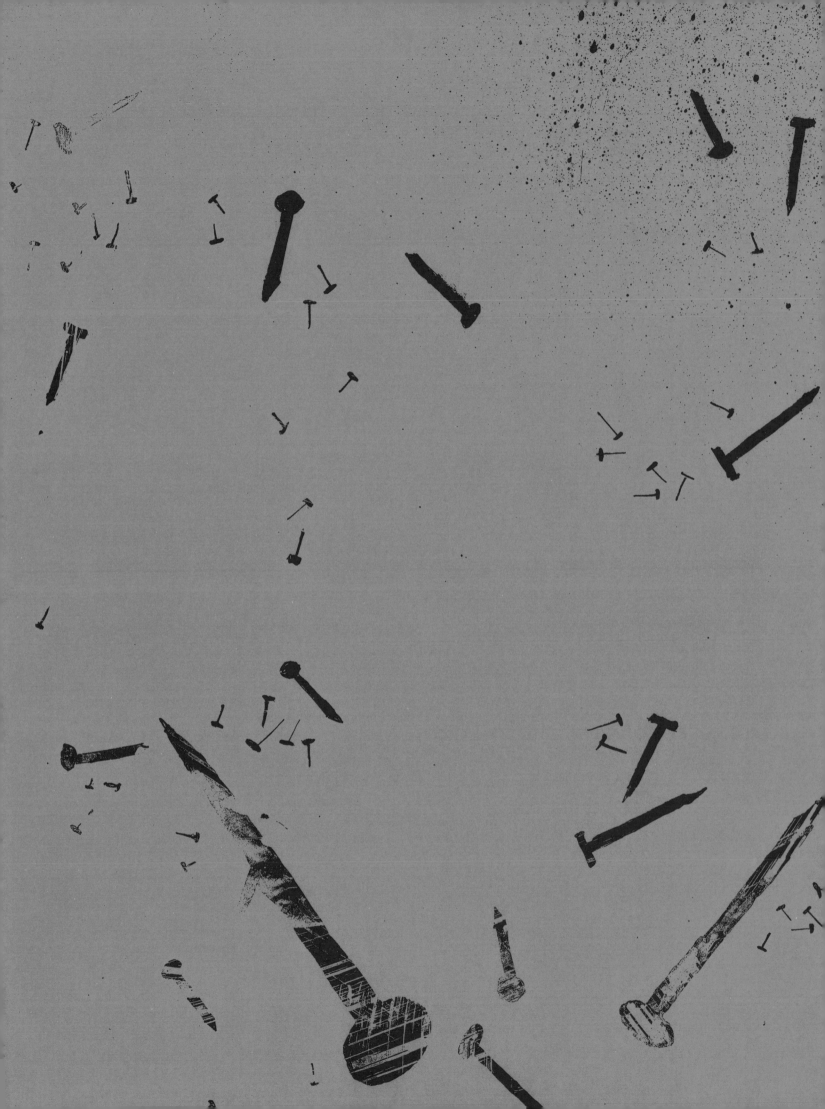